1/7/2011

2006

Day Trading the Currency Market

Founded in 1807, John Wiley & Sons is the oldest independent publishing company in the United States. With offices in North America, Europe, Australia, and Asia, Wiley is globally committed to developing and marketing print and electronic products and services for our customers' professional and personal knowledge and understanding.

The Wiley Trading series features books by traders who have survived the market's ever changing temperament and have prospered—some by reinventing systems, others by getting back to basics. Whether a novice trader, professional, or somewhere in-between, these books will provide the advice and strategies needed to prosper today and well into the future.

For a list of available titles, please visit our Web site at www.wileyfinance.com.

Day Trading the Currency Market

Technical and Fundamental Strategies To Profit from Market Swings

KATHY LIEN

WILEY

John Wiley & Sons, Inc.

Published by John Wiley & Sons, Inc., Hoboken, New Jersey.
Published simultaneously in Canada.

For general information on our other products and services or for technical support, please
contact our Customer Care Department within the United States at (800) 762-2974, outside
the United States at (317) 572-3993 or fax (317) 572-4002.

Wiley also publishes its books in a variety of electronic formats. Some content that appears
in print may not be available in electronic books. For more information about Wiley
products, visit our web site at www.wiley.com.

Library of Congress Cataloging-in-Publication Data:

Lien, Kathy, 1980–
    Day trading the currency market : technical and fundamental strategies to
profit from market swings / Kathy Lien.
        p.   cm.—(Wiley trading series)
    Includes index.
    ISBN-13: 978-0-471-71753-9 (cloth)
    ISBN-10: 0-471-71753-3 (cloth)
    1. Foreign exchange futures.   2. Foreign exchange market.   3. Speculation.
I. Title.   II. Series.
    HG3853.L54   2006
    332.4'5—dc22   2005016421

Printed in the United States of America.

10   9   8   7   6   5   4   3   2

Contents

Preface

L ooking for a good book on currency trading? After having taught
seminars across the country on how to trade currencies, I am repeatedly approached by avid traders who are serious about learning the
foreign exchange (FX) market and want recommendations for good currency trading books. *Day Trading the Currency Market* addresses this
need by not only providing technical and fundamental strategies for trading FX, but also by giving traders a more detailed insight into how the currency market works. This book is designed for both the beginner and the
advanced trader. There is something for every type of reader. In this book,
I try to accomplish two major goals—to touch on the major FX market basics or currency characteristics that all traders and particularly day
traders need to know, as well as to give you actionable strategies on which
to actually base some of your trading strategies. *Day Trading the Currency Market* goes beyond what every other currency trading book covers
and delves into such interesting topics as "What are the most market moving indicators for the U.S. dollar?" and "What are currency correlations
and how do traders use them?"

Here's a brief road map to whet your appetite on the topics covered.

FOREIGN EXCHANGE—THE FASTEST-GROWING MARKET OF OUR TIME

If you are wondering whether you should get into the FX market, take a
look at some of the reasons why the largest market in the world has always been the market of choice for the big players such as hedge funds
and institutional investors. Learn about why the FX market has exploded
over the past three years and the advantages that the FX spot market has

over the more traditional equities and futures markets—something that the most seasoned traders of the world have known for decades.

HISTORICAL EVENTS IN THE FX MARKET

How can you trade the currency market without knowing some of the major milestones that helped to shape the market into what it has become today? There are countless events that are still talked about and brought up despite the many years that have passed since they occurred. This chapter covers Bretton Woods, the end of the Bretton Woods, the Plaza Accord, George Soros and how he came to fame, the Asian financial crisis, the launch of the euro, and the burst of the technology bubble.

WHAT MOVES THE CURRENCY MARKET IN THE LONG TERM?

What moves the currency market is probably one of the best questions to ask for new traders. Currency movements can be dissected into short-term and long-term movements. This chapter covers some of the more macro longer-term factors that impact currency prices. The reason why this chapter was thrown in is to keep traders from losing sight of the bigger picture and how these longer-term factors on both a technical and a fundamental basis will always come back into play regardless of the shorter-term fluctuations. We also explore the different valuation models for forecasting currency rates, which can help more quantitative fundamental traders to develop their own methodologies for predicting currency movements.

WHAT MOVES THE CURRENCY MARKET IN THE SHORT TERM?

For day traders, knowing which pieces of U.S. data move the market the most is extremely valuable. System traders need to know when it is worthwhile to turn their systems off, while breakout traders will want to know where to place their big bets based on what economic releases typically set off the largest movements. This section not only ranks the importance of U.S. data, but it also reports on the knee-jerk reaction in pip values and whether there is usually a follow-through over the remainder of the day.

WHAT ARE THE BEST TIMES TO TRADE FOR INDIVIDUAL CURRENCY PAIRS?

Timing is everything in currency trading. In order to devise an effective and time-efficient investment strategy, it is important to note the amount of market activity around the clock in order to maximize the number of trading opportunities during a trader's own market hours. This section outlines the typical trading activity of major currency pairs in different time zones to see when they are the most volatile.

WHAT ARE CURRENCY CORRELATIONS AND HOW DO TRADERS USE THEM?

Everything in the currency market is interrelated to some extent, and knowing the direction and how strong the relationships between different currency pairs are can be used to the advantage of all traders. When trading in the FX market, one of the most important facts to remember in creating a strategy is that no currency pair is isolated. Knowing how closely correlated the currency pairs are in your portfolio is a great way to measure exposure and risk. Many traders may find themselves thinking that they are diversifying their portfolios by investing in different currency pairs, but few realize that many pairs actually have a tendency to move in the same direction or opposite to each other historically. The correlations between pairs can be strong or weak and last for weeks, months, or even years, which makes learning how to use and calculate correlation data extremely important.

TRADE PARAMETERS FOR DIFFERENT MARKET CONDITIONS

The most important first step for any trader, regardless of the market that you are trading in, is to create a trading journal. However, the FX trading journal is not just any trading journal. Aside from the typical listing of your trade ideas and executed trades with targets and stops, the FX trading journal also teaches you how to create a currency pair checklist that takes approximately 10 minutes to fill out and gives you a near immediate insight on the exact technical picture for each currency pair. Trading effectively means having a game plan, and we systematically dissect a game plan for you in this chapter, teaching you how to first profile a trading environment and then know which indicators to apply for that trading environment.

TECHNICAL TRADING STRATEGIES

This is the meat of the book for advanced traders. This section covers some of my favorite trading strategies for day traders and swing traders. Each strategy comes with rules and examples. They run the gamut of "Fading the Double Zeros" to the "Inside Day Breakout Play." Many of these strategies exploit specific characteristics of the FX market that have been observed across time. There are strategies for all types of traders—range, trend, and breakout.

FUNDAMENTAL TRADING STRATEGIES

The fundamental strategies section is more for medium-term swing traders who go not for 15 to 20 points but for 150 to 200 points or more. This section will teach you how to trade off commodity prices, fixed-income instruments, option volatilities, and risk reversals. It also covers intervention-based trades, macro-event-driven trades, and the secret moneymaking strategy used by hedge funds between 2002 and 2004, which is the leveraged carry trade.

PROFILES AND UNIQUE CHARACTERISTICS OF MAJOR CURRENCY PAIRS

The final section of this book is probably one of the most valuable, since it goes over the unique characteristics of each major currency pair: when they are most active, what drives their price action, and which economic data releases are most important. A broad economic overview of each currency is given, and a look into the central bank's monetary policy practices.

Acknowledgments

Thank you to my wonderful team for their invaluable research and support:

Boris Schlossberg

Richard Lee

Sam Shenker

Melissa Tuzzolo

Daniel Chen

Bosco Cheng

Jenny Tang

Vincent Ortiz

John Kicklighter

Ehren Goossens

And others:

Kristian Kerr

Randal Nishina

The Entire Staff at FXCM

CHAPTER 1

Foreign Exchange— The Fastest- Growing Market of Our Time

The foreign exchange market is the generic term for the worldwide institutions that exist to exchange or trade currencies. Foreign exchange is often referred to as "forex" or "FX." The foreign exchange market is an over-the-counter (OTC) market, which means that there is no central exchange and clearinghouse where orders are matched. FX dealers and market makers around the world are linked to each other around the clock via telephone, computer, and fax, creating one cohesive market.

Over the past few years, currencies have become one of the most popular products to trade. No other market can claim a 57 percent surge in volume over a three-year time frame. According to the Triennial Central Bank Survey of the foreign exchange market conducted by the Bank for International Settlements and published in September 2004, daily trading volume hit a record of $1.9 trillion, up from $1.2 trillion (or $1.4 trillion at constant exchange rates) in 2001. This is estimated to be approximately 20 times larger than the daily trading volume of the New York Stock Exchange and the Nasdaq combined. Although there are many reasons that can be used to explain this surge in activity, one of the most interesting is that the timing of the surge in volume coincides fairly well with the emergence of online currency trading for the individual investor.

EFFECTS OF CURRENCIES ON STOCKS AND BONDS

It is not the advent of online currency trading alone that has helped to increase the overall market's volume. With the volatility in the currency markets over the past few years, many traders are also becoming more aware of the fact that currency movements also impact the stock and bond markets. Therefore, if stocks, bonds, and commodities traders want to make more educated trading decisions, it is important for them to follow the currency markets as well. The following are some of the examples of how currency movements impacted stock and bond market movements in the past.

EUR/USD and Corporate Profitability

For stock market traders, particularly those who invest in European corporations that export a tremendous amount of goods to the United States, monitoring exchange rates are essential to predicting earnings and corporate profitability. Throughout 2003 and 2004, European manufacturers complained extensively about the rapid rise in the euro and the weakness in the U.S. dollar. The main culprit for the dollar's sell-off at the time was the country's rapidly growing trade and budget deficits. This caused the EUR/USD (euro-to-dollar) exchange rate to surge, which took a significant toll on the profitability of European corporations because a higher exchange rate makes the goods of European exporters more expensive to U.S. consumers. In 2003, inadequate hedging shaved approximately 1 billion euros from Volkswagen's profits, while Dutch State Mines (DSM), a chemicals group, warned that a 1 percent move in the EUR/USD rate would reduce profits by between 7 million and 11 million euros. Unfortunately, inadequate hedging is still a reality in Europe, which makes monitoring the EUR/USD exchange rate even more important in forecasting the earnings and profitability of European exporters.

Nikkei and U.S. Dollar

Traders exposed to Japanese equities also need to be aware of the developments that are occurring in the U.S. dollar and how they affect the Nikkei rally. Japan has recently come out of 10 years of stagnation. During this time, U.S. mutual funds and hedge funds were grossly underweight Japanese equities. When the economy began to rebound, these funds rushed in to make changes to their portfolios for fear of missing a great opportunity to take advantage of Japan's recovery. Hedge funds borrowed a lot of dollars in order to pay for increased exposure, but the problem was that their borrowings are very sensitive to U.S. interest rates and the Federal Reserve's monetary policy tightening cycle. Increased borrowing costs for the dollar could derail the Nikkei's rally because higher rates will raise the dollar's financing costs. Yet with the huge current account deficit, the Fed might need to continue raising rates to increase the attractiveness of dollar-denominated assets. Therefore, continual rate hikes coupled with slowing growth in Japan may make it less profitable for funds to be overleveraged and overly exposed to Japanese stocks. As a result, how the U.S. dollar moves also plays a role in the future direction of the Nikkei.

George Soros

In terms of bonds, one of the most talked-about men in the history of the FX markets is George Soros. He is notorious for being "the man who broke the Bank of England." This is covered in more detail in our history section (Chapter 2), but in a nutshell, in 1990 the U.K. decided to join the Exchange Rate Mechanism (ERM) of the European Monetary System in order to take part in the low-inflationary yet stable economy generated by the Germany's central bank, which is also known as the Bundesbank. This alliance tied the pound to the deutsche mark, which meant that the U.K. was subject to the monetary policies enforced by the Bundesbank. In the early 1990s, Germany aggressively increased interest rates to avoid the inflationary effects related to German reunification. However, national pride and the commitment of fixing exchange rates within the ERM prevented the U.K. from devaluing the pound. On Wednesday, September 16, 1992, also known as Black Wednesday, George Soros leveraged the entire value of his fund ($1 billion) and sold $10 billion worth of pounds to bet against the Exchange Rate Mechanism. This essentially "broke" the Bank of England and forced the devaluation of its currency. In a matter of 24 hours, the British pound fell approximately 5 percent or 5,000 pips. The Bank of England promised to raise rates in order to tempt speculators to buy pounds. As a result, the bond markets also experienced tremendous volatility, with the one-month U.K. London Interbank Offered Rate (LIBOR) increasing 1 percent and then retracing the gain over the next 24 hours. If bond traders were completely oblivious to what was going on in the currency markets, they probably would have found themselves dumbstruck in the face of such a rapid gyration in yields.

Chinese Yuan Revaluation and Bonds

For U.S. government bond traders, there has also been a brewing issue that has made it imperative to learn to monitor the developments in the currency markets. Over the past few years, there has been a lot of speculation about the possible revaluation of the Chinese yuan. Despite strong economic growth and a trade surplus with many countries, China has artificially maintained its currency within a tight trading band in order to ensure the continuation of rapid growth and modernization. This has caused extreme opposition from manufacturers and government officials from countries around the world, including the United States and Japan. It is estimated that China's fixed exchange rate regime has artificially kept the yuan 15 percent to 40 percent below its true value. In order to maintain a weak currency and keep the exchange rate within a tight band, the Chinese government has to sell the yuan and buy U.S. dollars each time its currency appreciates above the band's upper limit. China then uses these dollars to purchase U.S. Treasuries. This practice has earned China the status of being the world's second largest holder of U.S. Treasuries. Its demand has kept U.S. interest rates at historical lows. Even though China has made some changes to their currency regime, since then, the overall revaluation was modest, which means more is set to come. More revaluation spells trouble for the U.S. bond market, since it means that a big buyer may be pulling away. An announcement of this sort could send yields soaring and prices tumbling. Therefore, in order for bond traders to effectively manage risk, it is also important for them to follow the developments in the currency markets so that a shock of this type does not catch them by surprise.

COMPARING THE FX MARKET WITH FUTURES AND EQUITIES

Traditionally FX has not been the most popular market to trade because access to the foreign exchange market was primarily restricted to hedge funds, Commodity Trading Advisors who manage large amounts of capital, major corporations, and institutional investors due to regulation, capital requirements, and technology. One of the primary reasons why the foreign exchange market has traditionally been the market of choice for these large players is because the risk that a trader takes is fully customizable. That is, one trader could use a hundred times leverage while another may choose to not be leveraged at all. However, in recent years many firms have opened up the foreign exchange market to retail traders, providing leveraged trading as well as free instantaneous execution platforms, charts, and real-time news. As a result, foreign exchange trading has surged in popularity, increasing its attractiveness as an alternative asset class to trade.

Many equity and futures traders have begun to add currencies into the mix of products that they trade or have even switched to trading currencies exclusively. The reason why this trend is emerging is because these traders are beginning to realize that there are many attractive attributes to trading FX over equities or futures.

FX versus Equities

Here are some of the key attributes of trading spot foreign exchange compared to the equities market.

FX Market Key Attributes

- Foreign exchange is the largest market in the world and has growing liquidity.
- There is 24-hour around-the-clock trading.
- Traders can profit in both bull and bear markets.
- Short selling is permitted without an uptick, and there are no trading curbs.
- Instant executable trading platform minimizes slippage and errors.
- Even though higher leverage increases risk, many traders see trading the FX market as getting more bang for the buck.

Equities Market Attributes

- There is decent market liquidity, but it depends mainly on the stock's daily volume.
- The market is available for trading only from 9:30 a.m. to 4:00 p.m. New York time with limited after-hours trading.
- The existence of exchange fees results in higher costs and commissions.
- There is an uptick rule to short stocks, which many day traders find frustrating.
- The number of steps involved in completing a trade increases slippage and error.

The volume and liquidity present in the FX market, one of the most liquid markets in the world, have allowed traders to access a 24-hour market with low transaction costs, high leverage, the ability to profit in both bull and bear markets, minimized error rates, limited slippage, and no trading curbs or uptick rules. Traders can implement in the FX market the same strategies that they use in analyzing the equity markets. For fundamental traders, countries can be analyzed like stocks. For technical traders, the FX market is perfect for technical analysis, since it is already the most commonly used analysis tool by professional traders. It is therefore important to take a closer look at the individual attributes of the FX market to really understand why this is such an attractive market to trade.

Around-the-Clock 24-Hour Market   One of the primary reasons why the FX market is popular is because for active traders it is the ideal market to trade. Its 24-hour nature offers traders instant access to the markets at all hours of the day for immediate response to global developments. This characteristic also gives traders the added flexibility of determining their trading day. Active day traders no longer have to wait for the equities market to open at 9:30 a.m. New York time to begin trading. If there is a significant announcement or development either domestically or overseas between 4:00 p.m. New York time and 9:30 a.m. New York time, most day traders will have to wait for the exchanges to open at 9:30 a.m. to place trades. By that time, in all likelihood, unless you have access to electronic communication networks (ECNs) such as Instinet for premarket trading, the market would have gapped up or gapped down against you. All of the professionals would have already priced in the event before the average trader can even access the market.

In addition, most people who want to trade also have a full-time job during the day. The ability to trade after hours makes the FX market a much more convenient market for all traders. Different times of the day will offer different trading opportunities as the global financial centers around the world are all actively involved in foreign exchange. With the FX market, trading after hours with a large online FX broker provides the same liquidity and spread as at any other time of day.

As a guideline, at 5:00 p.m. Sunday, New York time, trading begins as the markets open in Sydney, Australia. Then the Tokyo markets open at 7:00 p.m. New York time. Next, Singapore and Hong Kong open at 9:00 p.m. EST, followed by the European markets in Frankfurt (2:00 a.m.) and then London (3:00 a.m.). By 4:00 a.m. the European markets are in full swing, and Asia has concluded its trading day. The U.S. markets open first in New York around 8:00 a.m. Monday as Europe winds down. By 5:00 p.m., Sydney is set to reopen once again.

The most active trading hours are when the markets overlap; for example, Asia and Europe trading overlaps between 2:00 a.m. and approximately 4:00 a.m., Europe and the United States overlap between 8:00 a.m. and approximately 11:00 a.m., while the United States and Asia overlap between 5:00 p.m. and 9:00 p.m.. During New York and London hours all of the currency pairs trade actively, whereas during the Asian hours the trading activity for pairs such as the GBP/JPY and AUD/JPY tend to peak.

Lower Transaction Costs   The existence of much lower transaction costs also makes the FX market particularly attractive. In the equities market, traders must pay a spread (i.e., the difference between the buy and sell price) and/or a commission. With online equity brokers, commissions can run upwards of $20 per trade. With positions of $100,000, average round-trip commissions could be as high as $120. The over-the-counter structure of the FX market eliminates exchange and clearing fees, which in turn lowers transaction costs. Costs are further reduced by the efficiencies created by a purely electronic marketplace that allows clients to deal directly with the market maker, eliminating both ticket costs and middlemen. Because the currency market offers around-the-clock liquidity, traders receive tight competitive spreads both intraday and at night. Equities traders are more vulnerable to liquidity risk and typically receive wider dealing spreads, especially during after-hours trading.

Low transaction costs make online FX trading the best market to trade for short-term traders. For an active equity trader who typically places 30 trades a day, at a $20 commission per trade you would have to pay up to $600 in daily transaction costs. This is a significant amount of money that would definitely take a large cut out of profits or deepen losses. The reason why costs are so high is because there are several people involved in an equity transaction. More specifically, for each trade there is a broker, the exchange, and the specialist. All of these parties need to be paid, and their payment comes in the form of commission and clearing fees. In the FX market, because it is decentralized with no exchange or clearinghouse (everything is taken care of by the market maker), these fees are not applicable.

Customizable Leverage Even though many people realize that higher leverage comes with risks, traders are humans and few of them find it easy to turn away the opportunity to trade on someone else's money. The FX market caters perfectly to these traders by offering the highest leverage available for any market. Most online currency firms offer 100 times leverage on regular-sized accounts and up to 200 times leverage on the miniature accounts. Compare that to the 2 times leverage offered to the average equity investor and the 10 times capital that is typically offered to the professional trader, and you can see why many traders have turned to the foreign exchange market. The margin deposit for leverage in the FX market is not seen as a down payment on a purchase of equity, as many perceive margins to be in the stock markets. Rather, the margin is a performance bond, or good faith deposit, to ensure against trading losses. This is very useful to short-term day traders who need the enhancement in capital to generate quick returns. Leverage is actually customizable, which means that the more risk-averse investor who feels comfortable using only 10 or 20 times leverage or no leverage at all can elect to do so. However, leverage is really a double-edged sword. Without proper risk management a high degree of leverage can lead to large losses as well.

Profit in Both Bull and Bear Markets   In the FX market, profit potentials exist in both bull and bear markets. Since currency trading always involves buying one currency and selling another, there is no structural bias to the market. Therefore, if you are long one currency, you are also short another. As a result, profit potentials exist equally in both upward-trending and downward-trending markets. This is different from the equities market, where most traders go long instead of short stocks, so the general equity investment community tends to suffer in a bear market.

No Trading Curbs or Uptick Rule   The FX market is the largest market in the world, forcing market makers to offer very competitive prices. Unlike the equities market, there is never a time in the FX markets when trading curbs would take effect and trading would be halted, only to gap when reopened. This eliminates missed profits due to archaic exchange regulations. In the FX market, traders would be able to place trades 24 hours a day with virtually no disruptions.

One of the biggest annoyances for day traders in the equity market is the fact that traders are prohibited from shorting a stock in a downtrend unless there is an uptick. This can be very frustrating as traders wait to join short sellers but are only left with continually watching the stock trend down before an uptick occurs. In the FX market, there is no such rule. If you want to short a currency pair, you can do so immediately; this allows for instant and efficient execution.

Online Trading Reduces Error Rates   In general, a shorter trade process minimizes errors. Online currency trading is typically a three-step process. A trader would place an order on the platform, the FX dealing desk would automatically execute it electronically, and the order confirmation would be posted or logged on the trader's trading station. Typically, these three steps would be completed in a matter of seconds. For an equities trade, on the other hand, there is generally a five-step process. The client would call his or her broker to place an order, the broker sends the order to the exchange floor, the specialist on the floor tries to match up orders (the broker competes with other brokers to get the best fill for the client), the specialist executes the trade, and the client receives a confirmation from the broker. As a result, in currency trades the elimination of a middleman minimizes the error rates and increases the efficiency of each transaction.

Limited Slippage   Unlike the equity markets, many online FX market makers provide instantaneous execution from real-time, two-way quotes. These quotes are the prices at which the firms are willing to buy or sell the quoted currency, rather than vague indications of where the market is trading, which aren't honored. Orders are executed and confirmed within seconds. Robust systems would never request the size of a trader's potential order, or which side of the market he's trading, before giving a bid/offer quote. Inefficient dealers determine whether the investor is a buyer or a seller, and shade the price to increase their own profit on the transaction.

The equity market typically operates under a "next best order" system, under which you may not get executed at the price you wish, but rather at the next best price available. For example, let's say Microsoft is trading at $52.50. If you enter a buy order at this price, by the time it reaches the specialist on the exchange floor the price may have risen to $53.25. In this case, you will not get executed at $52.50; you will get executed at $53.25, which is essentially a loss of three-quarters of a point. The price transparency provided by some of the better market makers ensures that traders always receive a fair price.

Perfect Market for Technical Analysis For technical analysts, currencies rarely spend much time in tight trading ranges and have the tendency to develop strong trends. Over 80 percent of volume is speculative in nature, and as a result the market frequently overshoots and then corrects itself. Technical analysis works well for the FX market and a technically trained trader can easily identify new trends and breakouts, which provide multiple opportunities to enter and exit positions. Charts and indicators are used by all professional FX traders, and candlestick charts are available in most charting packages. In addition, the most commonly used indicators—such as Fibonacci retracements, stochastics, moving average convergence/divergence (MACD), moving averages, (RSI), and support/resistance levels—have proven valid in many instances.

In the GBP/USD chart in Figure 1.1, it is clear that Fibonacci retracements, moving averages, and stochastics have at one point or another given successful trading signals. For example, the 50 percent retracement level has served as support for the GBP/USD throughout the month of January and for a part of February 2005. The moving average crossovers of the 10-day and 20-day simple moving averages also successfully forecasted the sell-off in the GBP/USD on March 21, 2005. Equity traders who focus on technical analysis have the easiest transition since they can implement in the FX market the same technical strategies that they use in the equities market.

FIGURE 1.1 GBP/USD Chart
(*Source:* eSignal. www.eSignal.com)

Analyze Stocks Like Countries Trading currencies is not difficult for fundamental traders, either. Countries can be analyzed just like stocks. For example, if you analyze growth rates of stocks, you can use gross domestic product (GDP) to analyze the growth rates of countries. If you analyze inventory and production ratios, you can follow industrial production or durable goods data. If you follow sales figures, you can analyze retail sales data. As with a stock investment, it is better to invest in the currency of a country that is growing faster and is in a better economic condition than other countries. Currency prices reflect the balance of supply and demand for currencies. Two of the primary factors affecting supply and demand of currencies are interest rates and the overall strength of the economy. Economic indicators such as GDP, foreign investment, and the trade balance reflect the general health of an economy and are therefore responsible for the underlying shifts in supply and demand for that currency. There is a tremendous amount of data released at regular intervals, some of which is more important than others. Data related to interest rates and international trade is looked at the most closely.

If the market has uncertainty regarding interest rates, then any bit of news relating to interest rates can directly affect the currency market. Traditionally, if a country raises its interest rate, the currency of that country will strengthen in relation to other countries as investors shift assets to that country to gain a higher return. Hikes in interest rates are generally bad news for stock markets, however. Some investors will transfer money out of a country's stock market when interest rates are hiked, causing the country's currency to weaken. Determining which effect dominates can be tricky, but generally there is a consensus beforehand as to what the interest rate move will do. Indicators that have the biggest impact on interest rates are the producer price index (PPI), consumer price index (CPI), and GDP. Generally the timing of interest rate moves is known in advance. They take place after regularly scheduled meetings by the Bank of England (BOE), the U.S. Federal Reserve (Fed), the European Central Bank (ECB), the Bank of Japan (BOJ), and other central banks.

The trade balance shows the net difference over a period of time between a nation's exports and imports. When a country imports more than it exports the trade balance will show a deficit, which is generally considered unfavorable. For example, if U.S. dollars are sold for other domestic national currencies (to pay for imports), the flow of dollars outside the country will depreciate the value of the dollar. Similarly, if trade figures show an increase in exports, dollars will flow into the United States and appreciate the value of the dollar. From the standpoint of a national economy, a deficit in and of itself is not necessarily a bad thing. If the deficit is greater than market expectations, however, then it will trigger a negative price movement.

FX versus Futures

The FX market holds advantages over not only the equity market, but also the futures market. Many futures traders have added currency spot trading to their portfolios. After recapping the key spot foreign exchange attributes, we compare the futures attributes.

FX Market Key Attributes

- It is the largest market in the world and has growing liquidity.
- There is 24-hour around-the-clock trading.
- Traders can profit in both bull and bear markets.
- Short selling is permitted without an uptick, and there are no trading curbs.
- Instant executable trading platform minimizes slippage and errors.
- Even though higher leverage increases risk, many traders see trading the FX market as getting more bang for the buck.

Futures Attributes

- Market liquidity is limited, depending on the month of the contract traded.
- The presence of exchange fees results in more costs and commissions.
- Market hours for futures trading are much shorter than for spot FX and are dependent on the product traded; each product may have different opening and closing hours, and there is limited after-hours trading.
- Futures leverage is higher than leverage for equities, but still only a fraction of the leverage offered in FX.
- There tend to be prolonged bear markets.
- Pit trading structure increases error and slippage.

Like they can in the equities market, traders can implement in the FX market the same strategies that they use in analyzing the futures markets. Most futures traders are technical traders, and as mentioned in the equities section, the FX market is perfect for technical analysis. In fact, it is the most commonly used analysis tool by professional traders. Let's take a closer look at how the futures market stacks up against the FX market.

Comparing Market Hours and Liquidity   The volume traded in the FX market is estimated to be more than five times that of the futures market. The FX market is open for trading 24 hours a day, but the futures market has confusing market hours that vary based on the product traded. For example, trading gold futures is open only between 7:20 a.m. and 1:30 p.m. on the New York Commodities Exchange (COMEX), whereas if you trade crude oil futures on the New York Mercantile Exchange, trading is open only between 8:30 a.m. and 2:10 p.m. These varying hours not only create confusion, but also make it difficult to act on breakthrough announcements throughout the remainder of the day.

In addition, if you have a full-time job during the day and can trade only after hours, futures would be a very inconvenient market product for you to trade. You would basically be placing orders based on past prices and not current market prices. This lack of transparency makes trading very cumbersome. With the FX market, if you choose to trade after hours through the right market makers, you can be assured that you would receive the same liquidity and spread as at any other time of day. In addition, each time zone has its own unique news and developments that could move specific currency pairs.

Low to Zero Transaction Costs In the futures market, traders must pay a spread and/or a commission. With futures brokers, average commissions can run close to $160 per trade on positions of $100,000 or greater. The over-the-counter structure of the FX market eliminates exchange and clearing fees, which in turn lowers transaction costs. Costs are further reduced by the efficiencies created by a purely electronic marketplace that allows clients to deal directly with the market maker, eliminating both ticket costs and middlemen. Because the currency market offers around-the-clock liquidity, traders receive tight, competitive spreads both intraday and at night. Futures traders are more vulnerable to liquidity risk and typically receive wider dealing spreads, especially during after-hours trading.

Low to zero transaction costs make online FX trading the best market to trade for short-term traders. If you are an active futures trader who typically places 20 trades a day, at $100 commission per trade, you would have to pay $2,000 in daily transaction costs. A typical futures trade involves a broker, a Futures Commission Merchant (FCM) order desk, a clerk on the exchange floor, a runner, and a pit trader. All of these parties need to be paid, and their payment comes in the form of commission and clearing fees, whereas the electronic nature of the FX market minimizes these costs.

No Limit Up or Down Rules/Profit in Both Bull and Bear Markets There is no limit down or limit up rule in the FX market, unlike the tight restriction on the futures market. For example, on the S&P 500 index futures, if the contract value falls more than 5 percent from the previous day's close, limit down rules will come in effect whereby on a 5 percent move the index is allowed to trade only at or above this level for the next 10 minutes. For a 20 percent decline, trading would be completely halted. Due to the decentralized nature of the FX market, there are no exchange-enforced restrictions on daily activity. In effect, this eliminates missed profits due to archaic exchange regulations.

Execution Quality and Speed/Low Error Rates The futures market is also known for inconsistent execution in terms of both pricing and execution time. Every futures trader has at some point in time experienced a half hour or so wait for a market order to be filled, only to then be executed at a price that may be far away from where the market was trading when the initial order was placed. Even with electronic trading and limited guarantees of execution speed, the prices for fills on market orders are far from certain. The reason for this inefficiency is the number of steps that are involved in placing a futures trade. A futures trade is typically a seven-step process:

1. The client calls his or her broker and places a trade (or places it online).
2. The trading desk receives the order, processes it, and routes it to the FCM order desk on the exchange floor.
3. The FCM order desk passes the order to the order clerk.
4. The order clerk hands the order to a runner or signals it to the pit.
5. The trading clerk goes to the pit to execute the trade.
6. The trade confirmation goes to the runner or is signaled to the order clerk and processed by the FCM order desk.
7. The broker receives the trade confirmation and passes it on to the client.

An FX trade, in comparison, is typically only a three-step process. A trader would place an order on the platform, the FX dealing desk would automatically execute it electronically, and the order confirmation would be posted or logged on the trader's trading station. The elimination of the additional parties involved in a futures trade increases the speed of the FX trade execution and decreases errors.

In addition, the futures market typically operates under a "next best order" system, under which traders frequently do not get executed at the initial market order price, but rather at the next best price available. For example, let's say a client is long five March Dow Jones futures contracts at 8800 with a stop order at 8700; if the price falls to this level, the order will most likely be executed at 8690. This 10-point difference would be attributed to slippage, which is very common in the futures market.

On most FX trading stations, traders execute directly off of real-time streaming prices. Barring any unforeseen circumstances, there is generally no discrepancy between the displayed price and the execution price. This holds true even during volatile times and fast-moving markets. In the futures market, in contrast, execution is uncertain because all orders must be done on the exchange, creating a situation where liquidity is limited by the number of participants, which in turn limits quantities that can be traded at a given price. Real-time streaming prices ensure that FX market orders, stops, and limits are executed with minimal slippage and no partial fills.

WHO ARE THE PLAYERS IN THE FX MARKET?

Since the foreign exchange market is an over-the-counter (OTC) market without a centralized exchange, competition between market makers prohibits monopolistic pricing strategies. If one market maker attempts to drastically skew the price, then traders simply have the option to find another market maker. Moreover, spreads are closely watched to ensure market makers are not whimsically altering the cost of the trade. Many equity markets, in contrast, operate in a completely different fashion; the New York Stock Exchange (NYSE), for instance, is the sole place where companies listed on the NYSE can have their stocks traded. Centralized markets are operated by what are referred to as *specialists*, while *market makers* is the term used in reference to decentralized marketplaces. (See Figures 1.2 and 1.3.) Since the NYSE is a centralized market, a stock traded on the NYSE can have only 1 bid/ask quote at all times. Decentralized markets, such as foreign exchange, can have multiple market makers—all of whom have the right to quote different prices. Let's look at how both centralized and decentralized markets operate.

Centralized Markets

By their very nature, centralized markets tend to be monopolistic: with a single specialist controlling the market, prices can easily be skewed to accommodate the interests of the specialist, not those of the traders. If, for example, the market is filled with sellers from whom the specialists must buy but no prospective buyers on the other side, the specialists will be forced to buy from the sellers and be unable to sell a commodity that is

FIGURE 1.2 Centralized Market Structure

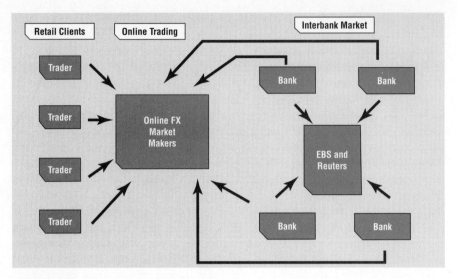

FIGURE 1.3 Decentralized Market Structure

being sold off and hence falling in value. In such a situation, the specialist may simply widen the spread, thereby increasing the cost of the trade and preventing additional participants from entering the market. Or specialists can simply drastically alter the quotes they are offering, thus manipulating the price to accommodate their own needs.

Hierarchy of Participants in Decentralized Market

While the foreign exchange market is decentralized and hence employs multiple market makers rather than a single specialist, participants in the FX market are organized into a hierarchy; those with superior credit access, volume transacted, and sophistication receive priority in the market.

At the top of the food chain is the interbank market, which trades the highest volume per day in relatively few (mostly G-7) currencies. In the interbank market, the largest banks can deal with each other directly, via interbank brokers or through electronic brokering systems like Electronic Brokering Services (EBS) or Reuters. The interbank market is a credit-approved system where banks trade based solely on the credit relationships they have established with one another. All the banks can see the rates everyone is dealing at; however, each bank must have a specific credit relationship with another bank in order to trade at the rates being offered.

Other institutions such as online FX market makers, hedge funds, and corporations must trade FX through commercial banks.

Many banks (small community banks, banks in emerging markets), corporations, and institutional investors do not have access to these rates because they have no established credit lines with big banks. This forces small participants to deal through just one bank for their foreign exchange needs, and often this means much less competitive rates for the participants further down the participant hierarchy. Those receiving the least competitive rates are customers of banks and exchange agencies.

Recently technology has broken down the barriers that used to stand between the end users of foreign exchange services and the interbank market. The online trading revolution opened its doors to retail clientele by connecting market makers and market participants in an efficient, low-cost manner. In essence, the online trading platform serves as a gateway to the liquid FX market. Average traders can now trade alongside the biggest banks in the world, with similar pricing and execution. What used to be a game dominated and controlled by the big boys is slowly becoming a level playing field where individuals can profit and take advantage of the same opportunities as big banks. FX is no longer an old boys club, which means opportunity abounds for aspiring online currency traders.

Dealing Stations—Interbank Market   The majority of FX volume is transacted primarily through the interbank market. The leading banks of the world trade with each other electronically over two platforms—the EBS and Reuters Dealing 3000-Spot Matching. Both platforms offer trading in the major currency pairs; however, certain currency pairs are more liquid and generally more frequently traded over either EBS or Reuters D3000. These two companies are continually trying to capture each other's market shares, but as a guide, here is the breakdown of which currencies are most liquid over the individual platforms:

EBS	**Reuters**
EUR/USD	GBP/USD
USD/JPY	EUR/GBP
EUR/JPY	USD/CAD
EUR/CHF	AUD/USD
USD/CHF	NZD/USD

Cross-currency pairs are generally not traded over either platform, but instead are calculated based on the rates of the major currency pairs and then offset using the "legs." For example, if an interbank trader had a client who wanted to go long AUD/JPY, the trader would most likely buy AUD/USD over the Reuters D3000 system and buy USD/JPY over EBS. The trader would then multiply these rates and provide the client with the respective AUD/JPY rate. These currency pairs are also known as synthetic currencies, and this helps to explain why spreads for cross currencies are generally wider than spreads for the major currency pairs.

CHAPTER 2

Historical Events in the FX Market

Before diving into the inner workings of currency trading, it is important for every trader to understand a few of the key milestones in the foreign exchange market, since even to this day they still represent events that are referenced repeatedly by professional forex traders.

BRETTON WOODS: ANOINTING THE DOLLAR AS THE WORLD CURRENCY (1944)

In July 1944, representatives of 44 nations met in Bretton Woods, New Hampshire, to create a new institutional arrangement for governing the international economy in the years after World War II. After the war, most agreed that international economic instability was one of the principal causes of the war, and that such instability needed to be prevented in the future. The agreement, which was developed by renowned economists John Maynard Keynes and Harry Dexter White, was initially proposed to Great Britain as a part of the Lend-Lease Act—an American act designed to assist Great Britain in postwar redevelopment efforts. After various negotiations, the final form of the Bretton Woods Agreement consisted of several key points:

1. The formation of key international authorities designed to promote fair trade and international economic harmony.

2. The fixing of exchange rates among currencies.

3. The convertibility between gold and the U.S. dollar, thus empowering the U.S. dollar as the reserve currency of choice for the world.

Of the three aforementioned parameters, only the first point is still in existence today. The organizations formed as a direct result of Bretton Woods include the International Monetary Fund (IMF), World Bank, and General Agreement on Tariffs and Trade (GATT), which are still in existence today and play a crucial role in the development and regulation of international economies. The IMF, for instance, initially enforced the price of $35 per ounce of gold that was to be fixed under the Bretton Woods system, as well as the fixing of exchange rates that occurred while Bretton Woods was in operation (and the financing required to ensure that fixed exchange rates would not create fundamental distortions in the international economy).

Since the demise of Bretton Woods, the IMF has worked closely with another progeny of Bretton Woods: the World Bank. Together, the two institutions now regularly lend funds to developing nations, thus assisting them in the development of a public infrastructure capable of supporting a sound mercantile economy that can contribute in an international arena. And, in order to ensure that these nations can actually enjoy equal and legitimate access to trade with their industrialized counterparts, the World Bank and IMF must work closely with GATT. While GATT was initially meant to be a temporary organization, it now operates to encourage the dismantling of trade barriers—namely tariffs and quotas.

The Bretton Woods Agreement was in operation from 1944 to 1971, when it was replaced with the Smithsonian Agreement, an international contract of sorts pioneered by U.S. President Richard Nixon out of the necessity to accommodate for Bretton Woods' shortcomings. Unfortunately, the Smithsonian Agreement possessed the same critical weakness: while it did not include gold/U.S. dollar convertibility, it did maintain fixed exchange rates—a facet that did not accommodate the ongoing U.S. trade deficit and the international need for a weaker U.S. dollar. As a result, the Smithsonian Agreement was short-lived.

Ultimately, the exchange rates of the world evolved into a free market, whereby supply and demand were the sole criteria that determined the value of a currency. While this did and still does result in a number of currency crises and greater volatility between currencies, it also allowed the market to become self-regulating, and thus the market could dictate the appropriate value of a currency without any hindrances.

As for Bretton Woods, perhaps its most memorable contribution to the international economic arena was its role in changing the perception regarding the U.S. dollar. While the British pound is still substantially stronger, and while the euro is a revolutionary currency blazing new frontiers in both social behavior and international trade, the U.S. dollar remains the world's reserve currency of choice for the time being. This is undeniably due largely in part to the Bretton Woods Agreement: by establishing dollar/gold convertibility, the dollar's role as the world's most accessible and reliable currency was firmly cemented. And thus, while Bretton Woods may be a doctrine of yesteryear, its impact on the U.S. dollar and international economics still resonates today.

END OF BRETTON WOODS: FREE MARKET CAPITALISM IS BORN (1971)

On August 15, 1971, it became official: the Bretton Woods system, a system used to fix the value of a currency to the value of gold, was abandoned once and for all. While it had been exorcised before, only to subsequently emerge in a new form, this final eradication of the Bretton Woods system was truly its last stand: no longer would currencies be fixed in value to gold, allowed to fluctuate only in a 1 percent range, but instead their fair valuation could be determined by free market behavior such as trade flows and foreign direct investment.

While U.S. President Nixon was confident that the end of the Bretton Woods system would bring about better times for the international economy, he was not a believer that the free market could dictate a currency's true valuation in a fair and catastrophe-free manner. Nixon, as well as most economists, reasoned that an entirely unstructured foreign exchange market would result in competing devaluations, which in turn would lead to the breakdown of international trade and investment. The end result, Nixon and his board of economic advisers reasoned, would be global depression.

Accordingly, a few months later, the Smithsonian Agreement was introduced. Hailed by President Nixon as the "greatest monetary agreement in the history of the world," the Smithsonian Agreement strived to maintain fixed exchange rates, but to do so without the backing of gold. Its key difference from the Bretton Woods system was that the value of the dollar could float in a range of 2.25 percent, as opposed to just 1 percent under Bretton Woods.

Ultimately, the Smithsonian Agreement proved to be unfeasible as well. Without exchange rates fixed to gold, the free market gold price shot up to \$215 per ounce. Moreover, the U.S. trade deficit continued to grow, and from a fundamental standpoint, the U.S. dollar needed to be devalued beyond the 2.25 percent parameters established by the Smithsonian Agreement. In light of these problems, the foreign exchange markets were forced to close in February 1972.

The forex markets reopened in March 1973, and this time they were not bound by a Smithsonian Agreement: the value of the U.S. dollar was to be determined entirely by the market, as its value was not fixed to any commodity, nor was its exchange rate fluctuation confined to certain parameters. While this did provide the U.S. dollar, and other currencies by default, the agility required to adapt to a new and rapidly evolving international trading environment, it also set the stage for unprecedented inflation. The end of Bretton Woods and the Smithsonian Agreement, as well as conflicts in the Middle East resulting in substantially higher oil prices, helped to create stagflation—the synthesis of unemployment and inflation—in the U.S. economy. It would not be until later in the decade, when Federal Reserve Chairman Paul Volcker initiated new economic policies and President Ronald Reagan introduced a new fiscal agenda, that the U.S. dollar would return to normal valuations. And by then, the foreign exchange markets had thoroughly developed, and were now capable of serving a multitude of purposes: in addition to employing a laissez-faire style of regulation for international trade, they also were beginning to attract speculators seeking to participate in a market with unrivaled liquidity and continued growth. Ultimately, the death of Bretton Woods in 1971 marked the beginning of a new economic era, one that liberated international trading while also proliferating speculative opportunities.

PLAZA ACCORD—DEVALUATION OF U.S. DOLLAR (1985)

After the demise of all the various exchange rate regulatory mechanisms that characterized the twentieth century—the gold standard, the Bretton Woods standard, and the Smithsonian Agreement—the currency market was left with virtually no regulation other than the mythical "invisible hand" of free market capitalism, one that supposedly strived to create economic balance through supply and demand. Unfortunately, due to a number of unforeseen economic events—such as the Organization of Petroleum Exporting Countries (OPEC) oil crises, stagflation throughout the 1970s, and drastic changes in the U.S. Federal Reserve's fiscal policy—supply and demand, in and of themselves, became insufficient means by which the currency markets could be regulated. A system of sorts was needed, but not one that was inflexible. Fixation of currency values to a commodity, such as gold, proved to be too rigid for economic development, as was also the notion of fixing maximum exchange rate fluctuations. The balance between structure and rigidity was one that had plagued the currency markets throughout the twentieth century, and while advancements had been made, a definitive solution was still greatly needed.

And hence in 1985, the respective ministers of finance and central bank governors of the world's leading economies—France, Germany, Japan, the United Kingdom, and the United States—convened in New York City with the hopes of arranging a diplomatic agreement of sorts that would work to optimize the economic effectiveness of the foreign exchange markets. Meeting at the Plaza Hotel, the international leaders came to certain agreements regarding specific economies and the international economy as a whole.

Across the world, inflation was at very low levels. In contrast to the stagflation of the 1970s—where inflation was high and real economic growth was low—the global economy in 1985 had done a complete 180-degree turn, as inflation was now low but growth was strong.

While low inflation, even when coupled with robust economic growth, still allowed for low interest rates—a circumstance developing countries particularly enjoyed—there was an imminent danger of protectionist policies like tariffs entering the economy. The United States was experiencing a large and growing current account deficit, while Japan and Germany were facing large and growing surpluses. An imbalance so fundamental in nature could create serious economic disequilibrium, which in turn would result in a distortion of the foreign exchange markets and thus the international economy.

The results of current account imbalances, and the protectionist policies that ensued, required action. Ultimately, it was believed that the rapid acceleration in the value of the U.S. dollar, which appreciated more than 80 percent against the currencies of its major trading partners, was the primary culprit. The rising value of the U.S. dollar helped to create enormous trade deficits. A dollar with a lower valuation, on the other hand, would be more conducive to stabilizing the international economy, as it would naturally bring about a greater balance between the exporting and importing capabilities of all countries.

At the meeting in the Plaza Hotel, the United States persuaded the other attendees to coordinate a multilateral intervention, and on September 22, 1985, the Plaza Accord was implemented. This agreement was designed to allow for a controlled decline of the dollar and the appreciation of the main antidollar currencies. Each country agreed to changes to its economic policies and to intervene in currency markets as necessary to get the dollar down. The United States agreed to cut its budget deficit and to lower interest rates. France, the United Kingdom, Germany, and Japan all agreed to raise interest rates. Germany also agreed to institute tax cuts while Japan agreed to let the value of the yen "fully reflect the underlying strength of the Japanese economy." However, the problem with the actual implementation of the Plaza Accord was that not every country adhered to its pledges. The United States in particular did not follow through with its initial promise to cut the budget deficit. Japan was severely hurt by the sharp rise in the yen, as its exporters were unable to remain competitive overseas, and it is argued that this eventually triggered a 10-year recession in Japan. The United States, in contrast, enjoyed considerable growth and price stability as a result of the agreement.

The effects of the multilateral intervention were seen immediately, and within two years the dollar had fallen 46 percent and 50 percent against the deutsche mark (DEM) and the Japanese yen (JPY), respectively. Figure 2.1 shows this depreciation of the U.S. dollar against the DEM and the JPY. The U.S. economy became far more export-oriented as a result, while other industrial countries like Germany and Japan as-

FIGURE 2.1 Plaza Accord Price Action

sumed the role of importing. This gradually resolved the current account deficits for the time being, and also ensured that protectionist policies were minimal and nonthreatening. But perhaps most importantly, the Plaza Accord cemented the role of the central banks in regulating exchange rate movement: yes, the rates would not be fixed, and hence would be determined primarily by supply and demand; but ultimately, such an invisible hand is insufficient, and it was the right and responsibility of the world's central banks to intervene on behalf of the international economy when necessary.

GEORGE SOROS—THE MAN WHO BROKE THE BANK OF ENGLAND

When George Soros placed a $10 billion speculative bet against the U.K. pound and won, he became universally known as "the man who broke the Bank of England." Whether you love him or hate him, Soros led the charge in one of the most fascinating events in currency trading history.

The United Kingdom Joins the Exchange Rate Mechanism

In 1979, a Franco-German initiative set up the European Monetary System (EMS) in order to stabilize exchange rates, reduce inflation, and prepare for monetary integration. The Exchange Rate Mechanism (ERM), one of the EMS's main components, gave each participatory currency a central exchange rate against a basket of currencies, the European Currency Unit (ECU). Participants (initially France, Germany, Italy, the Netherlands, Belgium, Denmark, Ireland, and Luxembourg) were then required to maintain their exchange rates within a 2.25 percent fluctuation band above or below each bilateral central rate. The ERM was an adjustable-peg system, and nine realignments would occur between 1979 and 1987. While the United Kingdom was not one of the original members, it would eventually join in 1990 at a rate of 2.95 deutsche marks to the pound and with a fluctuation band of +/– 6 percent.

Until mid-1992, the ERM appeared to be a success, as a disciplinary effect had reduced inflation throughout Europe under the leadership of the German Bundesbank. The stability wouldn't last, however, as international investors started worrying that the exchange rate values of several currencies within the ERM were inappropriate. Following German reunification in 1989, the nation's government spending surged, forcing the Bundesbank to print more money. This led to higher inflation and left the German central bank with little choice but to increase interest rates. But the rate hike had additional repercussions—because it placed upward pressure on the German mark. This forced other central banks to raise their interest rates as well, so as to maintain the pegged currency exchange rates (a direct application of Irving Fisher's interest rate parity theory). Realizing that the United Kingdom's weak economy and high unemployment rate would not permit the British government to maintain this policy for long, George Soros stepped into action.

Soros Bets Against Success of U.K. Involvement in ERM

The Quantum hedge fund manager essentially wanted to bet that the pound would depreciate because the United Kingdom would either devalue the pound or leave the ERM. Thanks to the progressive removal of capital controls during the EMS years, international investors at the time had more freedom than ever to take advantage of perceived disequilibriums, so Soros established short positions in pounds and long positions in marks by borrowing pounds and investing in mark-denominated assets. He also made great use of options and futures. In all, his positions accounted for a gargantuan $10 billion. Soros was not the only one; many other investors soon followed suit. Everyone was selling pounds, placing tremendous downward pressure on the currency.

At first, the Bank of England tried to defend the pegged rates by buying 15 billion pounds with its large reserve assets, but its sterilized interventions (whereby the monetary base is held constant thanks to open market interventions) were limited in their effectiveness. The pound was trading dangerously close to the lower levels of its fixed band. On September 16, 1992, a day that would later be known as Black Wednesday, the bank announced a 2 percent rise in interest rates (from 10 percent to 12 percent) in an attempt to boost the pound's appeal. A few hours later, it promised to raise rates again, to 15 percent, but international investors such as Soros could not be swayed, knowing that huge profits were right around the corner. Traders kept selling pounds in huge volumes, and the Bank of England kept buying them until, finally, at 7:00 p.m. that same day, Chancellor Norman Lamont announced Britain would leave the ERM and that rates would return to their initial level of 10 percent. The chaotic Black Wednesday marked the beginning of a steep depreciation in the pound's effective value.

Whether the return to a floating currency was due to the Soros-led attack on the pound or because of simple fundamental analysis is still debated today. What is certain, however, is that the pound's depreciation of almost 15 percent against the deutsche mark and 25 percent against the dollar over the next five weeks (as seen in Figure 2.2 and Figure 2.3) resulted in tremendous profits for Soros and other traders. Within a month, the Quantum Fund cashed in on approximately $2 billion by selling the now more expensive deutsche marks and buying back the now cheaper pounds. "The man who broke the Bank of England" showed how central banks can still be vulnerable to speculative attacks.

ASIAN FINANCIAL CRISIS (1997–1998)

Falling like a set of dominos on July 2, 1997, the relatively nascent Asian tiger economies created a perfect example in showing the interdependence of global capital markets and their subsequent effects throughout international currency forums. Based on several fundamental breakdowns, the cause of the contagion stemmed largely from shrouded lending practices, inflated trade deficits, and immature capital markets. Added together, the factors contributed to a "perfect storm"

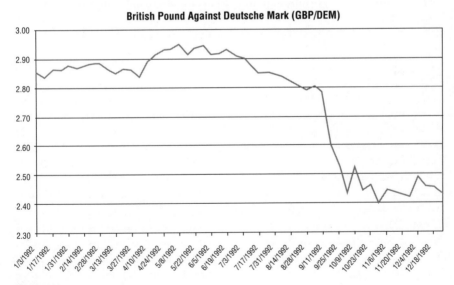

FIGURE 2.2 GBP/DEM After Soros

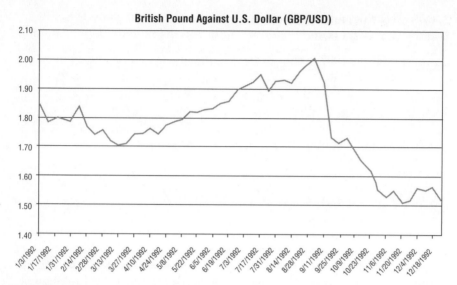

FIGURE 2.3 GBP/USD After Soros

that left major regional markets incapacitated and once-prized currencies devalued to significantly lower levels. With adverse effects easily seen in the equities markets, currency market fluctuations were negatively impacted in much the same manner during this time period.

The Bubble

Leading up to 1997, investors had become increasingly attracted to Asian investment prospects, focusing on real estate development and domestic equities. As a result, foreign investment capital flowed into the region as economic growth rates climbed on improved production in countries like Malaysia, the Philippines, Indonesia, and South Korea. Thailand, home of the baht, experienced a 13 percent growth rate in 1988 (falling to 6.5 percent in 1996). Additional lending support for a stronger economy came from the enactment of a fixed currency peg to the more formidable U.S. dollar. With a fixed valuation to the greenback, countries like Thailand could ensure financial stability in their own markets and a constant rate for export trading purposes with the world's largest economy. Ultimately, the region's national currencies appreciated as underlying fundamentals were justified, and speculative positions in expectation of further climbs in price mounted.

Ballooning Current Account Deficits and Nonperforming Loans

However, in early 1997, a shift in sentiment had begun to occur as international account deficits became increasingly difficult for respective governments to handle and lending practices were revealed to be detrimental to the economic infrastructure. In particular, economists were alerted to the fact that Thailand's current account deficit had ballooned in 1996 to $14.7 billion (it had been climbing since 1992). Although comparatively smaller than the U.S. deficit, the gap represented 8 percent of the country's gross domestic product. Shrouded lending practices also contributed heavily to these breakdowns, as close personal relationships of borrowers with high-ranking banking officials were well rewarded and surprisingly common throughout the region. This aspect affected many of South Korea's highly leveraged conglomerates as total nonperforming loan values skyrocketed to 7.5 percent of gross domestic product.

Additional evidence of these practices could be observed in financial institutions throughout Japan. After announcing a $136 billion total in questionable and nonperforming loans in 1994, Japanese authorities admitted to an alarming $400 billion total a year later. Coupled with a then crippled stock market, cooling real estate values, and dramatic slowdowns in the economy, investors saw opportunity in a depreciating yen, subsequently adding selling pressure to neighbor currencies. When Japan's asset bubble collapsed, asset prices fell by $10 trillion, with the fall in real estate prices accounting for nearly 65 percent of the total decline, which was worth two years of national output. This fall in asset prices sparked the banking crisis in Japan. It began in the early 1990s and then developed into a full-blown systemic crisis in 1997 following the failure of a number of high-profile financial institutions. In response, Japanese monetary authorities warned of potentially increasing benchmark interest rates in hopes of defending the domestic currency valuation. Unfortunately, these considerations never materialized and a shortfall ensued. Sparked mainly by an announcement of a managed float of the Thai baht, the slide snowballed as central bank reserves evaporated and currency price levels became unsustainable in light of downside selling pressure.

Currency Crisis

Following mass short speculation and attempted intervention, the aforementioned Asian economies were left ruined and momentarily incapacitated. The Thailand baht, once a prized possession, was devalued by as much as 48 percent, even slumping closer to a 100 percent fall at the turn of the New Year. The most adversely affected was the Indonesian rupiah. Relatively stable prior to the onset of a "crawling peg" with the Thai baht, the rupiah fell a whopping 228 percent from its previous high of 12,950 to the fixed U.S. dollar. These particularly volatile price actions are reflected in Figure 2.4. Among the majors, the Japanese yen fell approximately 23 percent from its high to its low against the U.S. dollar in 1997 and 1998, as shown in Figure 2.5.

The financial crisis of 1997–1998 revealed the interconnectivity of economies and their effects on the global currency markets. Additionally, it showed the inability of central banks to successfully intervene in currency valuations when confronted with overwhelming market forces along with the absence of secure economic fundamentals. Today, with the assistance of IMF reparation packages and the implementation of stricter requirements, Asia's four little dragons are churning away once again. With inflationary benchmarks and a revived exporting market, Southeast Asia is building back its once prominent stature among the world's industrialized economic regions. With the experience of evaporating currency reserves under their belts, the Asian tigers now take active initiatives to ensure that they have a large pot of reserves on hand in case speculators attempt to attack their currencies once again.

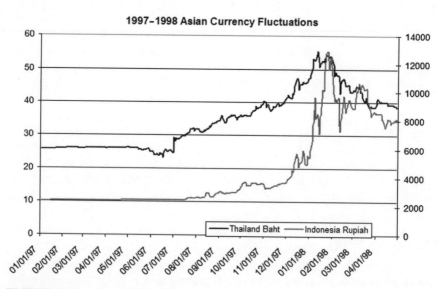

FIGURE 2.4 Asian Crisis Price Action

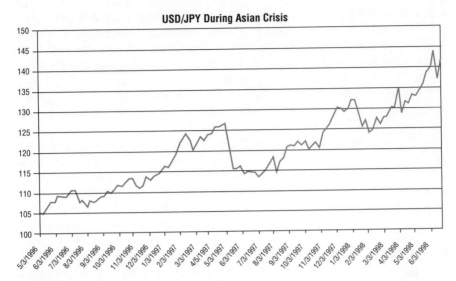

FIGURE 2.5 USD/JPY Asian Crisis Price Action

INTRODUCTION OF THE EURO (1999)

The introduction of the euro was a monumental achievement, marking the largest monetary changeover ever. The euro was officially launched as an electronic trading currency on January 1, 1999. The 11 initial member states of the European Monetary Union (EMU) were: Belgium, Germany, Spain, France, Ireland, Italy, Luxembourg, the Netherlands, Austria, Portugal, and Finland. Greece joined two years later. Each country fixed its currency to a specific conversion rate against the euro, and a common monetary policy governed by the European Central Bank (ECB) was adopted. To many economists, the system would ideally include all of the original 15 European Union (EU) nations, but the United Kingdom, Sweden, and Denmark decided to keep their own currencies for the time being. Euro notes and coins did not begin circulation until the first two months of 2002. In deciding whether to adopt the euro, EU members all had to weigh the pros and cons of such an important decision.

While ease of traveling is perhaps the most salient issue to EMU citizens, the euro also brings about numerous other benefits:

- It eliminates exchange rate fluctuations, thereby providing a more stable environment to trade within the euro area.

- The purging of all exchange rate risk within the zone allows businesses to plan investment decisions with greater certainty.
- Transaction costs diminish (mainly those relating to foreign exchange operations, hedging operations, cross-border payments, and the management of several currency accounts).
- Prices become more transparent as consumers and businesses can compare prices across countries more easily. This, in turn, increases competition.
- The huge single currency market becomes more attractive for foreign investors.
- The economy's magnitude and stability allow the ECB to control inflation with lower interest rates thanks to increased credibility.

Yet the euro is not without its limitations. Leaving aside political sovereignty issues, the main problem is that, by adopting the euro, a nation essentially forfeits any independent monetary policy. Since each country's economy is not perfectly correlated to the EMU's economy, a nation might find the ECB hiking interest rates during a domestic recession. This is especially true for many of the smaller nations. As a result, countries try to rely more heavily on fiscal policy, but the efficiency of fiscal policy is limited when it is not effectively combined with monetary policy. This inefficiency is only further exacerbated by the 3 percent of GDP limit on budget deficits, as stipulated by the Stability and Growth Pact.

Some concerns also exist regarding the ECB's effectiveness as a central bank. While its target inflation is slightly below 2 percent, the euro area's inflation edged above the benchmark from 2000 to 2002, and has of late continued to surpass the self-imposed objective. From 1999 to late 2002, a lack of confidence in the union's currency (and in the union itself) led to a 24 percent depreciation, from approximately $1.15 to the dollar in January 1999 to $0.88 in May 2000, forcing the ECB to intervene in foreign exchange markets in the last few months of 2000. Since then, however, things have greatly changed; the euro now trades at a premium to the dollar, and many analysts claim that the euro will someday replace the dollar as the world's dominant international currency. (Figure 2.6 shows a chart of the euro since it was launched in 1999.)

There are 10 more members slated to adopt the euro over the next few years. The enlargement, which will grow the EMU's population by one-fifth, is both a political and an economic landmark event: Of the new entrants, all but two are former Soviet republics, joining the EU after 15 years of restructuring. Once assimilated, these countries will become part of the world's largest free trade zone, a bloc of 450 million people. Consequently, the three largest accession countries, Poland, Hungary, and the

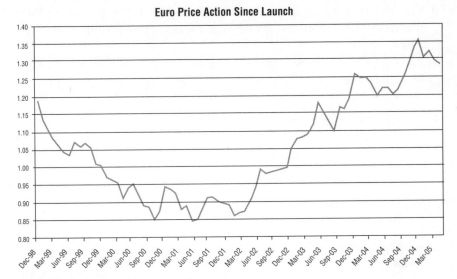

FIGURE 2.6 EUR/USD Price Since Launch

Czech Republic—which comprise 79 percent of new member combined GDP—are not likely to adopt the euro anytime soon. While euro members are mandated to cap fiscal deficits at 3 percent of GDP, each of these three countries currently runs a projected deficit at or near 6 percent. In a probable scenario, euro entry for Poland, Hungary, and the Czech Republic are likely to be delayed until 2009 at the earliest. Even smaller states whose economies at present meet EU requirements face a long process in replacing their national currencies. States that already maintain a fixed euro exchange rate—Estonia and Lithuania—could participate in the ERM earlier, but even on this relatively fast track, they would not be able to adopt the euro until 2007.

The 1993 the Maastricht Treaty set five main convergence criteria for member states to join the EMU.

Maastricht Treaty: Convergence Criteria

1. The country's government budget deficit could not be greater than 3 percent of GDP.
2. The country's government debt could not be larger than 60 percent of GDP.
3. The country's exchange rate had to be maintained within ERM bands without any realignment for two years prior to joining.

4. The country's inflation rate could not be higher than 1.5 percent above the average inflation rate of the three EU countries with the lowest inflation rates.

5. The country's long-term interest rate on government bonds could not be higher than 2 percent above the average of the comparable rates in the three countries with the lowest inflation.

CHAPTER 3

What Moves the Currency Market in the Long Term?

T here are two major ways to analyze financial markets: fundamental analysis and technical analysis. Fundamental analysis is based on underlying economic conditions, while technical analysis uses historical prices in an effort to predict future movements. Ever since technical analysis first surfaced, there has been an ongoing debate as to which methodology is more successful. Short-term traders prefer to use technical analysis, focusing their strategies primarily on price action, while medium-term traders tend to use fundamental analysis to determine a currency's proper valuation, as well as its probable future valuation.

Before implementing successful trading strategies, it is important to understand what drives the movements of currencies in the foreign exchange market. The best strategies tend to be the ones that combine both fundamental and technical analysis. Too often perfect technical formations have failed because of major fundamental events. The same occurs with fundamentals; there may be sharp gyrations in price action one day on the back of no economic news released, which suggests that the price action is random or based on nothing more than pattern formations. Therefore, it is very important for technical traders to be aware of the key economic data or events that are scheduled for release and, in turn, for fundamental traders to be aware of important technical levels on which the general market may be focusing.

FUNDAMENTAL ANALYSIS

Fundamental analysis focuses on the economic, social, and political forces that drive supply and demand. Those using fundamental analysis as a trading tool look at various macroeconomic indicators such as growth rates, interest rates, inflation, and unemployment. We list the most important economic releases in Chapter 10 as well as the most market-moving pieces of data for the U.S. dollar in Chapter 4. Fundamental analysts will combine all of this information to assess current and future performance. This requires a great deal of work and thorough analysis, as there is no single set of beliefs that guides fundamental analysis. Traders employing fundamental analysis need to continually keep abreast of news and announcements that can indicate potential changes to the economic, social, and political environment. All traders should have some awareness of the broad economic conditions before placing trades. This is especially important for day traders who are trying to make trading decisions based on news events because even though Federal Reserve monetary policy decisions are always important, if the rate move is already completely priced into the market, then the actual reaction in the EUR/USD, say, could be nominal.

Taking a step back, currency prices move primarily based on supply and demand. That is, on the most fundamental level, a currency rallies because there is demand for that currency. Regardless of whether the demand is for hedging, speculative, or conversion purposes, true movements are based on the need for the currency. Currency values decrease when there is excess supply. Supply and demand should be the real determinants for predicting future movements. However, how to predict supply and demand is not as simple as many would think. There are many factors that contribute to the net supply and demand for a currency, such as capital flows, trade flows, speculative needs, and hedging needs.

For example, the U.S. dollar was very strong (against the euro) from 1999 to the end of 2001, a situation primarily driven by the U.S. Internet and equity market boom and the desire for foreign investors to participate in these elevated returns. This demand for U.S. assets required foreign investors to sell their local currencies and purchase U.S. dollars. Since the end of 2001, when geopolitical uncertainty rose, the United States started cutting interest rates and foreign investors began to sell U.S. assets in search of higher yields elsewhere. This required foreign investors to sell U.S. dollars, increasing supply and lowering the dollar's value against other major currencies. The availability of funding or interest in buying a currency is a major factor that can impact the direction that a currency trades. It has been a primary determinant for the U.S. dollar between 2002 and 2005. Foreign official purchases of U.S. assets (also known as the Treasury international capital flow or TIC data) have become one of the most important economic indicators anticipated by the markets.

Capital and Trade Flows

Capital flows and trade flows constitute a country's balance of payments, which quantifies the amount of demand for a currency over a given period of time. Theoretically, a balance of payments equal to zero is required for a currency to maintain its current valuation. A negative balance of payments number indicates that capital is leaving the economy at a more rapid rate than it is entering, and hence theoretically the currency should fall in value.

This is particularly important in current conditions (at the time of this book's publication) where the United States is running a consistently large trade deficit without sufficient foreign inflow to fund that deficit. As a result of this very problem, the trade-weighted dollar index fell 22 percent in value between 2003 and 2005. The Japanese yen is another good example. As one of the world's largest exporters, Japan runs a very high trade surplus. Therefore, despite a zero interest rate policy that prevents capital flows from increasing, the yen has a natural tendency to trade higher based on trade flows, which is the other side of the equation. To be more specific, here is a detailed explanation of what capital and trade flows encompass.

Capital Flows: Measuring Currency Bought and Sold

Capital flows measure the net amount of a currency that is being purchased or sold due to capital investments. A positive capital flow balance implies that foreign inflows of physical or portfolio investments into a country exceed outflows. A negative capital flow balance indicates that there are more physical or portfolio investments bought by domestic investors than foreign investors. Let's look at these two types of capital flows—physical flows and portfolio flows.

Physical Flows   Physical flows encompass actual foreign direct investments by corporations such as investments in real estate, manufacturing, and local acquisitions. All of these require that a foreign corporation sell the local currency and buy the foreign currency, which leads to movements in the FX market. This is particularly important for global corporate acquisitions that involve more cash than stock.

Physical flows are important to watch, as they represent the underlying changes in actual physical investment activity. These flows shift in response to changes in each country's financial health and growth opportunities. Changes in local laws that encourage foreign investment also serve to promote physical flows. For example, due to China's entry into the World Trade Organization (WTO), its foreign investment laws have been relaxed. As a result of its cheap labor and attractive revenue opportunities (population of over 1 billion), corporations globally have flooded China with investments. From an FX perspective, in order to fund investments in China, foreign corporations need to sell their local currency and buy Chinese renminbi (RMB).

Portfolio Flows   Portfolio flows involve measuring capital inflows and outflows in equity markets and fixed income markets.

Equity Markets   As technology has enabled greater ease with respect to transportation of capital, investing in global equity markets has become far more feasible. Accordingly, a rallying stock market in any part of the world serves as an ideal opportunity for all, regardless of geographic location. The result of this has become a strong correlation between a country's equity markets and its currency: if the equity market is rising, investment dollars generally come in to seize the opportunity. Alternatively, falling equity markets could prompt domestic investors to sell their shares of local publicly traded firms to capture investment opportunities abroad.

The attraction of equity markets compared to fixed income markets has increased across the years. Since the early 1990s, the ratio of foreign transactions in U.S. government bonds over U.S. equities has declined from 10 to 1 to 2 to 1. As indicated in Figure 3.1, it is evident that the Dow Jones Industrial Average had a high correlation (of approximately 81 percent) with the U.S. dollar (against the deutsche mark) between 1994 and 1999. In addition, from 1991 to 1999 the Dow increased 300 percent, while the U.S. dollar index appreciated nearly 30 percent for the same time period. As a result, currency traders closely followed the global equity markets in an effort to predict short-term and intermediate-term equity-based capital flows. However, this relationship has shifted since the tech bubble burst in the United States, as foreign investors remained relatively risk-averse, causing a lower correlation between the performance of the U.S. equity market and the U.S. dollar. Nevertheless, a relationship does still exist, making it important for all traders to keep an eye on global market performances in search of intermarket opportunities.

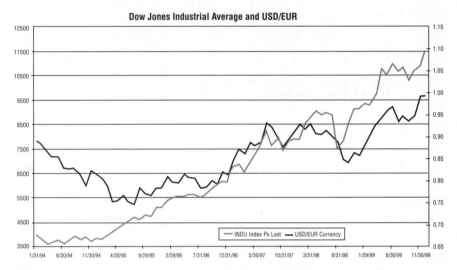

FIGURE 3.1 Dow Jones Industrial Average and USD/EUR

Fixed Income Markets Just as the equity market is correlated to exchange rate movement, so too is the fixed income market. In times of global uncertainty, fixed income investments can become particularly appealing, due to the inherent safety they possess. As a result, economies boasting the most valuable fixed income opportunities will be capable of attracting foreign investment—which will naturally first require the purchasing of the country's respective currency.

A good gauge of fixed income capital flows are the short- and long-term yields of international government bonds. It is useful to monitor the spread differentials between the yield on the 10-year U.S. Treasury note and the yields on foreign bonds. The reason is that international investors tend to place their funds in countries with the highest-yielding assets. If U.S. assets have one of the highest yields, this would encourage more investments in U.S. financial instruments, hence benefiting the U.S. dollar. Investors can also use short-term yields such as the spreads on two-year government notes to gauge short-term flow of international funds. Aside from government bond yields, federal funds futures can also be used to estimate movement of U.S. funds, as they price in the expectation of future Fed interest rate policy. Euribor futures, or futures on the Euro Interbank Offered Rate, are a barometer for the euro region's expected future interest rates and can give an indication of euro region future policy movements. We cover using fixed income products to trade FX further in Chapter 9.

Trade Flows: Measuring Exports versus Imports

Trade flows are the basis of all international transactions. Just as the investment environment of a given economy is a prime determinant of its currency valuation, trade flows represent a country's net trade balance. Countries that are net exporters—meaning they export more to international clients than they import from international producers—will experience a net trade surplus. Countries that are net exporters are more likely to have their currency rise in value, since from the perspective of international trade, their currency is being bought more than it is sold: international clients interested in buying the exported product/service must first buy the appropriate currency, thus creating demand for the currency of the exporter.

Countries that are net importers—meaning they make more international purchases than international sales—experience what is known as a trade deficit, which in turn has the potential to drive the value of the currency down. In order to engage in international purchases, importers must sell their currency to purchase that of the retailer of the good or service; accordingly, on a large scale this could have the effect of driving the currency down. This concept is important because it is a primary reason why many economists say that the dollar needs to continue to fall over the next few years to stop the United States from repeatedly hitting record high trade deficits.

To clarify this further, suppose, for example, that the U.K. economy is booming, and that its stock market is rallying as well. Meanwhile, in the United States, a lackluster economy is creating a shortage of investment opportunities. In such a scenario, the natural result would be for U.S. residents to sell their dollars and buy British pounds to take advantage of the rallying U.K. economy. This would result in capital outflow from the United States and capital inflow for the United Kingdom. From an exchange rate perspective, this would induce a fall in the USD coupled with a rise in the GBP as demand for USD declines and demand for GBP increases; in other words, the GBP/USD would rise.

For day and swing traders, a tip for keeping on top of the broader economic picture is to figure out how economic data for a particular country stacks up.

Trading Tip: Charting Economic Surprises

A good tip for traders is to stack up economic data surprises against price action to help explain and forecast the future movement in currencies. Figure 3.2 presents a sample of what can be done. The bar graph shows the percentages of surprise that economic indicators have compared to

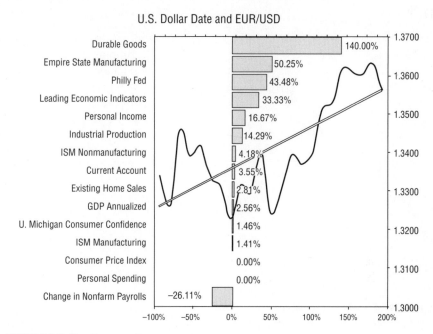

FIGURE 3.2 Charting Economic Surprises

consensus forecasts, while the dark line traces price action for the period during which the data was released; the white line is a simple price regression line. This charting can be done for all of the major currency pairs, providing a visual guide to understanding whether price action has been in line with economic fundamentals and helping to forecast future price action. This data is provided on a monthly basis on www.dailyfx.com, listed under Charting Economic Fundamentals.

According to the chart in Figure 3.2, in November 2004, there were 12 out of 15 positive economic surprises and yet the dollar sold off against the euro during the month of December, which was the month during which the economic data was released. Although this methodology is inexact, the analysis is simple and past charts have yielded some extremely useful clues to future price action. Figure 3.3 shows how the EUR/USD moved in the following month. As you can see, the EUR/USD quickly corrected itself during the month of January, indicating that the fundamental divergence of price action that occurred in December proved to be quite useful to dollar longs, who harvested almost 600 pips as the euro quickly retracted a large part of its gains in January. This method of analysis, called "variant perception," was invented by the legendary hedge fund

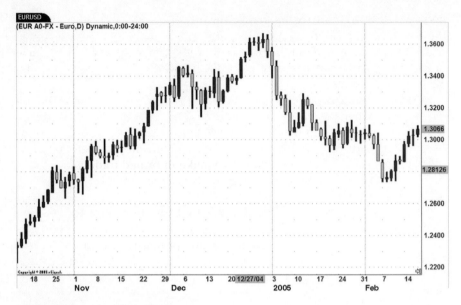

FIGURE 3.3   EUR/USD Chart
(*Source:* eSignal. www.eSignal.com)

manager Michael Steinhardt, who produced 24 percent average rates of return for 30 consecutive years.

While these charts rarely offer such clear-cut signals, their analytical value may also lie in spotting and interpreting the outlier data. Very large positive and negative surprises of particular economic statistics can often yield clues to future price action. If you go back and look at the EUR/USD charts, you will see that the dollar plunged between October and December. This was triggered by a widening of the current account deficit to a record high in October 2004. Economic fundamentals matter perhaps more in the foreign exchange market than in any other market, and charts such as these could provide valuable clues to price direction. Generally, the 15 most important economic indicators are chosen for each region and then a price regression line is superimposed over the past 20 days of price data.

TECHNICAL ANALYSIS

Prior to the mid-1980s, the FX market was primarily dominated by fundamental traders. However, with the rising popularity of technical analysis and the advent of new technologies, the influence of technical trading on the FX market has increased significantly. The availability of high leverage has led to an increased number of momentum or model funds, which have become important participants in the FX market with the ability to influence currency prices.

Technical analysis focuses on the study of price movements. Technical analysts use historical currency data to forecast the direction of future prices. The premise of technical analysis is that all current market information is already reflected in the price of each currency; therefore, studying price action is all that is required to make informed trading decisions. In addition, technical analysis works under the assumption that history tends to repeat itself.

Technical analysis is a very popular tool for short-term to medium-term traders. It works especially well in the currency markets because short-term currency price fluctuations are primarily driven by human emotions or market perceptions. The primary tool in technical analysis is charts. Charts are used to identify trends and patterns in order to find profit opportunities. The most basic concept of technical analysis is that markets have a tendency to trend. Being able to identify trends in their earliest stage of development is the key to technical analysis. Technical analysis integrates price action and momentum to construct a pictorial representation of past currency price action to predict future performance. Technical analysis tools such as Fibonacci retracement levels, moving averages, oscillators, candlestick charts, and Bollinger bands provide further information on the value of emotional extremes of buyers and sellers to direct traders to levels where greed and fear are the strongest. There are basically two types of markets, trending and range-bound; in the trade parameters section (Chapter 7), we attempt to identify rules that would help traders determine what type of market they are currently trading in and what sort of trading opportunities they should be looking for.

Is Technical Analysis or Fundamental Analysis Better?

Technical versus fundamental analysis is a longtime battle, and after many years there is still no winner or loser. Most traders abide by technical analysis because it does not require as many hours of study. Technical analysts can follow many currencies at one time. Fundamental analysts, in contrast, tend to specialize due to the overwhelming amount of data in the market. Technical analysis works well because the currency market tends to develop strong trends. Once technical analysis is mastered, it can be applied with equal ease to any time frame or currency traded.

FIGURE 3.4 USD/JPY September 11, 2001, Chart
(*Source:* eSignal. www.eSignal.com)

However, it is important to take into consideration both strategies, as fundamentals can trigger technical movements such as breakouts or trend reversals, while technical analysis can explain moves that fundamentals cannot, especially in quiet markets, such as resistance in trends. For example, as you can see in Figure 3.4, in the days leading up to September 11, 2001, USD/JPY had just broken out of a triangle formation and looked poised to head higher. However, as the chart indicates, instead of breaking higher as technicians may have expected, USD/JPY broke down following the terrorist attacks and ended up hitting a low of 115.81 from a high of 121.88 on September 10.

CURRENCY FORECASTING—WHAT BOOKWORMS AND ECONOMISTS LOOK AT

For more avid students of foreign exchange who want to learn more about fundamental analysis and valuing currencies, this section examines the different models of currency forecasting employed by the analysts of the major investment banks. There are seven major models for forecasting currencies: the balance of payments (BOP) theory, purchasing power parity (PPP), interest rate parity, the monetary model, the real interest rate differential model, the asset market model, and the currency substitution model.

Balance of Payments Theory

The balance of payments theory states that exchange rates should be at their equilibrium level, which is the rate that produces a stable current account balance. Countries with trade deficits experience a run on their foreign exchange reserves due to the fact that exporters to that nation must sell that nation's currency in order to receive payment. The cheaper currency makes the nation's exports less expensive abroad, which in turn fuels exports and brings the currency into balance.

What Is the Balance of Payments?   The balance of payments account is divided into two parts: the current account and the capital account. The current account measures trade in tangible, visible items such as cars and manufactured goods; the surplus or deficit between exports and imports is called the trade balance. The capital account measures flows of money, such as investments for stocks or bonds. Balance of payments data can be found on the web site of the Bureau of Economic Analysis (www.bea.gov).

Trade Flows   The trade balance of a country shows the net difference over a period of time between a nation's exports and imports. When a country imports more than it exports the trade balance is negative or is in a deficit. If the country exports more than it imports the trade balance is positive or is in a surplus. The trade balance indicates the redistribution of wealth among countries and is a major channel through which the macroeconomic policies of a country may affect another country.

In general, it is considered to be unfavorable for a country to have a trade deficit, in that it negatively impacts the value of the nation's currency. For example, if U.S. trade figures show greater imports than exports, more dollars flow out of the United States and the value of the U.S. currency depreciates. A positive trade balance, in comparison, will affect the dollar by causing it to appreciate against the other currencies.

Capital Flows   In addition to trade flows, there are also capital flows that occur among countries. They record a nation's incoming and outgoing investment flows such as payments for entire (or for parts of) companies, stocks, bonds, bank accounts, real estate, and factories. The capital flows are influenced by many factors, including the financial and economic climate of other countries. Capital flows can be in the form of physical or portfolio investments. In general, in developing countries, the composition of capital flows tends to be skewed toward foreign direct investment (FDI) and bank loans. For developed countries, due to the strength of the equity and fixed income markets, stocks and bonds appear to be more important than bank loans and FDI.

Equity Markets   Equity markets have a significant impact on exchange rate movements because they are a major place for high-volume currency movements. Their importance is considerable for the currencies of countries with developed capital markets where great amounts of capital inflows and outflows occur, and where foreign investors are major participants. The amount of the foreign investment flows in the equity markets is dependent on the general health and growth of the market, reflecting the well-being of companies and particular sectors. Movements of currencies occur when foreign investors move their money to a particular equity market. Thus they convert their capital in a domestic currency and push the demand for it higher, making the currency appreciate. When the equity markets are experiencing recessions, however, foreign investors tend to flee, thus converting back to their home currency and pushing the domestic currency down.

Fixed Income (Bond) Markets   The effect the fixed income markets have on currencies is similar to that of the equity markets and is a result of capital movements. The investor's interest in the fixed income market depends on the company's specifics and credit rating, as well as on the general health of the economy and the country's interest rates. The movement of foreign capital into and out of fixed income markets leads to change in the demand and supply for currencies, hence impacting the currencies' exchange rates.

Summary of Trade and Capital Flows   Determining and understanding a country's balance of payments is perhaps the most important and useful tool for those interested in fundamental analysis. Any international transaction gives rise to two offsetting entries, trade flow balance (current account) and capital flow balance (capital account). If the trade flow balance is a negative outflow, the country is buying more from foreigners than it sells (imports exceed exports). When it is a positive inflow, the country is selling more than it buys (exports exceed imports). The capital flow balance is positive when foreign inflows of physical or portfolio investments into a country exceed that country's outflows. A capital flow is negative when a country buys more physical or portfolio investments than are sold to foreign investors.

These two entries, trade and capital flow, when added together signify a country's balance of payments. In theory, the two entries should balance and add up to zero in order to provide for the maintenance of the status quo in a nation's economy and currency rates.

In general, countries might experience positive or negative trade, as well as positive or negative capital flow balances. In order to minimize the net effect of the two on the exchange rates, a country should try to maintain a balance between the two. For example, in the United States there is a substantial trade deficit, as more is imported than is exported. When the trade balance is negative, the country is buying more from foreigners than it sells and therefore it needs to finance its deficit. This negative trade flow might be offset by a positive capital flow into the country, as foreigners buy either physical or portfolio investments. Therefore, the United States seeks to minimize its trade deficit and maximize its capital inflows to the extent that the two balance out.

A change in this balance is extremely significant and carries ramifications that run deep into economic policy and currency exchange levels. The net result of the difference between the trade and capital flows, positive or negative, will impact the direction in which the nation's currency will move. If the overall trade and capital balance is negative it will result in a depreciation of the nation's currency, and if positive it will lead to an appreciation of the currency.

Clearly a change in the balance of payments carries a direct effect for currency levels. It is therefore possible for any investor to observe economic data relating to this balance and interpret the results that will occur. Data relating to capital and trade flows should be followed most closely. For instance, if an analyst observes an increase in the U.S. trade deficit and a decrease in the capital flows, a balance of payments deficit would occur and as a result an investor may anticipate a depreciation of the dollar.

Limitations of Balance of Payments Model   The BOP model focuses on traded goods and services while ignoring international capital flows. Indeed, international capital flows often dwarfed trade flows in the currency markets toward the end of the 1990s, though, and this often balanced the current accounts of debtor nations like the United States.

For example, in 1999, 2000, and 2001 the United States maintained a large current account deficit while the Japanese ran a large current account surplus. However, during this same period the U.S. dollar rose against the yen even though trade flows were running against the dollar.

The reason was that capital flows balanced trade flows, thus defying the BOP's forecasting model for a period of time. Indeed, the increase in capital flows has given rise to the asset market model.

Note: It is probably a misnomer to call this approach the balance of payments theory since it takes into account only the current account balance, not the actual balance of payments. However, until the 1990s capital flows played a very small role in the world economy so the trade balance made up the bulk of the balance of payments for most nations.

Purchasing Power Parity

The purchasing power parity theory is based on the belief that foreign exchange rates should be determined by the relative prices of a similar basket of goods between two countries. Any change in a nation's inflation rate should be balanced by an opposite change in that nation's exchange rate. Therefore, according to this theory, when a country's prices are rising due to inflation, that country's exchange rate should depreciate in order to return to parity.

PPP's Basket of Goods   The basket of goods and services priced for the PPP exercise is a sample of all goods and services covered by gross domestic product (GDP). It includes consumer goods and services, government services, equipment goods, and construction projects. More specifically, consumer items include food, beverages, tobacco, clothing, footwear, rents, water supply, gas, electricity, medical goods and services, furniture and furnishings, household appliances, personal transport equipment, fuel, transport services, recreational equipment, recreational and cultural services, telephone services, education services, goods and services for personal care and household operation, and repair and maintenance services.

Big Mac Index   One of the most famous examples of PPP is the *Economist*'s Big Mac Index. The Big Mac PPP is the exchange rate that would leave hamburgers costing the same in the United States as elsewhere, comparing these with actual rates signals if a currency is under- or overvalued. For example, in April 2002 the exchange rate between the United States and Canada was 1.57. In the United States a Big Mac cost $2.49. In Canada, a Big Mac cost $3.33 in local Canadian dollars (CAD), which works out to only $2.12 in U.S. dollars. Therefore, the exchange rate for USD/CAD is overvalued by 15 percent using this theory and should be only 1.34.

OECD Purchasing Power Parity Index   A more formal index is put out by the Organization for Economic Cooperation and Development. Under a joint OECD-Eurostat PPP program, the OECD and Eurostat share the responsibility for calculating PPPs. This latest information on which currencies are under- or overvalued against the U.S. dollar can be found on the OECD's web site at www.oecd.org. The OECD publishes a table that shows the price levels for the major industrialized countries. Each column states the number of specified monetary units needed in each of the countries listed to buy the same representative basket of consumer goods and services. In each case the representative basket costs 100 units in the country whose currency is specified. The chart that is then created compares the PPP of a currency with its actual exchange rate. The chart is updated weekly to reflect the current exchange rate. It is also updated about twice a year to reflect new estimates of PPP. The PPP estimates are taken from studies carried out by the OECD; however, they should not be taken as definitive. Different methods of calculation will arrive at different PPP rates.

According to the OECD information for September 2002, the exchange rate between the United States and Canada was 1.58 while the price level for the United States versus Canada was 122, which translates to an exchange rate of 1.22. Using this PPP model, the USD/CAD is once again greatly overvalued (by over 25 percent, not that far away from the Big Mac Index after all).

Limitations to Using Purchasing Power Parity   PPP theory should be used only for long-term fundamental analysis. The economic forces behind PPP will eventually equalize the purchasing power of currencies. However, this can take many years. A time horizon of 5 to 10 years is typical.

PPP's major weakness is that it assumes goods can be traded easily, without regard to such things as tariffs, quotas, or taxes. For example, when the United States announces new tariffs on imports the cost of domestic manufactured goods goes up; but those increases will not be reflected in the U.S. PPP tables.

There are other factors that must also be considered when weighing PPP: inflation, interest rate differentials, economic releases/reports, asset markets, trade flows, and political developments. Indeed, PPP is just one of several theories traders should use when determining exchange rates.

Interest Rate Parity

The interest rate parity theory states that if two different currencies have different interest rates then that difference will be reflected in the premium or discount for the forward exchange rate in order to prevent risk-less arbitrage.

For example, if U.S. interest rates are 3 percent and Japanese interest rates are 1 percent, then the U.S. dollar should depreciate against the Japanese yen by 2 percent in order to prevent riskless arbitrage. This future exchange rate is reflected into the forward exchange rate stated today. In our example, the forward exchange rate of the dollar is said to be at discount because it buys fewer Japanese yen in the forward rate than it does in the spot rate. The yen is said to be at a premium.

Interest rate parity has shown very little proof of working in recent years. Often currencies with higher interest rates rise due to the determination of central bankers trying to slow down a booming economy by hiking rates and have nothing to do with riskless arbitrage.

Monetary Model

The monetary model holds that exchange rates are determined by a nation's monetary policy. Countries that follow a stable monetary policy over time usually have appreciating currencies according to the monetary model. Countries that have erratic monetary policies or excessively expansionist policies should see the value of their currency depreciate.

How to Use the Monetary Model   There are several factors that influence exchange rates under this theory:

1. A nation's money supply.
2. Expected future levels of a nation's money supply.
3. The growth rate of a nation's money supply.

All of these factors are key to understanding and spotting a monetary trend that may force a change in exchange rates. For example, the Japanese economy has been slipping in and out of recession for over a decade. Interest rates are near zero, and annual budget deficits prevent the Japanese from spending their way out of recession, which leaves only one tool left at the disposal of Japanese officials determined to revive their economy: printing more money. By buying stocks and bonds, the Bank of Japan is increasing the nation's money supply, which produces inflation, which forces a change in the exchange rate. The example in Figure 3.5 illustrates the effect of money supply changes using the monetary model.

Indeed, it is in the area of excessive expansionary monetary policy that the monetary model is most successful. One of the few ways a coun-

FIGURE 3.5 Monetary Model

try can keep its currency from sharply devaluing is by pursuing a tight monetary policy. For example, during the Asian currency crisis the Hong Kong dollar came under attack from speculators. Hong Kong officials raised interest rates to 300 percent to halt the Hong Kong dollar from being dislodged from its peg to the U.S. dollar. The tactic worked perfectly as speculators were cleared out by such sky-high interest rates. The downside was the danger that the Hong Kong economy would slide into recession. But in the end the peg held and the monetary model worked.

Limitations of Monetary Model   Very few economists solely stand by this model anymore since it does not take into account trade flows and capital flows. For example, throughout 2002 the United Kingdom had higher interest rates, growth rates, and inflation rates than both the United States and the European Union, yet the pound appreciated in value against both the dollar and the euro. Indeed, the monetary model has greatly struggled since the dawn of freely floating currencies. The model holds that high interest rates signal growing inflation, which they often do, followed by a depreciating currency. But this does not take into account the capital inflows that would take effect as a result of higher interest yields or of an equity market that may be thriving in a booming economy—thus causing the currency to possibly appreciate.

In any case, the monetary model is one of several useful fundamental tools that can be employed in tandem with other models to determine the direction an exchange rate is heading.

Real Interest Rate Differential Model

The real interest rate differential theory states that exchange rate movements are determined by a nation's interest rate level. Countries that have high interest rates should see their currencies appreciate in value, while countries with low interest rates should see their currencies depreciate in value.

Basics of the Model   Once a nation raises its interest rates, international investors will discover that the yield for that nation's currency is more attractive and hence buy up that nation's currency. Figure 3.6 shows how well this theory held up in 2003 when interest rate spreads were near their widest levels in recent years.

The data from this graph shows a mixed result. The Australian dollar had the largest basis point spread and also had the highest return against the U.S. dollar, which seems to vindicate the model as investors bought up higher-yielding Aussie currency. The same can be said for the New Zealand dollar, which also had a higher yield than the U.S. dollar and gained 27 percent against USD. Yet the model becomes less convincing when comparing the euro, which gained 20 percent against the dollar (more than every currency except NZD) even though its basis point differential was only 100 points. The model then comes under serious question when comparing the British pound and the Japanese yen. The yen differential is –100 and yet it appreciates almost 12 percent against the dollar. Meanwhile, the British pound gained only 11 percent against the dollar even though it had a whopping 275-point interest rate differential.

Interest Rates vs. U.S.	Eurozone	Japan	U.K.	Canada	Australia	New Zealand
Central Bank Rate End of 2003	100	−100	275	175	425	400
% Change 2003 vs. USD	20%	12%	11%	21%	34%	27%

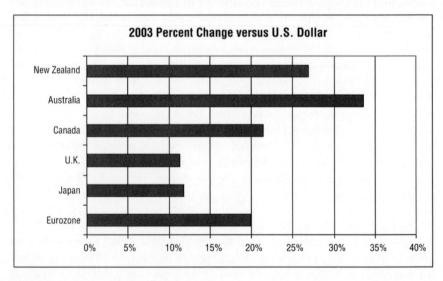

FIGURE 3.6   Real Interest Rate Model

This model also stresses that one of the key factors in determining the severity of an exchange rate's response to a shift in interest rates is the expected persistence of that shift. Simply put, a rise in interest rates that is expected to last for five years will have a much larger impact on the exchange rate than if that rise were expected to last for only one year.

Limitations to Interest Rate Model   There is a great deal of debate among international economists over whether there is a strong and statistically significant link between changes in a nation's interest rate and currency price. The main weakness of this model is that it does not take into account a nation's current account balance, relying on capital flows instead. Indeed, the model tends to overemphasize capital flows at the expense of numerous other factors: political stability, inflation, economic growth, and so on. Absent these types of factors, the model can be very useful since it is quite logical to conclude that an investor will naturally gravitate toward the investment vehicle that pays a higher reward.

Asset Market Model

The basic premise of this theory is that the flow of funds into other financial assets of a country such as equities and bonds increases the demand for that country's currency (and vice versa). As proof, advocates point out that the amount of funds that are placed in investment products such as stocks and bonds now dwarf the amount of funds that are exchanged as a result of the transactions in goods and services for import and export purposes. The asset market theory is basically the opposite of the balance of payments theory since it takes into account a nation's capital account instead of its current account.

A Dollar-Driven Theory   Throughout 1999, many experts argued that the dollar would fall against the euro on the grounds of the expanding U.S. current account deficit and an overvalued Wall Street. That was based on the rationale that non-U.S. investors would begin withdrawing their funds from U.S. stocks and bonds into more economically sound markets, which would weigh significantly on the dollar. Yet such fears have lingered since the early 1980s when the U.S. current account soared to a record high at the time of 3.5 percent of GDP.

Throughout the past two decades, the balance of payments approach in assessing the dollar's behavior has given way to the asset market approach. This theory continues to hold the most sway over pundits due to the enormity of U.S. capital markets. In May and June of 2002 the dollar plummeted more than a thousand points versus the yen at the same time equity investors fled U.S. equity markets due to the accounting scandals that were plaguing Wall Street. As the scandals subsided toward the end of 2002 the dollar rose 500 basis points from a low of 115.43 to close at 120.00 against the yen even though the current account balance remained in massive deficit the entire time.

Limitations to Asset Market Theory   The main limitation of the asset market theory is that it is untested and fairly new. It is frequently argued that over the long run there is no relationship between a nation's equity market performance and the performance of its currency. See Figure 3.7 for a comparison. Between 1986 and 2004, the S&P 500 index and the U.S. Dollar Index had a correlation of only 39 percent.

Also, what happens to a nation's currency when the stock market is trading sideways, stuck between bullish and bearish sentiments? That was the scenario in the United States for much of 2002, and currency traders found themselves going back to older moneymaking models, such as interest rate arbitrage, as a result. Only time will tell whether the asset market model will hold up or merely be a short-term blip on the currency forecasting radar.

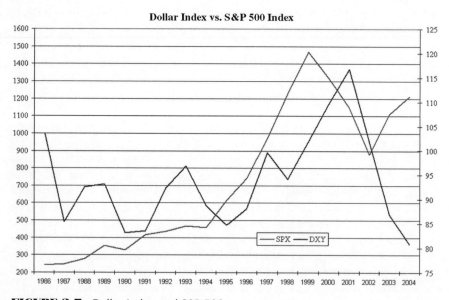

FIGURE 3.7   Dollar Index and S&P 500

Currency Substitution Model

This currency substitution model is a continuation of the monetary model since it takes into account a nation's investor flows. It posits that the shifting of private and public portfolios from one nation to another can have a significant effect on exchange rates. The ability of individuals to change their assets from domestic and foreign currencies is known as currency substitution. When this model is added to the monetary model, evidence shows that shifts in expectations of a nation's money supply can have a decided impact on that nation's exchange rates. Investors are looking at monetary model data and coming to the conclusion that a change in money flow is about to occur, thus changing the exchange rate, so they are investing accordingly, which turns the monetary model into a self-fulfilling prophecy. Investors who subscribe to this theory are merely jumping on the currency substitution model bandwagon on the way to the monetary model party.

Yen Example   In the monetary model example we showed that by buying stocks and bonds in the marketplace the Japanese government was basically printing yen (increasing the money supply). Monetary model theorists would conclude this monetary growth would in fact spark inflation (more yen chasing fewer products), decrease demand for the yen, and finally cause the yen to depreciate across the board. A currency substitution theorist would agree with this scenario and look to take advantage of this by shorting the yen or, if long the yen, by promptly getting out of the position. By taking this action, our yen trader is helping to drive the market precisely in that direction thus making the monetary model theory a fait accompli. The step-by-step process is illustrated in Figure 3.8.

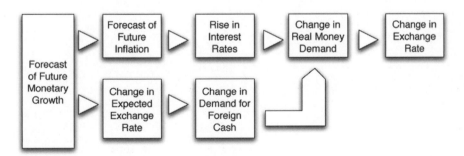

FIGURE 3.8   Currency Substitution Model

A. Japan announces new stock and bond buyback plan. Economists are now predicting Japan's money supply will dramatically increase.

B. Economists are also predicting a rise in inflation with the introduction of this new policy. Speculators expect a change in the exchange rate as a result.

C. Economists expect interest rates to rise also as inflation takes hold in the economy. Speculators start shorting the yen in anticipation of a change in the exchange rate.

D. Demand for the yen plummets as money flows easily through the Japanese economy and speculators dump yen in the markets.

E. The exchange rate for Japanese yen changes dramatically as the yen falls in value to foreign currencies, especially those that are easily substituted by investors (read: liquid yen crosses).

Limitations of Currency Substitution Model   Among the major, actively traded currencies this model has not yet shown itself to be a convincing, single determinant for exchange rate movements. While this theory can be used with more confidence in underdeveloped countries where hot money rushes in and out of emerging markets with enormous effect, there are still too many variables not accounted for by the currency substitution model. For example, using the earlier yen illustration, even though Japan may try to spark inflation with its securities buyback plan, it still has an enormous current account surplus that will continually prop up the yen. Also, Japan has numerous political land mines it must avoid in its own neighborhood, and should Japan make it clear it is trying to devalue its currency there will be enormous repercussions. These are just two of many factors the substitution model does not take into consideration. However, this model (like numerous other currency models) should be considered part of an overall balanced FX forecasting diet.

CHAPTER 4

What Moves the Currency Market in the Short Term?

For any type of trader, fundamental or technical, the importance of economic data cannot be underestimated. Having worked in the FX markets for many years, I have learned that even though there are many traders who claim to be pure technicians and do not factor fundamentals into their trading strategies, these same traders have also frequently stayed out of the markets ahead of key economic releases. In fact, many system traders turn their systems off ahead of big releases such as the U.S. nonfarm payrolls reports. On the other side of the spectrum, there are also technicians who do factor fundamentals into their trading strategies and wait only for key economic releases to put on breakout trades. As a result, it is important for any type of active market trader to know what the most important economic releases are for the U.S. dollar. Since 90 percent of all currency trades are against the U.S. dollar, the currency movements are naturally most sensitive to U.S. economic releases.

Based on a study that I conducted, the most significant movements in the dollar (against the euro) on the back of an economic release in 2004 occurred in the first 20 minutes of trading following the release. As shown in Table 4.1, the nonfarm payrolls report is hands down the most important piece of U.S. data. Throughout 2004, on average, the EUR/USD would move 124 pips (points in FX) in the first 20 minutes following the release. Excluding any release that came in within 10 percent of estimates, the average move was 133 pips. On a daily basis, the EUR/USD moved an average of 193 and 208 pips excluding nearly in-line

TABLE 4.1   Range of EUR/USD Following Economic Releases for 2004

First 20 Minutes	Average Range (Pips)	Total Daily Range	Average Range (Pips)
Nonfarm Payrolls	124	Nonfarm Payrolls	193
FOMC Decisions	74	FOMC Decisions	140
Trade Balance	64	TIC Data	132
Inflation (CPI)	44	Trade Balance	129
Retail Sales	43	Current Account	127
GDP	43	Durable Goods	126
Current Account	43	Retail Sales	125
Durable Goods	39	Inflation (CPI)	123
TIC Data	33	GDP	110

levels. On average, the EUR/USD moved 111 pips throughout the course of the trading day. On the other side of the spectrum is the gross domestic product (GDP) report, which results in an average move of only 43 pips in the first 20 minutes and 110 pips on a daily basis. The GDP ranking on the 20-minute table is higher than on the daily table because prices do retrace throughout the course of the day. The biggest 20-minute mover for the dollar may not be the most significant market mover for the entire trading. According to our own analysis of 20-minute and daily ranges, we have created the following rankings for economic data.

Top Market-Moving Indicators for Dollar as of 2004:
First 20 Minutes

1. Unemployment (nonfarm payrolls).
2. Interest rates (Federal Open Market Committee rate decisions).
3. Trade balance.
4. Inflation (consumer price index).
5. Retail sales.
6. Gross domestic product.
7. Current account.

8. Durable goods.

9. Foreign purchases of U.S. Treasuries (TIC data).

Daily

1. Unemployment (nonfarm payrolls).

2. Interest rates (FOMC rate decisions).

3. Foreign purchases of U.S. Treasuries (TIC data).

4. Trade balance.

5. Current account.

6. Durable goods.

7. Retail sales.

8. Inflation (consumer price index).

9. Gross domestic product.

You can compare the breakdowns of the average pip ranges for the EUR/USD that are shown in Table 4.1 with the average daily range for the EUR/USD in 2004, which was approximately 110 pips.

RELATIVE IMPORTANCE OF DATA CHANGES OVER TIME

With a dynamic market, one caveat is that the significance of economic data releases does change with time. According to a paper titled "Macroeconomic Implications of the Beliefs and Behaviors of Foreign Exchange Traders" written by Cheung and Chinn of the National Bureau of Economic Research (NBER) in 1992, the trade balance was the number one market-moving U.S. economic release on a 20-minute basis, while nonfarm payrolls (and unemployment data) was the third. In 1999, unemployment took the top place while the trade balance fell to the fourth. As indicated in the earlier table for 2004 (Table 4.1), the trade balance and inflation reports switched places with the trade balance being the third most market-moving indicator in 2004 instead of inflation, which took the ranking in 1997, while the significance of labor market data held steady. Intuitively, this makes sense since the market shifts its attention to different economic sectors and data based on the conditions of the domestic economy—for example, trade balances may be more important when a country is running unsustainable deficits, whereas an economy that has difficulty creating jobs will see unemployment data as more important.

FX Dealer Ranking of Importance of Economic Data: Changes over Time

As of 1997	As of 1992
1. Unemployment	1. Trade balance
2. Interest rates	2. Interest rates
3. Inflation	3. Unemployment
4. Trade balance	4. Inflation
5. GDP	5. GDP

Rankings are based on reaction one minute after data is released.

GROSS DOMESTIC PRODUCT—NO LONGER A BIG DEAL

Contrary to popular belief, the GDP report has also become one of the lesser important economic indicators on the U.S. calendar and has led to one of the smallest relative movements in the EUR/USD. One possible explanation is that GDP reports are less frequently released than other data used in the study (quarterly versus monthly), but in general the GDP data is more prone to ambiguity and misinterpretation. For example, surging GDP brought about by rising exports will be positive for the home currency; however, if GDP growth is a result of inventory buildup, the effect on the currency may actually be negative. Also, a large number of the components that comprise the GDP report are known in advance of the release.

HOW CAN YOU USE THIS TO YOUR BENEFIT?

For breakout traders, the knowledge of which data has the potential of leading to the largest average range can be useful in determining how to weight positions accordingly. For example, in Figure 4.1, which shows the daily EUR/USD chart, there is a triangle forming as prices consolidate significantly. A breakout trader would probably overweight positions ahead of the August 6, 2004, nonfarm payrolls release on the eve prior in the anticipation of a large breakout move following this release. In contrast, the third bar of the consolidation was the day of the GDP release. As you can see, the range was still comparatively tight, and given the knowledge that the average instantaneous 20-minute move off

FIGURE 4.1 EUR/USD Daily Chart
(*Source:* eSignal. www.eSignal.com)

of the GDP release is only a third of the nonfarm payrolls move, the same breakout players hoping for a large move off of that economic release should probably put on only 50 percent of the same position that they would have put on for a nonfarm payrolls–based breakout. The same guidelines apply for range traders or system traders. Nonfarm payrolls day would be a perfect day to stand on the sidelines and wait for prices to settle, whereas GDP day still provides an opportunity for solid range or systems-based trading.

Overall, knowing what economic indicator moves the market the most is very important for all traders. Knowing the 20-minute versus daily range is also very important because the exchange rate adjustment to economic news appears to be very swift. Any reaction beyond a 15-to-30-minute window after the data is released may be the result of investor overreaction or trading related to customer flow rather than news alone. The GDP is a perfect example—the 20-minute reaction ranking is higher than the daily ranking. It is also critical to stay abreast of which data the market deems important at any point in time because the market's focus changes from period to period; once-relevant data may end up having less of an effect on currency values later on, and vice versa.

Resource

"Macroeconomic Implications of the Beliefs and Behavior of Foreign Exchange Traders," www.georgetown.edu/faculty/evansm1/New%20Micro/chinn.pdf.

A DEEPER LOOK INTO THE FX MARKET

The next three chapters cover some of the unique studies that I have done on the FX market that provide some telling details for both the novice and the advanced trader. The topics are:

- What are the best times to trade for individual currency pairs?
- What are the most market-moving economic data?
- What are currency correlations and how do traders use them?

CHAPTER 5

What Are the Best Times to Trade for Individual Currency Pairs?

The foreign exchange market operates 24 hours a day and as a result it is impossible for a trader to track every single market movement and make an immediate response at all times. Timing is everything in currency trading. In order to devise an effective and time-efficient investment strategy, it is important to note the amount of market activity around the clock in order to maximize the number of trading opportunities during a trader's own market hours. Besides liquidity, a currency pair's trading range is also heavily dependent on geographical location and macroeconomic factors. Knowing what time of day a currency pair has the widest or narrowest trading range will undoubtedly help traders improve their investment utility due to better capital allocation. This chapter outlines the typical trading activity of major currency pairs in different time zones to see when they are the most volatile. Table 5.1 tabulates the average pip range for the different currency pairs during various time frames between 2002 and 2004.

ASIAN SESSION (TOKYO): 7 P.M.–4 A.M. EST

FX trading in Asia is conducted in major regional financial hubs; during the Asian trading session, Tokyo takes the largest market share, followed by Hong Kong and Singapore. Despite the flagging influence of the Japanese central bank on the FX market, Tokyo remains one of the most important

TABLE 5.1 Currency Pair Ranges

Currency Pairs (EST)	Asian Session	European Session	U.S. Session	U.S. & Europe Overlap	Europe & Asia Overlap
	7 P.M.–4 A.M.	2 A.M.–12 A.M.	8 A.M.–5 P.M.	8 A.M.–12 P.M.	2 A.M.–4 A.M.
EUR/USD	51	87	78	65	32
USD/JPY	78	79	69	58	29
GBP/USD	65	112	94	78	43
USD/CHF	68	117	107	88	43
EUR/CHF	53	53	49	40	24
AUD/USD	38	53	47	39	20
USD/CAD	47	94	84	74	28
NZD/USD	42	52	46	38	20
EUR/GBP	25	40	34	27	16
GBP/JPY	112	145	119	99	60
GBP/CHF	96	150	129	105	62
AUD/JPY	55	63	56	47	26

dealing centers in Asia. It is the first major Asian market to open, and many large participants often use the trade momentum there as the benchmark to gauge market dynamics as well as to devise their trading strategies. Trading in Tokyo can be thin from time to time; but large investment banks and hedge funds are known to try to use the Asian session to run important stop and option barrier levels. Figure 5.1 provides a ranking of the different currency pairs and their ranges during the Asian trading session.

For the more risk-tolerant traders, USD/JPY, GBP/CHF, and GBP/JPY are good picks because their broad ranges provide short-term traders with lucrative profit potentials, averaging 90 pips. Foreign investment banks and institutional investors, which hold mostly dollar-dominated assets, generate a significant amount of USD/JPY transactions when they enter the Japanese equity and bond markets. Japan's central bank, with more than $800 billion of U.S. Treasury securities, also plays an influential role in affecting the supply and demand of USD/JPY through its open market operations. Last but not least, large Japanese exporters are known to use the Tokyo trading hours to repatriate their foreign earnings, heightening the fluctuation of the currency pair. GBP/CHF and GBP/JPY remain highly volatile as central bankers and large players start to scale themselves into positions in anticipation of the opening of the European session.

For the more risk-averse traders, AUD/JPY, GBP/USD, and USD/CHF are good choices because they allow medium-term to long-term traders to

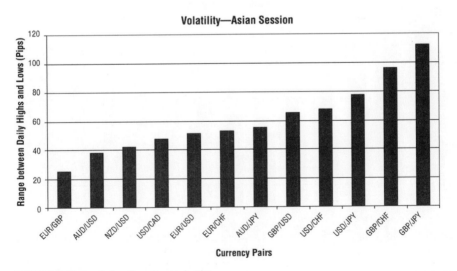

FIGURE 5.1 Asian Session Volatility

take fundamental factors into account when making a decision. The moderate volatility of the currency pairs will help to shield traders and their investment strategies from being prone to irregular market movements due to intraday speculative trades.

U.S. SESSION (NEW YORK): 8 A.M.–5 P.M. EST

New York is the second largest FX marketplace, encompassing 19 percent of total FX market volume turnover according to the 2004 Triennial Central Bank Survey of Foreign Exchange and Derivatives Market Activity in April 2004, published by the Bank for International Settlements (BIS). It is also the financial center that guards the back door of the world's FX market as trading activity usually winds down to a minimum from its afternoon session until the opening of the Tokyo market the next day. The majority of the transactions during the U.S. session are executed between 8 a.m. and noon, a period with high liquidity because European traders are still in the market.

For the more risk-tolerant traders, GBP/USD, USD/CHF, GBP/JPY, and GBP/CHF are good choices for day traders since the daily ranges average about 120 pips. (See Figure 5.2.) Trading activities in these currency

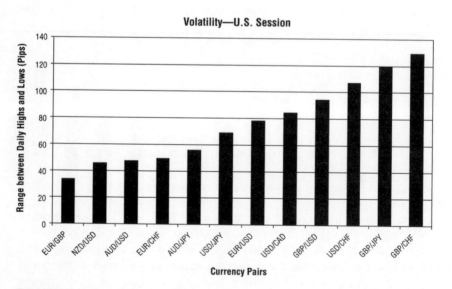

FIGURE 5.2 U.S. Session Volatility

pairs are particularly active because these transactions directly involve the U.S. dollar. When the U.S. equity and bond markets are open during the U.S. session, foreign investors have to convert their domestic currency, such as the Japanese yen, the euro, and the Swiss franc, into dollar-dominated assets in order to carry out their transactions. With the market overlap, GBP/JPY and GBP/CHF have the widest daily ranges.

Most currencies in the FX market are quoted with the U.S. dollar as the base and primarily traded against it before translating into other currencies. In the GBP/JPY case, for a British pound to be converted into Japanese yen, it has to be traded against the dollar first, then into yen. Therefore, a GBP/JPY trade involves two different currency transactions, GBP/USD and USD/JPY, and its volatility is ultimately determined by the correlations of the two derived currency pairs. Since GBP/USD and USD/JPY have negative correlations, which means their direction of movements are opposite to each other, the volatility of GBP/JPY is thus amplified. USD/CHF movement can also be explained similarly but has a greater intensity. Trading currency pairs with high volatility can be very lucrative, but it is also important to bear in mind that the risk involved is very high as well. Traders should continuously revise their strategies in response to market conditions because abrupt movements in exchange rates can easily stop out their trading orders or nullify their long-term strategies.

For the more risk-averse traders, USD/JPY, EUR/USD, and USD/CAD appear to be good choices since these pairs offer traders a decent amount of trading range to garner handsome profits with a smaller amount of risk. Their highly liquid nature allows an investor to secure profits or cut losses promptly and efficiently. The modest volatility of these pairs also provides a favorable environment for traders who want to pursue long-term strategies.

EUROPEAN SESSION (LONDON): 2 A.M.–12 P.M. EST

London is the largest and most important dealing center in the world, with a market share at more than 30 percent according to the BIS survey. Most of the dealing desks of large banks are located in London; the majority of major FX transactions are completed during London hours due to the market's high liquidity and efficiency. The vast number of market participants and their high transaction value make London the most volatile FX market of all. As shown in Figure 5.3, half of the 12 major pairs surpass the 80 pips line, the benchmark that we used to identify

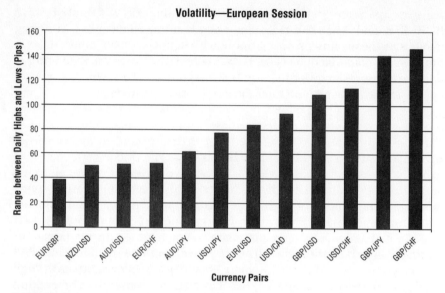

FIGURE 5.3 European Session Volatility

volatile pairs with GBP/JPY and GBP/CHF reaching as high as 140 and 146 pips respectively.

GBP/JPY and GBP/CHF are apt for the risk lovers. These two pairs have an average daily range of more than 140 pips and can be used to generate a huge amount of profits in a short period of time. Such high volatility for the two pairs reflects the peak of daily trade activity as large participants are about to complete their cycle of currency conversion around the world. London hours are directly connected to both the U.S. and the Asian sessions; as soon as large banks and institutional investors are finished repositioning their portfolios, they will need to start converting the European assets into dollar-denominated ones again in anticipation of the opening of the U.S. market. The combination of the two reconversions by the big players is the major reason for the extremely high volatility in the pairs.

For the more risk-tolerant traders, there are plenty of pairs to choose from. EUR/USD, USD/CAD, GBP/USD, and USD/CHF, with an average range of 100 pips, are ideal picks as their high volatilities offer an abundance of opportunity to enter the market. As mentioned earlier, trade between the European currencies and the dollars picks up again because the large participants have to reshuffle their portfolios for the opening of the U.S. session.

For the more risk-averse participants, the NZD/USD, AUD/USD, EUR/CHF, and AUD/JPY, with an average of about 50 pips, are good choices as these pairs provide traders with high interest incomes in additional to potential trade profits. These pairs allow investors to determine their direction of movements based on fundamental economic factors and be less prone to losses due to intraday speculative trades.

U.S.–EUROPEAN OVERLAP: 8 A.M.–12 P.M. EST

The FX markets tend to be most active when the hours of the world's two largest trading centers overlap. (See Figure 5.4.) The range of trading between 8 a.m. and noon EST constitutes on average 70 percent of the total average range of trading for all of the currency pairs during the European trading hours and 80 percent of the total average range of trading for all of the currency pairs during U.S. trading hours. Just these percentages alone tell day traders that if they are really looking for volatile price action and wide ranges and cannot sit at the screen all day, the time to trade is the U.S. and European overlap.

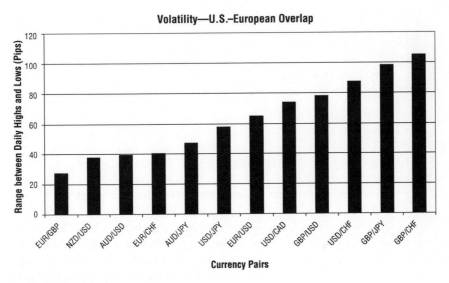

FIGURE 5.4 U.S.–European Overlap

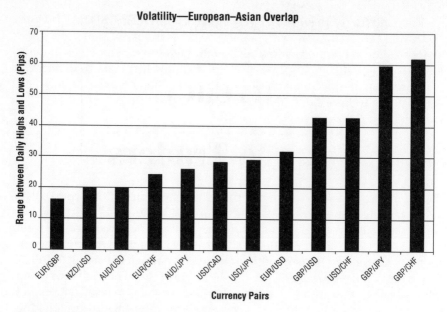

FIGURE 5.5 European–Asian Overlap

EUROPEAN–ASIAN OVERLAP: 2 A.M.–4 A.M. EST

The trade intensity in the European–Asian overlap is far lower than in any other session because of the slow trading during the Asian morning. (See Figure 5.5) Of course, the time period surveyed is relatively smaller as well. With trading extremely thin during these hours, risk-tolerant and risk-loving traders can take a two-hour nap or spend the time positioning themselves for a breakout move at the European or U.S. open.

CHAPTER 6

What Are Currency Correlations and How Do Traders Use Them?

hen trading in the FX market, one of the most important facts to remember in creating a strategy is that no currency pair is isolated. In many cases, foreign economic conditions, interest rates, and price changes affect much more than just a single pairing. Everything is interrelated in the forex market to some extent, and knowing the direction and how strong this relationship is can be used to your advantage; it has the potential to be a great trading tool. The bottom line is that unless you only want to trade one pair at a time, it can be very profitable to take into account how pairs move relative to one another. To do this, we can use correlation analysis. Correlations are calculations based on pricing data, and these numbers can help gauge the relationships that exist between different currency pairs. The information that the numbers give us can be a good aid for any trader who wants to diversify his or her portfolio, double up on positions without investing in the same currency pair, or just get an idea of how much risk their trades are opening them up to. If used correctly, this method has the potential to maximize gains, gauge exposure, and help prevent counterproductive trading.

POSITIVE/NEGATIVE CORRELATIONS: WHAT THEY MEAN AND HOW TO USE THEM

Knowing how closely correlated the currency pairs are in your portfolio is a great way to measure your exposure and risk. You might think that you're diversifying your portfolio by investing in different pairs, but many of them have a tendency to move in the same direction or opposite to one another. The correlations between pairs can be strong or weak and last for weeks, months, or even years. Basically, what a correlation number gives us is an estimate of how closely pairs move together or how opposite their actions are over a specified period of time. Any correlation calculation will be in decimal form; the closer the number is to 1, the stronger the connection between the two currencies. For example, by looking at the sample data in Table 6.1, we can see a +0.94 correlation between the EUR/USD and the NZD/USD over the last month. If you are not a fan of decimals, you can also think of the number as a percentage by multiplying it by 100 percent (in this case getting a 94 percent correlation between the EUR/USD and the NZD/USD). High decimals indicate currency pairs that closely mirror one another while lower numbers tell us that the pairs do not usually move in a parallel fashion. Therefore, because there is a high correlation in this particular pair, we can see that investing in both the EUR/USD and the NZD/USD is very similar to doubling up on a position. Likewise, it might not be the best idea to go long one of the currency pairs and short the other because a rally in one has a high likelihood of also setting off a rally in the other currency pair. While this would not make your profits and losses exactly zero because they have different pip values, the two do move in such a similar fashion that taking opposing positions could take a bite out of profits or even cause losses.

Positive correlations aren't the only way to measure similarities between pairings; negative correlations can be just as useful. In this case, instead of a very positive number, we are looking for a highly negative one. Just as on the positive side, the closer the number is to −1, the increasingly connected the two currencies movements are, this time in the opposite direction. Again we can use the EUR/USD as an example. While we just saw a strong positive correlation with the NZD/USD, the EUR/USD has a very negative relationship with the USD/CHF. Between these two currency pairs, the correlation has been −0.98 over the last year and −0.99 over the past month. This number indicates that these two pairings have a strong propensity to move in opposite directions. Therefore, taking contrary positions on the two pairs could act the same as taking the same position on two highly positive correlated pairs. In this instance, going long in one and shorting the other would be almost the same as doubling up on the position, and as a result, would also open your portfolio up to a higher amount of risk. However, deciding to go long or short on both would probably be counterproductive and lead to near zero profit and losses because the two currency pairs move in opposite directions so if one side of the trade became profitable, the other would usually result in losses.

TABLE 6.1 Correlation Table: Data for March 2005

EUR/USD	AUD/USD	USD/JPY	GBP/USD	NZD/USD	USD/CHF	USD/CAD
1 Month	0.94	−0.92	0.92	0.94	−0.99	−0.32
3 Month	0.47	−0.37	0.83	0.57	−0.98	−0.61
6 Month	0.74	−0.83	0.94	0.78	−0.96	−0.57
1 Year	0.85	−0.86	0.91	0.93	−0.98	−0.89

AUD/USD	EUR/USD	USD/JPY	GBP/USD	NZD/USD	USD/CHF	USD/CAD
1 Month	0.94	−0.91	0.95	0.96	−0.94	−0.17
3 Month	0.47	0.24	0.81	0.90	−0.44	−0.14
6 Month	0.74	−0.70	0.75	0.89	−0.70	−0.54
1 Year	0.85	−0.87	0.79	0.90	−0.78	−0.81

USD/JPY	EUR/USD	AUD/USD	GBP/USD	NZD/USD	USD/CHF	USD/CAD
1 Month	−0.92	−0.91	−0.88	−0.91	0.94	0.06
3 Month	−0.37	0.24	−0.08	0.15	0.40	0.12
6 Month	−0.83	−0.70	−0.75	−0.61	0.83	0.59
1 Year	−0.86	−0.87	−0.82	−0.84	0.83	0.80

GBP/USD	EUR/USD	AUD/USD	USD/JPY	NZD/USD	USD/CHF	USD/CAD
1 Month	0.92	0.95	−0.88	0.87	−0.95	−0.03
3 Month	0.83	0.81	−0.08	0.83	−0.82	−0.36
6 Month	0.94	0.75	−0.75	0.84	−0.88	−0.42
1 Year	0.91	0.79	−0.82	0.82	−0.90	−0.70

NZD/USD	EUR/USD	AUD/USD	USD/JPY	GBP/USD	USD/CHF	USD/CAD
1 Month	0.94	0.96	−0.91	0.87	−0.92	−0.29
3 Month	0.57	0.90	0.15	0.83	−0.53	−0.35
6 Month	0.78	0.89	−0.61	0.84	−0.69	−0.38
1 Year	0.93	0.90	−0.84	0.82	−0.88	−0.94

USD/CHF	EUR/USD	AUD/USD	USD/JPY	GBP/USD	NZD/USD	USD/CAD
1 Month	−0.99	−0.94	0.94	−0.95	−0.92	0.21
3 Month	−0.98	−0.44	0.40	−0.82	−0.53	0.55
6 Month	−0.96	−0.70	0.83	−0.88	−0.69	0.70
1 Year	−0.98	−0.78	0.83	−0.90	−0.88	0.87

(Continued)

TABLE 6.1 *(Continued)*

USD/CAD	EUR/USD	AUD/USD	USD/JPY	GBP/USD	NZD/USD	USD/CHF
1 Month	−0.32	−0.17	0.06	−0.03	−0.29	0.21
3 Month	−0.61	−0.14	0.12	−0.36	−0.35	0.55
6 Month	−0.57	−0.54	0.59	−0.42	−0.38	0.70
1 Year	−0.89	−0.81	0.80	−0.70	−0.94	0.84

Date		EUR/USD	AUD/USD	USD/JPY	GBP/USD	NZD/USD	USD/CHF	USD/CAD
03/29/2004–09/29/2004	6 Month Trailing	0.10	−0.28	0.69	0.68	−0.88	−0.60
04/29/2004–10/28/2004	6 Month Trailing	0.77	−0.67	0.47	0.84	−0.90	−0.78
05/31/2004–11/29/2004	6 Month Trailing	0.96	−0.88	0.61	0.88	−0.97	−0.89
06/30/2004–12/29/2004	6 Month Trailing	0.93	−0.94	0.87	0.94	−0.98	−0.85
07/30/2004–01/28/2005	6 Month Trailing	0.93	−0.93	0.92	0.95	−0.99	−0.86
08/31/2004–03/01/2005	6 Month Trailing	0.88	−0.91	0.96	0.91	−0.98	−0.80
09/30/2004–03/31/2005	6 Month Trailing	0.74	−0.83	0.95	0.79	−0.96	−0.58
	Average	0.76	−0.78	0.78	0.86	−0.95	−0.77

IMPORTANT FACT ABOUT CORRELATIONS: THEY CHANGE

Anyone who has ever traded the FX market knows that currencies are very dynamic; economic conditions, both sentiment and pricing change every day. Because of this, the most important aspect to remember when analyzing currency correlations is that they can easily change over time. The strong correlations that are calculated today might not be the same this time next month. Due to the constant reshaping of the forex environment, it is imperative to keep current if you decide to use this method for trading. For example, over a one-month period that we observed, the correlation between USD/CAD and USD/JPY was 0.06. This is a very low number and would indicate that the pairs do not really share any definitive relationship in their movements. However, if we look at the three-month data for the same time period, the number increases to 0.12 and then to 0.59 for six months and finally to 0.80 for a year. Therefore, for this particular example we can see that there was a blatant recent breakdown in the relationship between these two pairs. What was once a strongly positive association in the long run has almost totally deteriorated over the short term. On the other hand, the USD/CHF and AUD/USD pairing has shown a strengthening trend in the most recent data. The correlation between these two pairs started at –0.78 for the year and edged up to –0.94 for the last month. This suggests that there is an increasing probability that if one of the trades became profitable the other would incur a loss.

An even more dramatic example of the extent to which these numbers can change can be found in the GBP/USD and AUD/USD pairing; there was a –0.87 correlation between the two for the yearlong data. However, while these two tended to move in reasonably opposite directions in the long term, between January and March of 2005 they were actually positively correlated with a +0.24 reading. The major events that change the amount and even direction that pairs are correlated are usually associated with major economic happenings such as interest rate changes.

CALCULATING CORRELATIONS YOURSELF

Because correlations have the tendency to shift over time, the best way to keep current on the direction and strength of your pairings is to calculate them yourself. Although it might seem like a tricky concept, the actual process can be made quite easy. The simplest way to calculate the numbers is to use Microsoft Excel. In Excel, you can take the currency pairs that you want to derive a correlation from over a specific time period and just use the correlation function. The one-year, six-month, three-month, one-month, and six-month-trailing readings, gives the most comprehensive view of the similarities and differences between pairs; however, you can decide which or how many of these readings you want to analyze. Breaking down the process step-by-step, we'll find the correlation between the GBP/USD and the USD/CHF. First you'll need to get the pricing data for the two pairings. To keep organized, label one column GBP and the other CHF and then put in the weekly values of these currencies using the last price and pairing them with the USD for whatever time period you want to use. At the bottom of the two columns, go to an empty slot and type in =CORREL. Highlight all of the data in one of the pricing columns, type in a comma, and then do the same thing for the other currency; the number produced is your correlation. Although it is not necessary to update your numbers every day, updating them once every couple of weeks or at the very least once a month is generally a good idea.

CHAPTER 7

Trade Parameters for Different Market Conditions

After having gone through the emergence of the foreign exchange market, who the major players are, significant historical milestones, and what moves the markets, it is time to cover some of my favorite strategies for trading currencies. However, before I even begin going over these strategies, the most important first step for any trader, regardless of the market that you are trading in, is to create a trading journal.

KEEPING A TRADING JOURNAL

Through my experience, I have learned that being a successful trader is not about finding the holy grail of indicators that can perfectly forecast movements 100 percent of the time, but instead to develop discipline. I cannot overemphasize the importance of keeping a trading journal as the primary first step to becoming a successful and professional trader. While working on the interbank FX trading desk at J. P. Morgan and then on the cross-markets trading desk after the merger with Chase, the trading journal mentality was ingrained into the minds of every dealer and proprietary trader on the trading floors, regardless of rank. The reason was simple: the bank was providing the capital for trading and we needed to be held accountable, especially since each transaction involved millions of dollars. For every trade that was executed, we needed to have a solid rationale as well as justification for the choice of entry and exit levels. More specifically, you had to know where to place your exit points before you placed the trade to approximate worst-case losses and to manage risk.

With this sort of accountability, the leading banks of the world are able to breed successful and professional traders. For individual traders, this practice is even more important because you are trading with your own money and not someone else's. For interbank traders, when it comes down to the bottom line, it is someone else's money that they are trading with and regardless of how poorly they might have performed over the prior two weeks, they will still be receiving a paycheck twice a month. At a bank, traders have plenty of time to make the money back without any disruptions to their daily way of life—unless of course they lose $1 million in one day. As an individual trader you do not have this luxury. When you are trading with your own money, each dollar earned or lost is your money. Therefore, even though you should be trading only with risk capital, or money that would not otherwise be used for rent or groceries, one way or the other, the pain is felt. To avoid repeating the same mistakes and taking large losses, I cannot stress enough the importance of keeping a trading journal. The journal is designed to ensure that as a trader you take only calculated losses and you learn from each one of your mistakes. The trading journal setup that I recommend is broken up into three parts:

1. Currency Pair Checklist.
2. Trades That I Am Waiting For.
3. Existing or Completed Trades.

Currency Pair Checklist

The first section of your trading journal should consist of a spreadsheet that can be printed out and completed every day. This purpose of this checklist is to get a feel for the market and to identify trades. It should list all of the currency pairs that are offered for trading in the left column, followed by three columns for the current, high, and low prices and then a series of triggers laid out as a row on the right-hand side. Newer traders probably want to start off with following only the four major currency pairs, which are the EUR/USD, USD/JPY, USD/CHF, and GBP/USD, and then gradually add in the crosses. Although the checklist that I have created is fairly detailed, I find that it is a very useful daily exercise and should take no more than 20 minutes to complete once the appropriate indicators are saved on the charts. The purpose of this checklist is to get a clear visual of which currencies are trending and which are range trading. Comprehending the big picture is the first step to trading successfully. Too often I have seen traders fail because they lose sight of the overall environment that they are trading in. The worst thing to do is to trade blindly. Trying to pick tops or bottoms in a strong trend or buying breakouts in a range-bound environment can lead to significant losses. You can see in Figure 7.1 of the EUR/USD that trying to pick tops in this pair would have led to more than three years of frustrating and unsuccessful trading. For trending environments, traders will find a higher success rate by buying on retracements in an uptrend or selling on rallies in a downtrend. Picking tops and bottoms should be a strategy that is used only in clear range-trading environments, and even then traders need to be careful of contracting ranges leading to breakout scenarios.

A simplified version of the daily market overview sheet that I use is shown in Table 7.1. As you can see in the table, the first two columns after the daily high and low prices are the levels of the 10-day high and low. Listing these prices helps to identify where current prices are within previous price action. This helps traders gauge whether we are pressing toward a 10-day high or low or if we are simply trapped in the middle of the range. Yet just the prices alone do not provide enough information to determine if we are in a trending or a range-bound environment. The next five indicators provide a checklist for determining a trending environment. The more X marks in this section, the stronger the trend.

FIGURE 7.1   EUR/USD Three-Year Chart
(*Source:* eSignal. www.eSignal.com)

TABLE 7.1 Currency Checklist

March 30, 2005—7:30 AM EST

Currency Pair	Current Price	Daily High	Daily Low	10-day High	10-day Low	Trending					Range				
						ADX (14) above 25	Crosses Bollinger	Crosses 50-day	Crosses 100-day	Crosses 200-day	ADX (14) below 25	RSI (14) Greater	RSI (14) Less than	Stochastics > 70	Stochastics < 30
EUR/USD	1.3050	1.3275	1.2998	1.3250	1.2876	X					X				
GBP/USD	1.9150	1.9160	1.9100	1.9160	1.8935				X			X		X	
USD/JPY	106.45							X							
USD/CHF	1.1855														
AUD/USD	0.7126														
NZD/USD	0.7150														
USD/CAD	1.1975														
EUR/JPY															
EUR/GBP															
EUR/CHF															
AUD/JPY															
CHF/JPY															
GBP/JPY															
GBP/CHF															
AUD/CAD															
EUR/CAD															
AUD/NZD															

The first column in the trending indicator group is the "ADX (14) above 25." ADX is the Average Directional Index, which is the most popularly used indicator for determining the strength of a trend. If the index is above 25, this indicates that a trend has developed. Generally speaking, the greater the number, the stronger the trend. The next column uses Bollinger bands. When strong trends develop, the pair will frequently tag and cross either the upper or lower Bollinger band. The next three trend indicators are the longer-term simple moving averages (SMAs). A break above or below these moving averages may also be indicative of a trending environment. With moving averages, crossovers in the direction of the trend can be used as a further confirmation. If there are two or more Xs in this section, traders should be looking for opportunities to buy on dips in an uptrend or sell on rallies in a downtrend rather than selling at the top and buying back at the bottom of the range.

The last section of the trading journal is the range group. The first indicator is once again ADX, but this time, we are looking for ADX below 25, which would suggest that the currency pair's trend is weak. Next, we look at the traditional oscillators, the Relative Strength Index (RSI), and stochastics. If the ADX is weak and there is significant technical resistance above, provided by indicators such as moving averages or Fibonacci retracement levels, and RSI and/or stochastics are at overbought or oversold levels, we identify an environment that is highly conducive to range trading.

Of course, the market overview sheet is not foolproof, and just because you have numerous X marks in either the trend group or the range group doesn't mean that a trend will not fade or a breakout will not occur. Yet what this spreadsheet will do is certainly prevent traders from trading blindly and ignoring the broader market conditions. It will provide traders with a launching pad from which to identify the day's trading opportunities.

Trades That I Am Waiting For

The next section in the trading journal lists the possible trades for the day. Based on an initial overview of the charts, this section is where you should list the trades that you are waiting to make. A sample entry would be:

April 5, 2005

Buy AUD/USD on a break of 0.7850 (previous day high).
Stop at 0.7800 (50-day SMA).

Target 1—0.7925 (38.2% Fibonacci retracement of Nov.–Mar. bull wave).

Target 2—0.8075 (upper Bollinger).

Target 3—10-day trailing low.

Therefore, as soon as your entry level is reached, you know exactly how you want to take action and where to place your stops and limits. Of course, it is also important to take a quick glance at the market to make sure that the trading conditions that you were looking for are still intact. For example, if you were looking for a strong breakout with no retracement to occur at the entry level, when it does break, you want to make sure that the scenario that you were looking for plays out. This exercise is used to help you develop a plan of action to tackle your trading day. Before every battle, warriors regroup to go over the plan of attack; in trading you want to have the same mentality. Plan and prepare for the worst-case scenario and know your plan of attack for the day!

Existing or Completed Trades

This section is developed and used to enforce discipline and to learn from your mistakes. At the end of each trading day, it is important to review this section to understand why certain trades resulted in losses and others resulted in profits. The purpose of this section is to identify trends. I will use a completely unrelated example to explain why this is important. On a normal day, most people will subconsciously inject a lot of "ums" or "uhs" into their daily conversation. However, I bet most of these people do not even realize that they are even doing it until someone records one of their conversations and plays it back to them. This is one of the ways that professional presenters and newscasters train to kick the habit of using placeholder words. Having worked with more than 65,000 traders, too often have I seen these traders repeatedly make the same mistakes. This could be taking profits too early, letting losses run, getting emotional about trading, ignoring economic releases, or getting into a trade prematurely. Having a record of previous trades is like keeping a recording of your conversations. When you flip back to the trades that you have completed, you have a perfect map of what strategies have or have not been profitable for you. The reason why a journal is so important is because it minimizes the emotional component of trades. I frequently see novice traders take profits early but let losses run. The following are two samples of trade journal entries that could provide learning opportunities:

February 12, 2005

Trade: Short 3 lots of EUR/USD @ 1.3045.

Stop: 1.3095 (former all-time high).

Target: 1.2900.

Result: Trade closed on Feb. 13, 2005—stopped out of the 3 lots @ 1.3150 (–105 pips).

Comments: Got margin call! EUR/USD broke the all-time high, but I thought it was going to reverse, and did not stick to stop—kept letting losses run, until eventually margin call closed out all positions. Note to self: *Make sure stick to stops!*

April 3, 2005

Trade: Long 2 lots of USD/CAD @ 1.1945.

Stop: 1.1860 (strong technical support—confluence of 50-day moving average and 68% Fibonacci retracement of Feb.-Mar. rally).

Target: First lot @ 1.2095 (upper Bollinger and 5 pips shy of 1.2100 psychological resistance).

Second lot @ 1.2250 (former head and shoulders support turned resistance, 100-day SMA).

Result: Trade closed on Apr. 5, 2005—stopped out of the 2 lots at 1.1860 (–85 pips).

Comments: USD/CAD did not continue uptrend and was becoming overbought; I didn't see that ADX was weakening and falling from higher levels and that there was also a divergence in stochastics. Note to self: *Make sure to look for divergences next time!*

Unlike many traders, I believe the best trades are where both the technical and fundamental pictures are telling the same story. In line with this premise, I prefer to stay out of trades that contradict my fundamental outlook. For example, if there is a bullish formation in both the GBP/USD and the AUD/USD due to U.S. dollar weakness, but the Bank of England has finished raising interest rates, while the Reserve Bank of Australia has full intentions of raising rates to tame the strength of the Australian economy, I would most likely choose to express my bearish dollar view in the AUD/USD rather than the GBP/USD. My bias for choosing the AUD/USD over the GBP/USD would be even stronger if the AUD/USD already offered a higher interest rate differential than the GBP/USD. Too often have I seen technicals thwarted by fundamentals, so now I always incorporate both into my trading strategy. I use a combination of technical, fundamental, and positioning and am generally also a trend follower. I also typically use a top-down approach that involves the following:

1. First I will take an overall technical survey of the market and pick the currency pairs that have retraced to attractive levels for entry in order to participate in a medium-term trend.

2. For currencies with a dollar component (i.e., not the crosses), I determine if my initial technical view for that pair coincides with my fundamental view on the dollar as well as my view on how upcoming U.S. releases may impact trading for the day. The reason why I look at the dollar specifically is because 90 percent of all currency trades involve the dollar, which makes U.S. fundamentals particularly important.

3. If it is a cross-currency pair such as GBP/JPY, I will proceed by determining if the technical view coincides with the fundamental outlook using Fibonacci retracements, ADX, moving averages, oscillators, and other technical tools.

4. Then I like to look at positioning using the FXCM Speculative Sentiment index to see if it supports the trade.

5. If I am left with two equally compelling trade ideas, I will choose the one with a positive interest rate differential.

HAVE A TOOLBOX—USE WHAT WORKS FOR THE CURRENT MARKET ENVIRONMENT

Once you have created a trading journal, it is time to figure out which indicators to use on your charts. The reason why a lot of traders fail is because they neglect to realize that their favorite indicators are not foolproof. Buying when stochastics are in oversold territory and selling when they are in overbought territory is a strategy that is used quite often by range traders with a great deal of success, but once the market stops range trading and begins trending, then relying on stochastics could lead to a tremendous amount of losses. In order to become consistently profitable, successful traders need to learn how to be adaptable.

One of the most important practices that every trader must understand is to be conscious of the environment that they are trading in.

Every trader needs to have some sort of checklist that will help them to classify their trading environment so that they can determine whether the market is trending or range-bound. Defining trade parameters is one of the most important disciplines of trading. Too many traders have tried to pick the top within a trend, only to wind up with consistently unprofitable trades.

Although defining trade parameters is important to traders in any market (currencies, futures, equities), it is particularly important in the currency market since over 80 percent of the volume is speculative in nature. This means that currencies can spend a very long time in a certain trading environment. Also, the currency market obeys technical analysis particularly well given its large scale and number of participants.

There are basically two types of trading environments, which means that at any point in time an instrument is either range trading or trending. The first step every trader needs to take is to define the current trading environment. The shortest time frame that traders should use in step one is daily charts, even if you are trading on a five-minute time frame.

STEP ONE—PROFILE TRADING ENVIRONMENT

There are many different ways that traders can determine whether a currency pair is range trading or trending. Of course, many people do it visually, but having set rules will help to keep traders out of trends that may be fading or to prevent traders from getting into a range trade in the midst of a possible breakout. Table 7.2 outlines some of rules that I look for in order to classify a currency pair's trading environment.

TABLE 7.2 Trend/Range Trading Rules

Trade	Rules	Indicators
Range	• ADX < 20 • Decreasing implied volatility • Risk reversals near choice or flipping between favoring calls and puts	Bollinger bands, ADX, options
Trend	• ADX > 25 • Momentum consistent with trend direction • Risk reversals strongly bid for put or call	Moving averages, ADX, options, momentum

Range

Look for:

ADX (Average Directional Index) Less Than 20   The average directional index is one of the primary technical indicators used to determine the strength of a trend. When ADX is less than 20, this suggests that the trend is weak, which is generally characteristic of a range-bound market. An ADX less than 20 and trending downward provides a further confirmation that the trend not only is weak, but will probably stay in a range trading environment for a while longer.

Decreasing Implied Volatility   There are many ways to analyze volatility. What I like to do is actually track short-term versus long-term volatility. When short-term volatility is falling, especially after a burst above long-term volatility, it is usually indicative of a reversion to range trading scenarios. Volatility usually blows out when a currency pair experiences sharp, quick moves. It contracts when ranges are narrow and the trading is very quiet in the markets. The lazy man's version of the way I track volatility is Bollinger bands, which provide a fairly decent measure for determining volatility conditions. A narrow Bollinger band suggests that ranges are small and there is low volatility in the markets, while wide Bollinger bands are reflective of large ranges and a highly volatile environment. In a range trading environment, we are looking for fairly narrow Bollinger bands ideally in a horizontal formation similar to the USD/JPY chart in Figure 7.2.

Risk Reversals Flipping between Calls and Puts   A risk reversal consists of a pair of options, a call and a put, on the same currency. Risk reversals have both the same expiration (one month) and the same sensitivity to the underlying spot rate. They are quoted in terms of the difference in volatility between the two options. While in theory these options should have the same implied volatility, in practice these volatilities often differ in the market. Risk reversals can be seen as having a market polling function. A number strongly in favor of calls or puts indicates that the market prefers calls over puts. The reverse is true if the number is strongly in favor of puts versus calls. Thus, risk reversals can be used as a substitute for gauging positions in the FX market. In an ideal environment, far out-of-the-money calls and puts should have the same volatility. However, this is rarely the case since there is generally a sentiment bias in the markets that is reflected in risk reversals. In range-bound environments, risk reversals tend to flip between favoring calls and puts at nearly zero

FIGURE 7.2 USD/JPY Bollinger Band Chart
(*Source:* eSignal. www.eSignal.com)

(or equal), indicating that there is indecision among bulls and bears and there is no strong bias in the markets.

What Does a Risk Reversal Table Look Like? According to the risk reversals shown in Table 7.3, we can see that the market is strongly favoring yen calls (JC) and dollar puts over the long term. EUR/USD short-term risk reversals are near zero, which is what you are looking for when profiling a range-bound environment. The most readily available free resource that I know of for up-to-date risk reversals is the IFR news plug-in which can be found on the FX Trading Station at www.fxcm.com.

Trend

Look for:

ADX (Average Directional Index) Greater Than 20 As mentioned earlier when we talked about range trading conditions, the Average Directional Index is one of the primary technical indicators used to determine the strength of a trend. In a trending environment, we look for ADX to be greater than 25 and rising. However, if ADX is greater than 25 but sloping downward, especially off of the extreme 40 level, you have to be

TABLE 7.3 Risk Reversals

14:40 GMT April 19th
1 Month to 1 Year Risk Reversal

Currency	1M R/R	3M R/R	6M R/R	1 YR R/R
USD/JPY	0.3/0.6 JC	0.7/1.0 JC	1.1/1/3 JC	1.3/1.6 JC
EUR/USD	0.1/0.3 EC	0.0/0.3 EC	0.0/0.3 EC	0.1/0.4 EC
GBP/USD	0.0/0.3 SP	0.0/0.3 SC	0.0/0.3 SC	0.0/0.3 SC
USD/CHF	0.2/0.2 CC	0.0/0.3 CC	0.0/0.4 CC	0.1/0.5 CC

JC = Japanese Yen Call
EC = Euro Call
SP = Sterling Put
SC = Sterling Call
CC = Swiss Call

careful of aggressive trend positioning since the downward slope may indicate that the trend is waning.

Momentum Consistent with Trend Direction In addition to using ADX, I also recommend looking for a confirmation of a trending environment through momentum indicators. Traders should look for momentum to be consistent with the direction of the trend. Most currency traders will look for oscillators to point strongly in the direction of the trend. For example, in an uptrend, trend traders will look for the moving averages, RSI, stochastics, and moving average convergence/divergence (MACD) to all point strongly upward. In a downtrend, they will look for these same indicators to point downward. Some currency traders use the momentum index, but only to a lesser extent. One of the strongest momentum indicators is a perfect order in moving averages. A perfect order is when the moving averages line up perfectly; that is, for an uptrend, the 10-day SMA is greater than the 20-day SMA, which is greater than the 50-day SMA. The 100-day SMA and the 200-day SMA are below the shorter-term moving averages. In a downtrend, a perfect order would be when the shorter-term moving averages stack up below the longer-term moving averages.

Options (Risk Reversals) With a trending environment, we are looking for risk reversals to strongly favor calls or puts. When one side of the market is laden with interest, it is usually indicative of a strongly trending environment or that a contra-trend move may be brewing if risk reversals are at extreme levels.

STEP TWO—DETERMINE TRADING TIME HORIZON

Once you have determined that a currency pair is either range-bound or trending, it is time to determine how long you plan on holding the trade. The following is a set of guidelines and indicators that I use for trading different time frames. Not all of the guidelines need to be met, but the more guidelines that are met, the more solid the trading opportunity.

Intraday Range Trade

Rules

1. Use hourly charts to determine entry points and daily charts to confirm that a range trade exists on a longer time frame.
2. Use oscillators to determine entry point within range.
3. Look for short-dated risk reversals to be near choice.
4. Look for reversal in oscillators (RSI or stochastics at extreme point).
5. It is a stronger trade when prices fail at key resistance or hold key support levels (use Fibonacci retracement points and moving averages).

Indicators Stochastics, MACD, RSI, Bollinger bands, options, Fibonacci retracement levels.

Medium-Term Range Trade

Rules

1. Use daily charts.
2. There are two ways to range trade in the medium term: position for upcoming range trading opportunities or get involved in existing ranges:

   Upcoming range opportunities: Look for high-volatility environments, where short-term implied volatilities are significantly higher than longer-term volatilities; seek reversion back to the mean environments.
   Existing ranges: Use Bollinger bands to identify existing ranges.

3. Look for reversals in oscillators such as RSI and stochastics.
4. Make sure ADX is below 25 and ideally falling.

5. Look for medium-term risk reversals near choice.

6. Confirm with price action—failure at key range resistances and bounces on key range supports (using traditional technical indicators).

Indicators   Options, Bollinger bands, stochastics, MACD, RSI, Fibonacci retracement levels.

Medium-Term Trend Trade

Rules

1. Look for developing trend on daily charts and use weekly charts for confirmation.

2. Refer back to the characteristics of a trending environment—look for those parameters to be met.

3. Buy breakout/retracement scenarios on key Fibonacci levels or moving averages.

4. Look for no major resistance levels in front of trade.

5. Look for candlestick pattern confirmation.

6. Look for moving average confluence to be on same side of trade.

7. Enter on a break of significant high or low.

8. The ideal is to wait for volatilities to contract before getting in.

9. Look for fundamentals to also be supportive of trade—growth and interest rates. You want to see a string of economic surprises or disappointments, depending on directional bias.

Indicators   ADX, parabolic stop and reversal (SAR), RSI, Ichimoku clouds (a Japanese formation), Elliott waves, Fibonacci.

Medium-Term Breakout Trade

Rules

1. Use daily charts.

2. Look for contraction in short-term volatility to a point where it is sharply below long-term volatility.

3. Use pivot points to determine whether a break is a true break or a false break.

4. Look for moving average confluences to be supportive of trade.

Indicators   Bollinger bands, moving averages, Fibonacci.

RISK MANAGEMENT

Although risk management is one of the simpler topics to grasp, it seems to be the hardest to follow for most traders. Too often we have seen traders turn winning positions into losing positions and solid strategies result in losses instead of profits. Regardless of how intelligent and knowledgeable traders may be about the markets, their own psychology will cause them to lose money. What could be the cause of this? Are the markets really so enigmatic that few can profit? Or is there simply a common mistake that many traders are prone to make? The answer is the latter. And the good news is that the problem, while it can be an emotionally and psychologically challenging one, is ultimately fairly easy to grasp and solve.

Most traders lose money simply because they have no understanding of or place no importance on *risk management*. Risk management involves essentially knowing how much you are willing to risk and how much you are looking to gain. Without a sense of risk management, most traders simply hold on to losing positions for an extremely long amount of time, but take profits on winning positions far too prematurely. The result is a seemingly paradoxical scenario that in reality is all too common: the trader ends up having more winning positions than losing ones, but ends up with a negative profit/loss (P/L). So, what can traders do to ensure they have solid risk management habits? There are a few key guidelines that all traders, regardless of their strategy or what they are trading, should keep in mind.

Risk-Reward Ratio

Traders should look to establish a risk-reward ratio for every trade they place. In other words, they should have an idea of how much they are willing to lose, and how much they are looking to gain. Generally, the risk-reward ratio should be at least 1:2, if not more. Having a solid risk-reward ratio can prevent traders from entering positions that ultimately are not worth the risk.

Stop-Loss Orders

Traders should also employ stop-loss orders as a way of specifying the maximum loss they are willing to accept. By using stop-loss orders, traders can avoid the common predicament of being in a scenario where they have many winning trades but a single loss large enough to eliminate any trace of profitability in the account. Trailing stops to lock in profits are particularly useful. A good habit of more successful traders is to employ the rule of moving your stop to break even as soon as your position has profited by the same amount that you initially risked through the stop order. At the same time, some traders may also choose to close a portion of their position.

For those looking to add to a winning position or go with a trend, the best strategy is to treat the new transaction as if it were a new trade of its own, independent of the winning position. If you are going to add to a winning position, perform the same analysis of the chart that you would if you had no position at all. If a trade continues to go in your favor, you can also close out part of the position while trailing your stop higher on the remaining lots that you are holding. Try thinking about your risk and reward on each separate lot that you have bought if they are at different entry points as well. If you buy a second lot 50 pips above your first entry point, don't use the same stop price on both, but manage the risk on the second lot independently from the first.

Using Stop-Loss Orders to Manage Risk   Given the importance of money management to successful trading, using the stop-loss order is imperative for any trader looking to succeed in the currency market. The stop-loss order allows traders to specify the maximum loss they are willing to accept on any given trade. If the market reaches the rate the trader specifies in his/her stop-loss order, then the trade will be closed immediately. As a result, using stop-loss orders allows you to know how much you are risking at the time you enter the trade.

There are two parts to successfully using a stop-loss order: (1) initially placing the stop at a reasonable level and (2) trailing the stop—meaning moving it forward toward profitability—as the trade progresses in your favor.

Placing the Stop-Loss   There are two recommended ways of placing a stop-loss order.

Two-Day Low Method   These volatility-based stops involve placing your stop-loss order approximately 10 pips below the two-day low of the pair. For example, if the low on the EUR/USD's most recent candle was 1.1200 and the previous candle's low was 1.1100, then the stop should be placed around 1.1090—10 pips below the two-day low—if a trader is looking to get long.

Parabolic Stop and Reversal (SAR)   Another form of volatility-based stop is the parabolic SAR, an indicator that is found on many currency trading charting applications. The FX Power Charts, for instance, offer this indicator, freely available to all course subscribers (www.fxcm.com). Parabolic SAR is a volatility-based indicator that graphically displays a small dot at the point on the chart where the stop should be placed. Figure 7.3 is an example of a chart with parabolic SAR placed on it.

There is no magic formula that works best in every situation, but the following is an example of how these stops could be used. Upon entering a long position, determine where support is and place a stop 20 pips below support. For example, let's say this is 60 pips below the entry point.

If the trade earns a profit of 60 pips, close half of the position in a market order, then move the stop up to the entry point. At this time, trail the stop 60 pips behind the moving market price. If the parabolic SAR moves up so that it is above the entry point, you could switch to using the parabolic SAR as the stop level. Of course, during the day, there can be other signals that could prompt you to move your stop. If the price breaks through a new resistance level, that resistance then becomes support. You can place a stop 20 pips below that support level, even if it is only 30 to 40 pips away from the current price. The underlying principle you have to use is to find a point to place your stop where you would no longer want to be in the trade once the price reaches that level. Usually the stop falls at a point where the price goes below support.

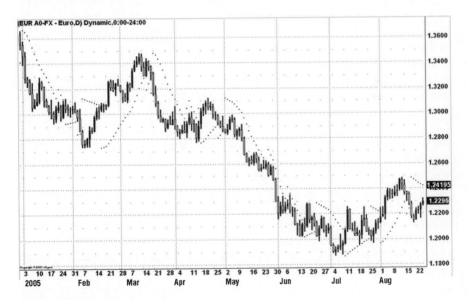

FIGURE 7.3 Parabolic SAR
(*Source:* eSignal. www.eSignal.com)

PSYCHOLOGICAL OUTLOOK

Aside from employing proper risk management strategies, one of the other most crucial yet overlooked elements of successful trading is maintaining a healthy psychological outlook. At the end of the day, traders who are unable to cope with the stress of market fluctuations will not stand the test of time—no matter how skilled they may be at the more scientific elements of trading.

Emotional Detachment

Traders must make trading decisions based on strategies independent of fear and greed. One of the premier attributes good traders have is that of emotional detachment: while they are dedicated and fully involved in their trades, they are not emotionally married to them; they accept losing, and make their investment decisions on an intellectual level. Traders who are emotionally involved in trading often make substantial errors, as they tend to whimsically change their strategy after a few losing trades, or become overly carefree after a few winning trades. A good trader must be emotionally balanced, and must base all trading decisions on strategy—not fear or greed.

Know When to Take a Break

In the midst of a losing streak, consider taking a break from trading before fear and greed dominate your strategy.

Not every trade can be a winning one. As a result, traders must be psychologically capable of coping with losses. Most traders, even successful ones, go through stretches of losing trades. The key to being a successful trader, though, is being able to come through a losing stretch unfazed and undeterred. If you are going through a bad stretch, it may be time to take a break from trading. Often, taking a few days off from watching the market to clear your mind can be the best remedy for a losing streak. Continuing to trade relentlessly during a tough market condition can breed greater losses as well as ruin your psychological trading condition. Ultimately, it's always better to acknowledge your losses rather than continue to fight through them and pretend that they don't exist. Make no mistake about it: regardless of how much you study, practice, or trade, there will be losing trades throughout your entire career. The key is to make them small enough that you can live to trade another day, while allowing your winning trades to stay open. You can overcome a lot of bad luck with proper money management techniques. This is why we stress a 2:1 reward-to-risk ratio, as well as why I recommend not risking more than 2 percent of your equity on any single trade.

Whether you are trading forex, equities, or futures, there are 10 trading rules that successful traders should live by:

1. Limit your losses.
2. Let your profits run.
3. Keep position sizes within reason.
4. Know your risk-reward ratio.
5. Be adequately capitalized.
6. Don't fight the trend.
7. Never add to losing positions.
8. Know market expectations.
9. Learn from your mistakes—keep a trading journal.
10. Have a maximum loss or retracement in profits.

CHAPTER 8

Technical Trading Strategies

MULTIPLE TIME FRAME ANALYSIS

In order to trade successfully on an intraday basis, it is important to be selective. Trend trading is one of the most popular strategies employed by global macro hedge funds. Although there are many traders who prefer to range trade, the big profit potentials tend to lie in trades that capture and participate in big market movements. It was once said by Mark Boucher, a hedge fund manager of Midas Trust Fund and a former number one money manager as ranked by Nelson MarketPlace's World's Best Money Managers, that 70 percent of a market's moves occurs 20 percent of the time. This makes multiple time frame analysis particularly important because no trader wants to lose sight of the overall big picture. A great comparison is taking a road trip from Chicago to Florida. There are certainly going to be a lot of left and right turns during the road trip, but the driver needs to be aware throughout the whole trip that he or she is headed south. In trading, looking for opportunities to buy in an uptrend or sell in a downtrend tends to be much more profitable than trying to pick tops and bottoms.

The most common form of multiple time frame analysis is to use daily charts to identify the overall trend and then to use the hourly charts to determine specific entry levels.

The AUD/USD chart in Figure 8.1 is a daily chart of the Australian dollar against the U.S. dollar. As you can see, the Australian dollar has been trending higher since January 2002. Range or contrarian traders who continually looked to pick tops would have been faced with at least three

FIGURE 8.1 AUD/USD Multiple Time Frame Daily Chart
(*Source:* eSignal. www.eSignal.com)

years of unprofitable and difficult trading, particularly when the currency pair was hitting record highs in late 2003 into early 2004. This area would have certainly attracted many traders looking to pick a top or to fade the trend. Despite a dip in late 2004, the AUD/USD has remained strong going into 2005, which would have made it very difficult for medium-term range players to trade.

Instead, the more effective trading strategy is to actually take a position in the direction of the trend. In the AUD/USD example, this would have involved looking for opportunities to buy on dips. Figure 8.2 is an hourly chart with Fibonacci retracements drawn from the February 2004 all-time high and the low of June 17, 2004. Rather than looking for opportunities to sell, we use the 76 percent Fibonacci retracement level as key support zones to go long the Australian dollar. The horizontal line in Figure 8.2 represents the Fibonacci retracement level. What we did therefore was use the daily charts to get a gauge of the overall trend and then used the hourly charts to pinpoint entry levels.

Let's take a look at another example, this one of the British pound. Figure 8.3 is the daily chart of the GBP/USD for January 2002 to May 2005. Like traders of the Australian dollar, traders trying to pick tops in the GBP/USD would have also faced at least three years of difficult trading, particularly when the GBP/USD was making 10-year highs in January

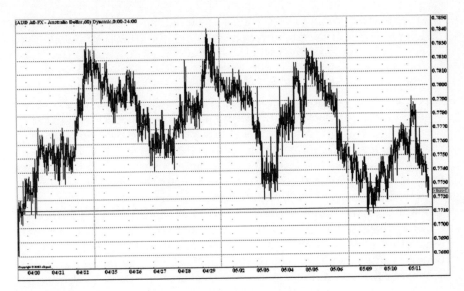

FIGURE 8.2 AUD/USD Multiple Time Frame Hourly Chart
(*Source:* eSignal. www.eSignal.com)

FIGURE 8.3 GBP/USD Multiple Time Frame Daily Chart
(*Source:* eSignal. www.eSignal.com)

2004. This level would have certainly attracted many skeptics looking to pick tops. To the frustration of those who did, the GBP/USD rallied up to 10 percent beyond its 10-year highs post January, which means that those top pickers would have incurred significant losses.

Taking a look at the hourly chart for the GBP/USD, we want to look for opportunities to buy on dips rather than sell on rallies. Figure 8.4 shows two Fibonacci retracement levels drawn from the September 2004 and December 2004 bull wave. Those levels held pretty well on retracements between four-tenths and four-fourteenths while the 23.6 percent Fibonacci level offered an opportunity for breakout trading rather than a significant resistance level. In that particular scenario, keeping in mind the bigger picture would have shielded traders from trying to engage in reversal plays at those levels.

Multiple time frame analysis can also be employed on a shorter-term basis. Let us take a look at an example using CHF/JPY. First we start with our hourly chart of CHF/JPY, which is shown in Figure 8.5. Using Fibonacci retracements, we see on our hourly charts that prices have failed at the 38.2 percent retracement of the December 30, 2004, to February 9, 2005, bear wave numerous times. This indicates that the pair is contained within a weeklong downtrend below those levels. Therefore, we want to use our 15-minute charts to look for entry levels to participate in the overall downtrend. However, in order to increase the success of this trade, we want to make sure that CHF/JPY is also in a downtrend on a daily basis.

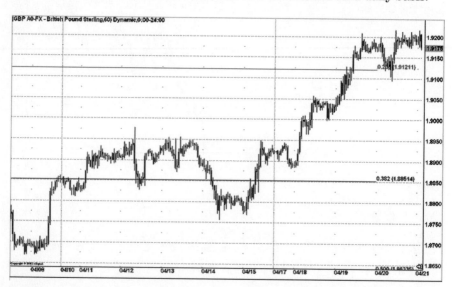

FIGURE 8.4   GBP/USD Multiple Time Frame Hourly Chart
(*Source:* eSignal. www.eSignal.com)

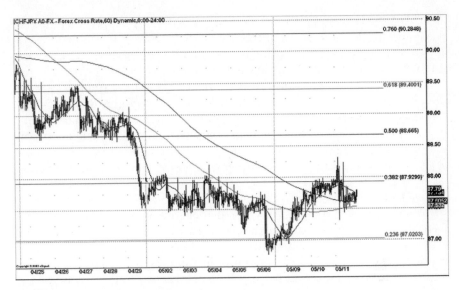

FIGURE 8.5 CHF/JPY Multiple Time Frame Hourly Chart
(*Source:* eSignal. www.eSignal.com)

Taking a look at Figure 8.6, we see that CHF/JPY is indeed trading below the 200-day simple moving average with the 20-day SMA crossing below the 100-day SMA. This confirms the bearish momentum in the currency pair. So as a day trader, we move on to the 15-minute chart to pinpoint entry levels. Figure 8.7 is the 15-minute chart; the horizontal line is the 38.2 percent Fibonacci retracement of the earlier downtrend. We see that CHF/JPY broke above the horizontal line on May 11, 2005; however, rather than buying into a potential breakout trade, the bearish big picture reflected on the hourly and daily charts suggests a contrarian trade at this point. In fact, there were two instances shown in Figure 8.7 where the currency pair broke above the Fibonacci level only to then trade significantly lower. Disciplined day traders would use those opportunities to fade the breakout.

The importance of multiple time frame analysis cannot be overestimated. Thinking about the big picture first will keep traders out of numerous dangerous trades. The majority of new traders in the market are range traders for the simple fact that buying at the low and selling at the high is an easy concept to grasp. Of course, this strategy does work, but traders also need to be mindful of the trading environment that they are participating in. Looking back to Chapter 7, traders should try to range trade only when the conditions for a range-bound market are met. The most im-

FIGURE 8.6 CHF/JPY Multiple Time Frame Daily Chart
(*Source:* eSignal. www.eSignal.com)

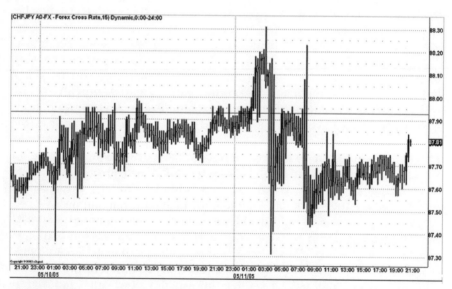

FIGURE 8.7 CHF/JPY Multiple Time Frame 15-Minute Chart
(*Source:* eSignal. www.eSignal.com)

portant condition (but certainly not the only one) is to look for ADX to be less than 25 and ideally trending downward.

FADING THE DOUBLE ZEROS

One of the most widely overlooked yet lucrative areas of trading is market structure. Developing a keen understanding of micro structure and dynamics allows traders to gain an unbelievable advantage and is probably one of the most reliable tactics for profiting from intraday fluctuations. Developing a feel for and understanding of market dynamics is key to profitably taking advantage of short-term fluctuations. In foreign exchange trading this is especially critical, as the primary influence of intraday price action is order flow. Given the fact that most individual traders are not privy to sell-side bank order flow, day traders looking to profit from short-term fluctuations need to learn how to identify and anticipate price zones where large order flows should be triggered. This technique is very efficient for intraday traders as it allows them to get on the same side as the market maker.

When trading intraday, it is impossible to look for bounces off of every support or resistance level and expect to be profitable. The key to successful intraday trading requires that we be more selective and enter only at those levels where a reaction is more likely. Trading off psychologically important levels such as the double zeros or round numbers is one good way of identifying such opportunities. Double zeros represent numbers where the last two digits are zeros—for example, 107.00 in the USD/JPY or 1.2800 in the EUR/USD. After noticing how many times a currency pair would bounce off of double zero support or resistance levels intraday despite the underlying trend, we have noticed that the bounces are usually much bigger and more relevant than rallies off other areas. This type of reaction is perfect for intraday FX traders as it gives them the opportunity to make 50 pips while risking only 15 to 20 pips.

Implementing this methodology is not difficult, but it does require individual traders to develop a solid feel for dealing room and market participant psychology. The idea behind why this methodology works is simple. Large banks with access to conditional order flow have a very distinct advantage over other market participants. The banks' order books give them direct insight into potential reactions at different price levels. Dealers will often use this strategic information themselves to put on short-term positions for their own accounts.

Market participants as a whole tend to put conditional orders near or around the same levels. While stop-loss orders are usually placed just beyond the round numbers, traders will cluster their take-profit orders at the round number. The reason why this occurs is because traders are humans and humans tend to think in round numbers. As a result, take-profit orders have a very high tendency of being placed at the double zero level. Since the FX market is a nonstop continuous market, speculators also use stop and limit orders much more frequently than in other markets. Large banks with access to conditional order flow, like stops and limits, actively seek to exploit these clusterings of positions to basically gun stops. The strategy of fading the double zeros attempts to put traders on the same side as market makers and basically positions traders for a quick contra-trend move at the double zero level.

This trade is most profitable when there are other technical indicators that confirm the significance of the double zero level.

Strategy Rules

Long

1. First, locate a currency pair that is trading well below its intraday 20-period simple moving average on a 10- or 15-minute chart.
2. Next, enter a long position several pips below the figure (no more than 10).
3. Place an initial protective stop no more than 20 pips below the entry price.
4. When the position is profitable by double the amount that you risked, close half of the position and move your stop on the remaining portion of the trade to breakeven. Trail your stop as the price moves in your favor.

Short

1. First, locate a currency pair that is trading well above its intraday 20-period simple moving average on a 10- or 15-minute chart.
2. Next, short the currency pair several pips above the figure (no more than 10).
3. Place an initial protective stop no more than 20 pips above the entry price.
4. When the position is profitable by double the amount that you risked, close half of the position and move your stop on the remaining portion of the trade to breakeven. Trail your stop as the price moves in your favor.

Market Conditions

This strategy works best when the move happens without any major economic number as a catalyst—in other words, in quieter market conditions. It is used most successfully for pairs with tighter trading ranges, crosses, and commodity currencies. This strategy does work for the majors but under quieter market conditions since the stops are relatively tight.

Further Optimization

The psychologically important round number levels have even greater significance if they coincide with a key technical level. Therefore the strategy tends to have an even higher probability of success when other important support or resistance levels converge at the figure, such as moving averages, key Fibonacci levels, and Bollinger bands, just to name a few.

Examples

So let us take a look at some of the examples of this strategy in action. The first example that we will go over is Figure 8.8, a 15-minute chart of the EUR/USD. According to the rules of the strategy, we see that the EUR/USD broke down and was trading well below its 20-period moving average. Prices continued to trend lower, moving toward 1.2800, which is our double zero number. In accordance with the rules, we place an entry order a few pips below the breakeven number at 1.2795. Our order is triggered and we put our stop 20 pips away at 1.2775. The currency pair hits a low of 1.2786 before moving higher. We then sell half of the position when the currency pair rallies by double the amount that we risked at 1.2835. The stop on the remaining half of the position is then moved to breakeven at 1.2795. We proceed to trail the stop. The trailing stop can be done using a variety of methods including a monetary or percentage basis. We choose to trail the stop by a two-bar low for a really short-term trade and end up getting out of the other half of the position at 1.2831. Therefore on this trade we earned 40 pips on the first position and 36 pips on the second position.

The next example is for USD/JPY. In Figure 8.9, we see that USD/JPY is trading well below its 20-period moving average on a 10-minute chart and is headed toward the 105 double zero level. This trade is particularly strong because the 105 level is very important in USD/JPY. Not only is it a psychologically important level, but it also served as an important support and resistance level throughout 2004 and into early 2005. The 105 level is also the 23.6 percent Fibonacci retracement of the May 14, 2004, high and

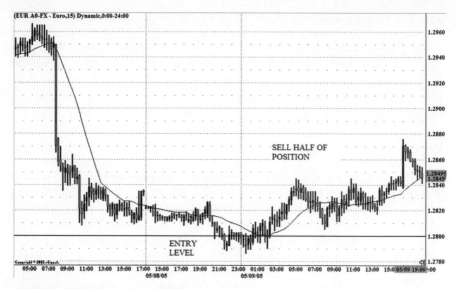

FIGURE 8.8   EUR/USD Double Zeros Example
(*Source:* eSignal. www.eSignal.com)

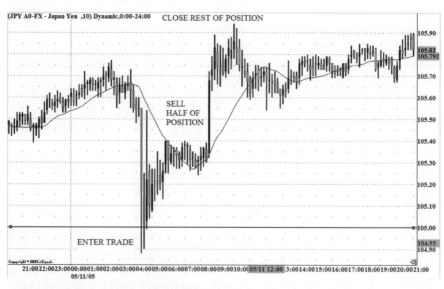

FIGURE 8.9   USD/JPY Double Zeros Example
(*Source:* eSignal. www.eSignal.com)

January 17, 2005, low. All of this provides a strong signal that lots of speculators may have taken profit orders at that level and that a contra-trend trade is very likely. As a result, we place our limit order a few pips below 105.00 at 104.95. The trade is triggered and we place our stop at 104.75. The currency pair hits a low of 104.88 before moving higher. We then sell half of our position when the currency pair rallies by double the amount that we risked at 105.35. The stop on the remaining half of the position is then moved to breakeven at 104.95. We proceed to trail the stop by a five-bar low to filter out noise on the shorter time frame. We end up selling the other half of the position at 105.71. As a result on this trade, we earned 40 pips on the first position and 76 pips on the second position. The reason why this second trade was more profitable than the one in the first example is because the double zero level was also a significant technical level.

Making sure that the double zero level is a significant level is a key element of filtering for good trades. The next example, shown in Figure 8.10, is USD/CAD on a 15-minute chart. The great thing about this trade is that it is a triple zero level rather than just a double zero level. Triple zero levels hold even more significance than double zero levels because of their less frequent occurrence. In Figure 8.10, we see that USD/CAD is also trading well below its 20-period moving average and heading toward 1.2000. We look to go long a few pips below the double zero level at

FIGURE 8.10 USD/CAD Double Zeros Example
(*Source:* eSignal. www.eSignal.com)

1.1995. We place our stop 20 pips away at 1.1975. The currency pair hits a low of 1.1980 before moving higher. We then sell half of our position when the currency pair rallies by double the amount that we risked at 1.2035. The stop on the remaining half of the position is then moved to breakeven at 1.1995. We proceed to trail the stop once again by the two-bar low and end up exiting the second half of the position at 1.2081. As a result, we earned 40 pips on the first position and 86 pips on the second position. Once again, this trade worked particularly well because 1.2000 was a triple zero level.

Although the examples covered in this chapter are all to the long side, the strategy also works to the short side.

WAITING FOR THE REAL DEAL

The lack of volume data in the FX market has forced day traders to develop different strategies that rely less on the level of demand and more on the micro structure of the market. One of the most common characteristics that day traders try to exploit is the market's 24-hour around-the-clock nature. Although the market is open for trading throughout the course of the day, the extent of market activity during each trading session can vary significantly.

Traditionally, trading tends to be the quietest during the Asian market hours, as we indicated in Chapter 4. This means that currencies such as the EUR/USD and GBP/USD tend to trade within a very tight range during these hours. According to the Bank for International Settlements' Triennial Central Bank Survey of the FX market published in September 2004, the United Kingdom is the most active trading center, capturing 31 percent of total volume. Adding in Germany, France, and Switzerland, European trading as a whole accounts for 42 percent of total FX trading. The United States, on the other hand, is second only to the United Kingdom for the title of most active trading center, but that amounts to only approximately 19 percent of total turnover. This makes the London open exceptionally important because it gives the majority of traders in the market an opportunity to take advantage of events or announcements that may have occurred during late U.S. trading or in the overnight Asian session. This becomes even more critical on days when the Federal Open Market Committee (FOMC) of the Federal Reserve meets to discuss and announce monetary policy because the announcement occurs at 2:15 p.m. New York time, which is past the London close.

The British pound trades most actively against the U.S. dollar during the European and London trading hours. There is also active trading during the U.S./European overlap, but besides those time frames, the pair tends to trade relatively lightly because the majority of GBP/USD trading is done through U.K. and European market makers. This provides a great opportunity for day traders to capture the initial directional intraday real move that generally occurs within the first few hours of trading in the London session. This strategy exploits the common perception that U.K. traders are notorious stop hunters. This means that the initial movement at the London open may not always be the real one. Since U.K. and European dealers are the primary market makers for the GBP/USD, they have tremendous insight into the extent of actual supply and demand for the pair. The trading strategy of waiting for the real deal first sets up when interbank dealing desks survey their books at the onset of trading and use their client data to trigger close stops on both sides of the markets to gain the pip differential. Once these stops are taken out and the books are cleared, the real directional move in the GBP/USD will begin to occur, at which point we look for the rules of this strategy to be met before entering into a long or short position. This strategy works best following the U.S. open or after a major economic release. With this strategy you are looking to wait for the noise in the markets to settle down and to trade the real market price action afterward.

Strategy Rules

Long

1. Early European trading in GBP/USD begins around 1:00 a.m. New York time. Look for the pair to make a new range low of at least 25 pips above the opening price (the range is defined as the price action between the Frankfurt and London power hour of 1 a.m. New York time to 2 a.m. New York time).
2. The pair then reverses and penetrates the high.
3. Place an entry order to buy 10 pips above the high of the range.
4. Place a protective stop no more than 20 pips away from your entry.
5. If the position moves lower by double the amount that you risked, cover half and trail a stop on the remaining position.

Short

1. GBP/USD opens in Europe and trades more than 25 pips above the high of the Frankfurt and London power hour.
2. The pair then reverses and penetrates the low.

3. Place an entry order to sell 10 pips below the low of the range.

4. Place a protective stop no more than 20 pips away from your entry.

5. If the position moves lower by double the amount that you risked, cover half and trail a stop on the remaining position.

Examples

Let us go ahead and take a look at some examples of this strategy in action. Figure 8.11 is a textbook example of the strategy of waiting for the real deal. We see that the GBP/USD breaks upward on the London open, reaching a high of 1.8912 approximately two hours into trading. The currency pair then begins to trend lower ahead of the U.S. market open and we position for the trade by putting an entry order to short 10 pips below the Frankfurt open to the London open range of 1.8804 at 1.8794. Our stop is then placed 20 pips higher at 1.8814, while our take-profit order is placed at 1.8754, which is double the amount risked. Once the take-profit order on the first lot is fulfilled, we move the stop to breakeven at 1.8794 and trail the stop by the two-bar high. The second lot eventually gets stopped out at 1.8740, and we end up earning 40 pips on the first position and 54 pips on the second position.

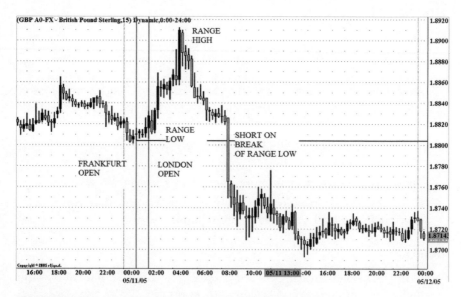

FIGURE 8.11 GBP/USD May 2005 Real Deal Example
(*Source:* eSignal. www.eSignal.com)

The next example is shown in Figure 8.12. In this example, we also see the GBP/USD break upward on the London open, reaching a high of 1.8977 right at the U.S. open. The currency pair then begins to trend lower during the early U.S. session, breaking the Frankfurt open to the London open range low of 1.8851. Our entry point is 10 pips below that level at 1.8841. Our short position is triggered, and we place our stop 20 pips higher at 1.8861 and the first take-profit level at 1.8801, which is double the amount risked. Once our limit order is triggered, we move the stop to breakeven at 1.8841 and trail the stop by the two-bar high. The second lot gets stopped out at 1.8789, and we end up earning 40 pips on the first position and 52 pips on the second position.

The third example is shown in Figure 8.13. In this example, we also see the GBP/USD break upward on the London open, reaching a high of 1.9023 right before the U.S. FOMC meeting. The currency pair then breaks lower on the back of the meeting, penetrating the Frankfurt open to the London open range low of 1.8953. Our entry order is already placed 10 pips below that level at 1.8943. Our short position is triggered and we place our stop 20 pips higher at 1.8963 and the first take-profit level at 1.8903, which is double the amount risked. Once our limit order is triggered, we move the stop to breakeven at 1.8943 and trail the stop by the

FIGURE 8.12 GBP/USD April 2005 Real Deal Example
(*Source:* eSignal. www.eSignal.com)

FIGURE 8.13 GBP/USD March 2005 Real Deal Example
(*Source:* eSignal. www.eSignal.com)

two-bar high. The second lot gets stopped out at 1.8853, and we end up earning 40 pips on the first position and 90 pips on the second position.

INSIDE DAY BREAKOUT PLAY

Throughout this book, volatility trading has been emphasized as one of the most popular strategies employed by professional traders. There are many ways to interpret changes in volatilities, but one of the simplest strategies is actually a visual one and requires nothing more than a keen eye. Although this is a strategy that is very popular in the world of professional trading, new traders are frequently amazed by its ease, accuracy, and reliability. Breakout traders can identify inside days with nothing more than a basic candlestick chart.

An inside day is defined as a day where the daily range has been contained within the prior day's trading range, or, in other words, the day's high and low do not exceed the previous day's high and low. There need to be at least two inside days before the volatility play can be implemented. The more inside days, the higher the likelihood of an upside surge in volatility, or a breakout scenario. This type of strategy is best employed on daily charts, but the longer the time frame, the more significant the breakout opportunity. Some traders use the inside day strategy on hourly charts, which does work to some success, but identifying inside days on daily charts tends to lead to an even greater probability of success. For day traders looking for inside days on hourly charts, chances of a solid breakout increase if the contraction precedes the London or U.S. market opens. The key is to predict a valid breakout and not get caught in a false breakout move. Traders using the daily charts could look for breakouts ahead of major economic releases for the specific currency pair. This strategy works with all currencies pairs, but has less frequent instances of false breakouts in the tighter range pairs such as the EUR/GBP, USD/CAD, EUR/CHF, EUR/CAD, and AUD/CAD.

Strategy Rules

Long

1. Identify a currency pair where the daily range has been contained within the prior day's range for at least two days (we are looking for multiple inside days).
2. Buy 10 pips above the high of the previous inside day.
3. Place a stop and reverse order for two lots at least 10 pips below the low of the nearest inside day.
4. Take profit when prices reach double the amount risked or begin to trail the stop at that level.

Protect against false breakouts: If the stop and reverse order is triggered, place a stop at least 10 pips *above the high* of the nearest inside day and protect any profits larger than what you risked with a trailing stop.

Short

1. Identify a currency pair where the daily range has been contained within the prior day's range for at least two days (we are looking for multiple inside days).
2. Sell 10 pips below the low of the previous inside day.
3. Place a stop and reverse order for two lots at least 10 pips above the high of the nearest inside day.
4. Take profit when prices reach double the amount risked or begin to trail the stop at that level.

Protect against false breakouts: If the stop and reverse order is triggered, place a stop at least 10 pips *below the low* of the nearest inside day and protect any profits larger than what you risked with a trailing stop.

Further Optimization

For further optimization, technical formations can be used in conjunction with the visual identification to place a higher weight on a specific direction of the breakout. For example, if the inside days are building and contracting toward the top of a recent range such as a bullish ascending triangle formation, the breakout has a higher likelihood of occurring to the upside. The opposite scenario is also true: if inside days are building and contracting toward the bottom of a recent range and we begin to see that a bearish descending triangle is in formation, the breakout has a higher likelihood of occurring to the downside. Aside from triangles, other technical factors that can be considered include significant support and resistance levels. For example, if there are significant Fibonacci and moving average support zones resting below the inside day levels, this indicates either a higher likelihood of an upside breakout or at least a higher probability of a false breakout to the downside.

Examples

Let us take a look at a few examples. Figure 8.14 is a daily chart of the euro against the British pound, or the EUR/GBP. The two inside days are identified on the chart and it is clear visually that both of those days' ranges, including the highs and lows, are contained within the previous day's range. In accordance with our rules, we place an order to go long 10 pips above the high of the previous inside day at 0.6634 and an order to sell 10 pips below the low of the previous inside day at 0.6579. Our long order gets triggered two bars after the most recent inside day. We then proceed to place a stop and reverse order 10 pips below the low of the most recent inside day at 0.6579. So basically, we went long at 0.6634 with a stop at 0.6579, which means that we are risking 45 pips. When prices reach our target level of double the amount risked (90 pips) or 0.6724, we have two choices—either close out the entire trade or begin trailing the stop. More conservative traders should probably square positions at this point, while more aggressive traders could look for more profit potential. We choose to close out the trade for a 90-pip profit, but those who stayed in and weathered a bit of volatility could have taken advantage of another 100 pips of profits three weeks later.

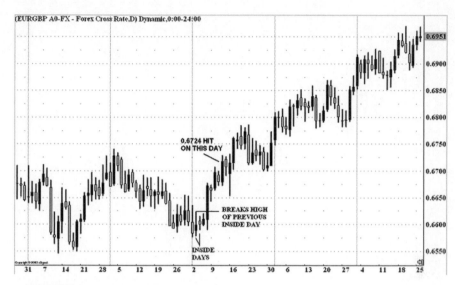

FIGURE 8.14 EUR/GBP Inside Day Chart
(*Source:* eSignal. www.eSignal.com)

Figure 8.15 is another example of inside day trading, this time using the daily chart of the New Zealand dollar against the U.S. dollar (NZD/USD). The difference between this example and the previous one is that our stop and reverse order actually gets triggered, indicating that the first move was a false breakout. The two inside days are labeled on the chart. In accordance with our rules, after identifying the inside days, we place an order to buy on the break of the high of the previous inside day and an order to sell on the break of the low of the previous inside day. The high on the first or previous inside day is 0.6628. We place an order to go long at 0.6638 or to go short at 0.6618. Our long order gets triggered on the first day of the break at 0.6638 and we place a stop and reverse order 10 pips below the low of the most recent inside day (or the daily candle before the breakout), which is 0.6560. However, instead of continuing the breakout, the pair reverses and we close our first position at 0.6560 with a 78-pip loss. We then enter into a new short position with the reverse order at 0.6560. The new stop is then 10 pips above the high of the most recent inside day at 0.6619. When NZD/USD moves by double the initial amount risked, conservative traders can take profit on the entire position while aggressive traders can trail the stop using various methods, which may be dependent on how wide the trading range is. In this example, since the daily trading range is fairly wide, we choose to close the position once the

FIGURE 8.15 NZD/USD Inside Day Chart
(*Source:* eSignal. www.eSignal.com)

price reaches our limit of 0.6404 for a profit of 156 pips and a total profit
on the entire trade of 78 pips.

The final example uses technicals to help determine a directional bias
of the inside day breakout. Figure 8.16 is a daily chart of EUR/CAD. The inside days are once again identified directly on the chart. The presence of
higher lows suggests that the breakout could very well be to the upside.
Adding in the MACD histogram to the bottom of the chart, we see that the
histogram is also in positive territory right when the inside days are forming. As such, we choose to opt for an upside breakout trade based on technical indicators. In accordance with the rules, we go long 10 pips above the
high of the previous inside day at 1.6008. Our short trade gets triggered
first, but then our stop and reverse order kicks in. Our long trade is then
triggered and we place our new stop order 10 pips below the low of the
most recent inside day at 1.5905. When prices move by double the amount
that we risked to 1.6208, we exit the entire position for a 200-pip profit.

With the inside day breakout strategy, the risk is generally pretty high
if done on daily charts, but the profit potentials following the breakout are
usually fairly large as well. More aggressive traders can also trade more
than one position, which would allow them to lock in profits on the first
half of the position when prices move by double the amount risked and
then trail the stop on the remaining position. Generally these breakout

FIGURE 8.16 EUR/CAD Inside Day Chart
(*Source:* eSignal. www.eSignal.com)

trades are precursors to big trends, and using trailing stops would allow traders to participate in the trend move while also banking some profits.

THE FADER

More often than not, traders will find themselves faced with a potential breakout scenario, position for it, and then only end up seeing the trade fail miserably and have prices revert back to range trading. In fact, even if prices do manage to break out above a significant level, a continuation move is not guaranteed. If this level is very significant, we frequently see interbank dealers or other traders try to push prices beyond those levels momentarily in order to run stops. Breakout levels are very significant levels, and for this very reason there is no hard-and-fast rule as to how much force is needed to carry prices beyond levels into a sustainable trend.

Trading breakouts at key levels can involve a lot of risk and as a result, false breakout scenarios appear more frequently than actual breakout scenarios. Sometimes prices will test the resistance level once, twice, or even three times before breaking out. This has fostered the development of a large contingent of contra-trend traders who look only to fade breakouts in the currency markets. Yet fading every breakout can also result in some significant losses because once a real breakout occurs, the trend is generally strong and long-lasting. So what this boils down to is that traders need a methodology for screening out consolidation patterns for trades that have a higher potential of resulting in a false breakout. The following rules provide a good basis for screening such trades. The fader strategy is a variation of the waiting for the real deal strategy. It uses the daily charts to identify the range-bound environment and the hourly charts to pinpoint entry levels.

Strategy Rules

Long

1. Locate a currency pair whose 14-period ADX is less than 35. Ideally the ADX should also be trending downward, indicating that the trend is weakening further.
2. Wait for the market to break below the previous day's low by at least 15 pips.
3. Place an entry order to buy 15 pips above the previous day's high.
4. After getting filled, place your initial stop no more than 30 pips away.
5. Take profit on the position when prices increase by double your risk, or 60 pips.

Short

1. Locate a currency pair whose 14-period ADX is less than 35. Ideally the ADX should also be trending downward, indicating that the trend is weakening further.
2. Look for a move above the previous day's high by at least 15 pips.
3. Place an entry order to sell 15 pips below the previous day's low.
4. Once filled, place the initial protective stop no more than 30 pips above your entry.
5. Take profits on the position when it runs 60 pips in your favor.

Further Optimization

The false breakout strategy works best when there are no significant economic data scheduled for release that could trigger sharp unexpected movements. For example, prices often consolidate ahead of the U.S. non-farm payrolls release. Generally speaking, they are consolidating for a reason and that reason is because the market is undecided and is either positioned already or wants to wait to react following that release. Either way, there is a higher likelihood that any breakout on the back of the release would be a real one and not one that you want to fade. This strategy works best with currency pairs that are less volatile and have narrower trading ranges.

Examples

Figure 8.17 is an hourly chart of the EUR/USD. Applying the rules just given, we see that the 14-period ADX dips below 35, at which point we begin looking for prices to break below the previous day's low of 1.2166 by 15 pips. Once that occurs, we look for a break back above the previous day's high of 1.2254 by 15 pips, at which point we enter into position at 1.2269. The stop is placed 30 pips below the entry price at 1.2239, with the limit exit order placed 60 pips above the entry at 1.2329. The exit order gets triggered a few hours later for a total profit of 60 pips with a risk of 30 pips.

Figure 8.18 is an example of the fader trading strategy on the short side. Applying the rules to the hourly chart of the GBP/USD, we see that

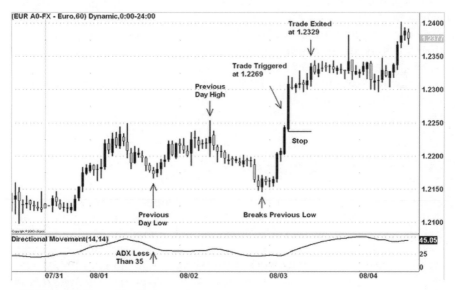

FIGURE 8.17 EUR/USD Fader Chart
(*Source:* eSignal. www.eSignal.com)

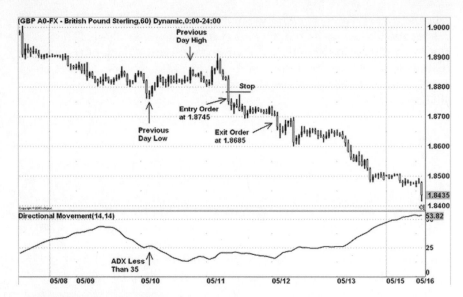

FIGURE 8.18   GBP/USD Fader Chart
(*Source:* eSignal. www.eSignal.com)

the 14-period ADX dips below 35, at which point we begin to look for prices to break 15 pips above the previous day's high of 1.8865 or below the previous day's low of 1.8760. The break above occurs first, at which time we look for prices to reverse and break back below the previous day's low. A few hours later, the break occurs and we sell 15 pips below the previous day's low at 1.8745. We then place our stop 30 pips away at 1.8775 with a take profit order 60 pips lower at 1.8685. The limit exit order gets triggered, and, as indicated on the chart, the trade was profitable.

FILTERING FALSE BREAKOUTS

Trading breakouts can be a very rewarding but frustrating endeavor as many breakouts have a tendency to fail. A major reason why this occurs frequently in the foreign exchange market is because the market is much more technically driven than many of the other markets and as a result there are many market participants who intentionally look to break pairs out in order to suck in other nonsuspecting traders. In an effort to filter out potential false breakouts, a price action screener should be used to identify those breakouts that have a higher probability of success. The rules behind this strategy are specifically developed to take advantage of strong trending markets that make new highs that then proceed to fail by taking out a recent low and then reverse again to make other new highs. This type of setup tends to have a very high success rate as it allows traders to enter strongly trending markets after weaker players have been flushed out, only to have real money players reenter the market and push the pair up to make major highs.

Strategy Rules

Long

1. Look for a currency pair that is making a 20-day high.
2. Look for the pair to reverse over the next three days to make a two-day low.
3. Buy the pair if it takes out the 20-day high within three days of making the two-day low.
4. Place the initial stop a few pips below the original two-day low that was identified in step 2.
5. Protect any profits with a trailing stop or take profit by double the amount risked.

Short

1. Look for a currency pair that is making a 20-day low.
2. Look for the pair to reverse over the next three days to make a two-day high.
3. Sell the pair if it trades below the 20-day low within three days of making the two-day high.
4. Risk up to a few ticks above the original two-day high that was identified in step 2.
5. Protect profits with a trailing stop or take profit by double the amount risked.

Examples

Take a look at our first example in Figure 8.19. The daily chart of the GBP/USD shows that the currency pair made a new 20-day high on November 17 at 1.8631. This means that the currency pair gets onto our radar screens and we prepare to look for the pair to make a new two-day low and then rally back beyond the previous 20-day high of 1.8631 over the next three days. We see this occur on November 23, at which time we enter a few pips above the high at 1.8640. We then place our stop a few pips below the two-day low of 1.8472 at 1.8465. As the currency moves in our favor, we have two choices: either to take profits by double the amount that we risked, which would be 336 pips in profits, or to use a trailing stop such as a two-bar low. We decide to trail by the two-bar low and end up getting out of the position at 1.9362 on December 8 for a total profit of 722 pips in two weeks.

Figure 8.20 shows another example of this strategy in the works. The daily chart of USD/CAD shows that the currency pair made a new 20-day high on April 21 at 1.3636. This means that the currency pair is now on our radar screens and we are looking for the pair to make a new two-day low and then retrace back below the previous 20-day high of 1.3636 over the next three days. We see this occur on April 23, at which time we enter a few pips above the high at 1.3645. We then place our stop a few pips below the original two-day low of 1.3514 at 1.3505. As the currency moves in our favor, we have two choices: either to take profits by double the amount that we risked, which would be 280 pips in profits, or to use a trailing stop such as a two-bar low. Using a two-bar low trailing stop, the trade would have been closed at 1.3686 for a 41-pip profit. Alternatively, the 280-pip limit would have been executed on May 10.

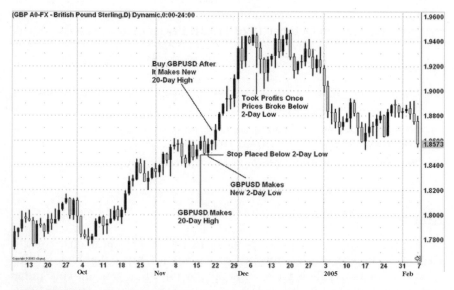

FIGURE 8.19   GBP/USD Filtering False Breakouts Chart
(*Source:* eSignal. www.eSignal.com)

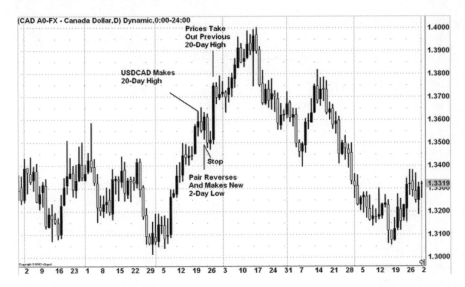

FIGURE 8.20 USD/CAD Filtering False Breakouts Chart
(*Source:* eSignal. www.eSignal.com)

Our last example is on the short side. Figure 8.21 is a daily chart of USD/JPY. The chart illustrates that USD/JPY made a new 20-day low on October 11 below 109.30. The currency pair then proceeded to make a new two-day high on October 13 of 110.21. Prices then reversed over the next two days to break below the original 20-day low, at which point our sell order at 109.20 (a few pips below the 20-day low) was triggered. We placed our stop a few pips above the two-day high at 110.30. As the currency moves in our favor, we have two choices: either to take profits by double the amount that we risked, which would be 220 pips in profits, or to use a trailing stop such as a two-bar high. The two-bar profit would have the trade exited at 106.76 on November 2, while the 220-pip profit would have the trade exited at 107.00 on October 25.

CHANNEL STRATEGY

Channel trading is less exotic but nevertheless works very well with currencies. The primary reason is because currencies rarely spend much time in tight trading ranges and have the tendency to develop strong trends. By just going through a few charts, traders can see that channels can easily be identified and occur frequently. A common scenario would be channel

FIGURE 8.21   USD/JPY Filtering False Breakouts Chart
(*Source:* eSignal. www.eSignal.com)

trading during the Asian session and a breakout in either the London or the U.S. session. There are many instances where economic releases are triggers for a break of the channel. Therefore it is imperative that traders keep on top of economic releases. If a channel has formed, a big U.S. number is expected to be released, and the currency pair is at the top of a channel, the probability of a breakout is high, so traders should be looking to buy the breakout, not fade it.

Channels are created when we draw a trend line and then draw a line that is parallel to the trend line. Most if not all of the price activity of the currency pair should fall between the two channel lines. We will seek to identify situations where the price is trading within a narrow channel, and then trade in the direction of a breakout from the channel. This strategy will be particularly effective when used prior to a fundamental market event such as the release of major economic news, or when used just prior to the open of a major financial market.

Here are the rules for long trades using this technique.

1. First, identify a channel on either an intraday or a daily chart. The price should be contained within a narrow range.
2. Enter long as the price breaks above the upper channel line.

3. Place a stop just under the upper channel line.

4. Trail your stop higher as the price moves in your favor.

Examples

Let us now examine a few examples. The first is a USD/CAD 15-minute chart shown in Figure 8.22. The total range of the channel is approximately 30 pips. In accordance with our strategy, we place entry orders 10 pips above and below the channel at 1.2395 and 1.2349. The order to go long gets triggered first and almost immediately we place a stop order 10 pips under the upper channel line at 1.2375. USD/CAD then proceeds to rally and reaches our target of double the range at 1.2455. A trailing stop also could have been used, similar to the ones that we talked about in our risk management section in Chapter 7.

The next example, shown in Figure 8.23, is a 30-minute chart of EUR/GBP. The total range between the two lines is 15 pips. In accordance with our strategy, we place entry orders 10 pips above and below the channel at 0.6796 and 0.6763. The order to go long gets triggered first and almost immediately we place a stop order 10 pips under the upper

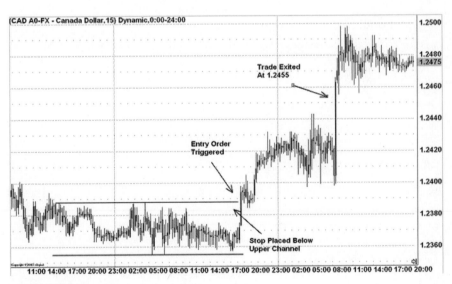

FIGURE 8.22 USD/CAD Channel Example
(*Source:* eSignal. www.eSignal.com)

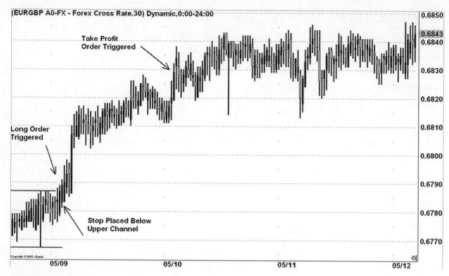

FIGURE 8.23 EUR/GBP Channel Example
(*Source:* eSignal. www.eSignal.com)

channel line at 0.6776. EUR/GBP then proceeds to rally and reaches our
target of double the range at 0.6826.

Figure 8.24 is a 5-minute chart of the EUR/USD. The total range between the two lines is 13 pips over the course of four hours. The channel
actually also occurs between the European and U.S. open ahead of the
U.S. retail sales report. In accordance with our strategy, we place entry
orders 10 pips above and below the channel at 1.2785 and 1.2752. The order to go short gets triggered first, and almost immediately we place a
stop order 10 pips above the lower channel line at 1.2772. The EUR/USD
then proceeds to sell off significantly and hits our target of double the
range of 26 pips. More aggressive traders also could have trailed their
stops to take advantage of what eventually became a much more exten-
sive move lower.

PERFECT ORDER

A perfect order in moving averages is defined as a set of moving averages
that are in sequential order. For an uptrend, a perfect order would be a
situation in which the 10-day simple moving average (SMA) is at a higher

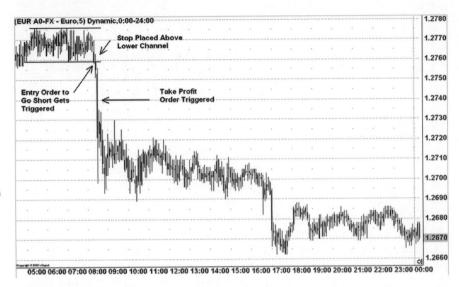

FIGURE 8.24 EUR/USD Channel Example
(*Source:* eSignal. www.eSignal.com)

price level than the 20-day SMA, which is higher than the 50-day SMA. Meanwhile, the 100-day SMA would be below the 50-day SMA, while the 200-day SMA would be below the 100-day SMA. In a downtrend, the opposite is true, where the 200-day SMA is at the highest level and the 10-day SMA is at the lowest level. Having the moving averages stacked up in sequential order is generally a strong indicator of a trending environment. Not only does it indicate that the momentum is on the side of the trend, but the moving averages also serve as multiple levels of support. To optimize the perfect order strategy, traders should also look for ADX to be greater than 20 and trending upward. Entry and exit levels are difficult to determine with this strategy, but we generally want to stay in the trade as long as the perfect order holds and exit once the perfect order no longer holds. Perfect orders do not happen often, and the premise of this strategy is to capture the perfect order when it first happens.

The perfect order seeks to take advantage of a trending environment near the beginning of the trend. Here are the rules for using this technique.

1. Look for a currency pair with moving averages in perfect order.
2. Look for ADX pointing upward, ideally greater than 20.

3. Buy five candles after the initial formation of the perfect order (if it still holds).

4. The initial stop is the low on the day of the initial crossover for longs and the high for shorts.

5. Exit the position when the perfect order no longer holds.

Examples

Figure 8.25 is a daily chart of the EUR/USD. On October 27, 2004, moving averages in the EUR/USD formed a sequential perfect order. We enter into the position five candles after the initial formation at 1.2820. Our initial stop is at the October 27, 2004 low of 1.2695. The pair continues to trend higher, and we exit the position when the perfect order no longer holds and the 10-day SMA moves below the 20-day SMA. This occurs on December 22, 2005, when prices open at 1.3370. The total profit on this trade is 550 pips. We risked 125 pips on the trade.

The next example is USD/CHF. In Figure 8.26, the perfect order occurs on November 3, 2004. In accordance with our rules, we enter into the trade five candles after the initial formation at 1.1830. Our stop is at the November 3, 2004 high (for a short trade) of 1.1927. The pair then proceeds to continue to trend lower, and we exit the position when the per-

FIGURE 8.25   EUR/USD Perfect Order Example
(*Source:* eSignal. www.eSignal.com)

FIGURE 8.26 USD/CHF Perfect Order Example
(*Source:* eSignal. www.eSignal.com)

FIGURE 8.27 USD/CAD Perfect Order Example
(*Source:* eSignal. www.eSignal.com)

fect order no longer holds and the 20-day SMA moves below the 10-day SMA. This occurs on December 16, 2005, when prices open at 1.1420. The total profit on this trade is 410 pips. We risked 97 pips.

Figure 8.27 is a perfect order formation in the USD/CAD. The formation materialized on September 30, 2004. We count five bars forward and enter into the position at 1.2588 with a stop at 1.2737. The pair then proceeds to sell off and we look to exit the position when the perfect order formation no longer holds. This occurs on December 9, 2005, at which time we buy back our position at 1.2145 for a 443-pip profit while risking 149 pips.

CHAPTER 9

Fundamental Trading Strategies

PICKING THE STRONGEST PAIRING

When trading currencies, many traders make the mistake of shaping opinions around only one specific currency without taking into account the relative strength and weakness of both of the currencies in the pair that they are trading. In the FX market, this neglect of foreign economic conditions has the potential to greatly hinder the profitability of a trade. It also increases the odds of a loss. When trading against a strong economy, there is more room for failure; the currency you want to trade could flop badly, leaving you stuck against a currency more likely to appreciate. Likewise, there is an augmented chance that the other currency could strengthen, resulting in a trade with negligible gains. Therefore, finding strong economy/weak economy pairings is a good strategy to use when attempting to maximize returns.

Take for example March 22, 2005—the U.S. Federal Reserve upped its risk for inflation in its Federal Open Market Committee (FOMC) statement, causing every major currency pair to tank against the dollar. Along with this, a slew of positive U.S. economic data further reinforced the dollar's strength. While you probably could have gained on any long dollar trade at that point, in some of the pairs the dollar appreciation had much more staying power than in others. For example, after the initial bloodbath, the pound did show a rebound in the weeks after the Fed's meeting, while the yen depreciated for a longer period of time. The reason is because at the time, Britain's economy had been exhibiting a consistent, impressive amount of economic growth, which, after the compulsive dollar frenzy, helped it gain back some substantial ground within a matter of a few weeks. The rebound in the British pound against the dollar can be seen in Figure 9.1. After hitting a low of 1.8595 on March 28, the pair proceeded to rebound back toward its pre-FOMC level of 1.9200 over the next three weeks.

On the other hand, the Japanese yen saw a depreciation over a much longer period of time with a continual upward movement in the USD/JPY pair well into the middle of April. This price action can be seen in Figure 9.2. After the FOMC meeting, the dollar proceeded to strengthen another 300 pips over the next two weeks. Part of the reason for the differences in these movements was that market watchers did not have much faith in the Japanese economy, which had been teetering on the edge of recession and showing no signs of positive economic expansion. Therefore, the dollar strength had a much higher impact and an increased amount of staying power with the struggling yen than with the consistently strong pound.

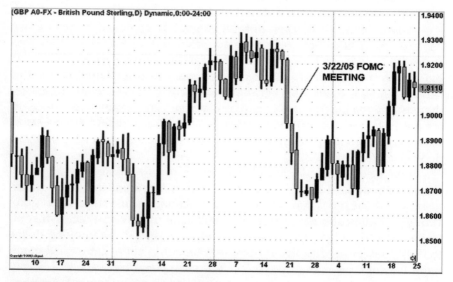

FIGURE 9.1 GBP/USD Post Fed Meeting
(*Source:* eSignal. www.eSignal.com)

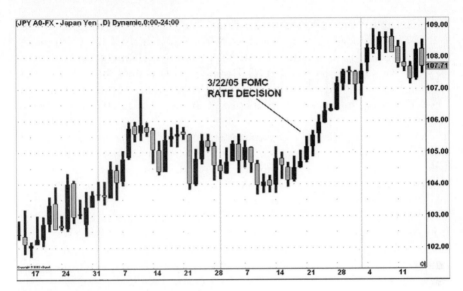

FIGURE 9.2 USD/JPY Post Fed Meeting
(*Source:* eSignal. www.eSignal.com)

Of course, interest rates as well as other geopolitical macro events are also important, but when weighing two equally compelling trades, finding the best strong economy and weak economy pairing can lead to higher chances of success. Examining crosses of the majors during this time period shows another way that knowledge of the strength of different currency pairings can be used to increase profitability. For example, take a look at Figure 9.3 and Figure 9.4. Following the FOMC meeting on March 22, both AUD/JPY and EUR/JPY sold off, but AUD/JPY rebounded much quicker than EUR/JPY. One of the reasons why this might have occurred could very well be the strong economy/weak economy comparison. The Eurozone economy experienced very weak growth in 2003, 2004, and into 2005. Australia, on the other hand, performed much better and throughout 2004 and the first half of 2005 Australia offered one of the highest interest rates of the industrialized world. As a result, as indicated in Figure 9.3, the currency pair rebounded much quicker than EUR/JPY post FOMC. This is why when looking for a trade, it is important to keep strong economy/weak economy pairings in mind.

FIGURE 9.3 AUD/JPY Post Fed Meeting
(*Source:* eSignal. www.eSignal.com)

FIGURE 9.4 EUR/JPY Post Fed Meeting
(*Source:* eSignal. www.eSignal.com)

LEVERAGED CARRY TRADE

The leveraged carry trade strategy is one of the favorite trading strategies of global macro hedge funds and investment banks. It is the quintessential global macro trade. In a nutshell, the carry trade strategy entails going long or buying a high-yielding currency and selling or shorting a low-yielding currency. Aggressive speculators will leave the exchange rate exposure unhedged, which means that the speculator is betting that the high-yielding currency is going to appreciate in addition to earning the interest rate differential between the two currencies. For those who hedge the exchange rate exposure, although interest rate differentials tend to be rather small, on the scale of 1 to 5 percent, if traders factor in 5 to 10 times leverage, the profits from interest rates alone can be substantial. Just think about it: A 2.5 percent interest rate differential becomes 25 percent on 10 times leverage. Leverage can also be very risky if not managed properly because it can exacerbate losses. Capital appreciation generally occurs when a number of traders see this same opportunity and also pile into the trade, which ends up rallying the currency pair.

In foreign exchange trading, the carry trade is an easy way to take advantage of this basic economic principle that money is constantly flowing in and out of different markets, driven by the economic law of supply and demand: markets that offer the highest returns on investment will in general attract the most capital. Countries are no different—in the world of international capital flows, nations that offer the highest interest rates will generally attract the most investment and create the most demand for their currencies.. A very popular trading strategy, the carry trade is simple to master. If done correctly, it can earn a high return without an investor taking on a lot of risk. However, carry trades do come with some risk. The chances of loss are great if you do not understand how, why, and when carry trades work best.

How Do Carry Trades Work?

The way a carry trade works is to buy a currency that offers a high interest rate while selling a currency that offers a low interest rate. Carry trades are profitable because an investor is able to earn the difference in interest—or spread—between the two currencies.

An example: Assume that the Australian dollar offers an interest rate of 4.75 percent, while the Swiss franc offers an interest rate of 0.25 percent. To execute the carry trade, an investor buys the Australian dollar and sells the Swiss franc. In doing so, he or she can earn a profit of 4.50

percent (4.75 percent in interest earned minus 0.25 percent in interest paid), as long as the exchange rate between Australian dollars and Swiss francs does not change. This return is based on zero leverage. Five times leverage equals a 22.5 percent return on just the interest rate differential. To illustrate, take a look at the following example and Figure 9.5 to see how an investor would actually execute the carry trade:

Executing the Carry Trade

Buy AUD and sell CHF (long AUD/CHF).

Long AUD position: investor earns 4.75 percent.

Short CHF position: investor pays 0.25 percent.

With spot rate held constant, profit is 4.50 percent, or 450 basis points.

If the currency pair also increased in value due to other traders identifying this opportunity, the carry trader would earn not only yield but also capital appreciation.

To summarize: A carry trade works by buying a currency that offers a high interest rate while selling a currency that offers a low interest rate.

Why Do Carry Trades Work?

Carry trades work because of the constant movement of capital into and out of countries. Interest rates are a big reason why some countries attract a great deal of investment as opposed to others. If a country's economy is doing well (high growth, high productivity, low unemployment,

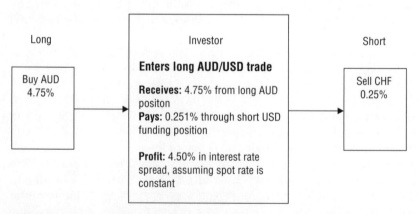

FIGURE 9.5 Leveraged Carry Trade Example

rising incomes, etc.), it will be able to offer those who invest in the country a higher return on investment. Another way to make this point is to say that countries with better growth prospects can afford to pay a higher rate of interest on the money that is invested in them.

Investors prefer to earn higher interest rates, so investors who are interested in maximizing their profits will naturally look for investments that offer them the highest rate of return. When making a decision to invest in a particular currency, an investor is more likely to choose the one that offers the highest rate of return, or interest rate. If several investors make this exact same decision, the country will experience an inflow of capital from those seeking to earn a high rate of return.

What about countries that are not doing well economically? Countries that have low growth and low productivity will not be able to offer investors a high rate of return on investment. In fact, there are some countries that have such weak economies that they are unable to offer any return on investment, meaning that interest rates are zero or very close to it.

This difference between countries that offer high interest rates versus countries that offer low interest rates is what makes carry trades possible.

Let's take another look at the previous carry trade example, but in a slightly more detailed way:

Imagine an investor in Switzerland who is earning an interest rate of 0.25 percent per year on her bank deposit of Swiss francs. At the same time, a bank in Australia is offering 4.75 percent per year on a deposit of Australian dollars. Seeing that interest rates are much higher with the Australian bank, this investor would like to find a way to earn this higher rate of interest on her money.

Now imagine that the investor could somehow trade her deposit of Swiss francs paying 0.25 percent for a deposit of Australian dollars paying 4.75 percent. What she has effectively done is to sell her Swiss franc deposit and buy an Australian dollar deposit. After this transaction she now owns an Australian dollar deposit that pays her 4.75 percent in interest per year, 4.50 percent more than she was earning with her Swiss franc deposit.

In essence, this investor has just done a carry trade by "buying" an Australian dollar deposit, and "selling" a Swiss franc deposit.

The net effect of millions of people doing this transaction is that capital flows out of Switzerland and into Australia as investors take their Swiss francs and trade them in for Australian dollars. Australia is able to attract more capital because of the higher rates it offers. This inflow of capital increases the value of the currency (see Figure 9.6).

To summarize: Carry trades are made possible by the differences in

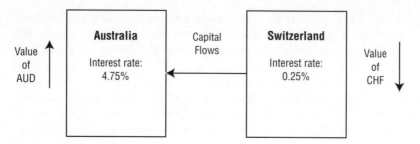

FIGURE 9.6   Effects of a Carry Trade: AUD/CHF Carry Trade Example 1

interest rates between countries. Because they prefer to earn higher interest rates, investors will look to buy and hold high-interest-rate-paying currencies.

When Do Carry Trades Work Best?

Carry trades work better during certain times than others. In fact, carry trades are the most profitable when investors as a group have a very specific attitude toward risk.

How Much Risk Are You Willing to Take?   People's moods tend to change over time—sometimes they may feel more daring and willing to take chances, while other times they may be more timid and prone to being conservative. Investors, as a group, are no different. Sometimes they are willing to make investments that involve a good amount of risk, while other times they are more fearful of losses and look to invest in safer assets.

In financial jargon, when investors as a whole are willing to take on risk, we say that they have *low risk aversion* or, in other words, are in risk-seeking mode. In contrast, when investors are drawn to more conservative investments and are less willing to take on risk, we say that they have *high risk aversion*.

Carry trades are the most profitable when investors have low risk aversion. This statement makes sense when you consider what a carry trade involves. To recap, a carry trade involves buying a currency that pays a high interest rate while selling a currency that pays a low interest rate. In buying the high-interest-rate currency, the investor is taking a risk—there is a good deal of uncertainty around whether the economy of the country will continue to perform well and be able to pay high interest rates. Indeed, there is a clear chance that something might happen to prevent the country from paying this high interest rate. Ultimately, the investor must be willing to take this chance.

If investors as a whole were not willing to take on this risk, then capital would never move from one country to another, and the carry trade opportunity would not exist. Therefore, in order to work, carry trades require that investors as a group have low risk aversion, or are willing to take the risk of investing in the higher-interest-rate currency.

To summarize: Carry trades have the most profit potential during times when investors are willing to take the risk of investing in high-interest-paying currencies.

When Will Carry Trades Not Work?

So far we have shown that a carry trade will work best when investors have low risk aversion. What happens when investors have high risk aversion?

Carry trades are the least profitable when investors have high risk aversion. When investors have high risk aversion, they are less willing as a group to take chances with their investments. Therefore, they would be less willing to invest in riskier currencies that offer higher interest rates. Instead, when investors have high risk aversion they would actually prefer to put their money in "safe haven" currencies that pay lower interest rates. This would be equivalent to doing the exact opposite of a carry trade—in other words, investors are buying the currency with the low interest rate and selling the currency with the high interest rate.

Going back to our earlier example, assume the investor suddenly feels uncomfortable holding a foreign currency, the Australian dollar. Now, instead of looking for the higher interest rate, she is more interested in keeping her investment safe. As a result, she swaps her Australian dollars for more familiar Swiss francs.

The net effect of millions of people doing this transaction is that capital flows out of Australia and into Switzerland as investors take their Australian dollars and trade them in for Swiss francs. Because of this high investor risk aversion, Switzerland attracts more capital due to the safety its currency offers despite the lower interest rates. This inflow of capital increases the value of the Swiss franc (see Figure 9.7).

To summarize: Carry trades will be the least profitable during times when investors are unwilling to take the risk of investing in high-interest-paying currencies.

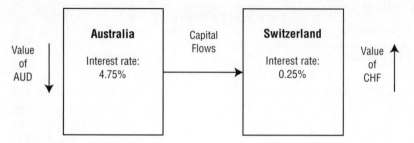

FIGURE 9.7 Effects of a Carry Trade When Investors Have High Risk Aversion: AUD/CHF Carry Trade Example 2

Importance of Risk Aversion

Carry trades will generally be profitable when investors have low risk aversion, and unprofitable when investors have high risk aversion. Therefore, before placing a carry trade it is critical to be aware of the risk environment—whether investors as a whole have high or low risk aversion—and when it *changes*.

Increasing risk aversion is generally beneficial for low-interest-rate-paying currencies: Sometimes the mood of investors will change rapidly—investors' willingness to make risky trades can change dramatically from one moment to the next. Often these large shifts are caused by significant global events. When investor risk aversion does rise quickly, the result is generally a large capital inflow into low-interest-rate-paying "safe haven" currencies (see Figure 9.6).

For example, in the summer of 1998 the Japanese yen appreciated against the dollar by over 20 percent in the span of two months, due mainly to the Russian debt crisis and Long-Term Capital Management hedge fund bailout. Similarly, just after the September 11, 2001, terrorist attacks the Swiss franc rose by more than 7 percent against the dollar over a 10-day period.

These sharp movements in currency values often occur when risk aversion quickly changes from low to high. As a result, when risk aversion shifts in this way, a carry trade can just as quickly turn from being profitable to unprofitable. Conversely, as investor risk aversion goes from high to low, carry trades become more profitable, as detailed in Figure 9.8.

How do you know if investors as a whole have high or low risk aversion? Unfortunately, it is difficult to measure investor risk aversion with a single number. One way to get a broad idea of risk aversion levels is to look at the different yields that bonds pay. The wider the difference, or

Carry Trade Profitability		
(−) ←————————————————————→ (+)		
High Risk Aversion	**Risk Neutral**	**Low Risk Aversion**
1. Investors less willing to take risks, remove funds from risky currencies. 2. Capital flows out of riskier high-interest currencies and into low-interest safe-haven currencies. 3. Low-interest currencies appreciate as investors get out of risky trades.		1. Investors more willing to take greater risks. 2. Capital flows away from low-interest currencies and into those that pay higher interest rates. 3. Low-interest currencies tend to remain weak, used in financing risky trades.

FIGURE 9.8 Risk Aversion and Carry Trade Profitability

spread, between bonds of different credit ratings, the higher the investor risk aversion. Bond yields can be found in most financial newspapers. In addition, several large banks have developed their own measures of risk aversion that signal when investors are willing to take risks and when they are not.

Other Things to Bear in Mind When Considering a Carry Trade

While risk aversion is one of the most important things to consider before making a carry trade, it is not the only one. The following are some additional issues to be aware of.

Low-Interest-Rate Currency Appreciation By entering into a carry trade, an investor is able to earn a profit from the interest rate difference, or spread, between a high-interest-rate currency and a low-interest-rate currency. However, the carry trade can turn unprofitable if for some reason (like the earlier risk aversion example) the low-interest-rate currency appreciates by a large amount.

Aside from increases in investor risk aversion, improving economic conditions within a low-interest-paying country can also cause its currency to appreciate. An ideal carry trade involves a low-interest currency whose economy is weak and has low expectations for growth. If the economy were to improve, however, the country might then be able to offer investors a higher rate of return through increased interest rates. If this were to occur—again using the earlier example, say that Switzerland increased the interest rates it offered—then investors may take advantage of these higher rates by investing in Swiss francs. As seen in Figure 9.7, an appreciation of the Swiss franc would negatively affect the profitability of the Australian dollar–Swiss franc carry trade. (At the very least, higher interest rates in Switzerland would negatively affect the carry trade's profitability by lowering the interest rate spread.)

To give another example, this same sequence of events may currently be unfolding for the Japanese yen. Given its zero interest rates, the Japanese yen has for a very long time been an ideal low-interest-rate currency to use in carry trades (known as "yen carry trades"). This situation, however, may be changing. Increased optimism about the Japanese economy has recently led to an increase in the Japanese stock market. Increased investor demand for Japanese stocks and currency has caused the yen to appreciate, and this yen appreciation negatively affects the profitability of carry trades like Australian dollar (high interest rate) versus Japanese yen.

If investors continue to buy the yen, the "yen carry trade" will grow more and more unprofitable. This further illustrates the fact that when the low-interest-rate currency in a carry trade (the currency being sold) appreciates, it negatively affects the profitability of the carry trade.

Trade Balances   Country trade balances (the difference between imports and exports) can also affect the profitability of a carry trade. We have shown that when investors have low risk aversion, capital will flow from the low-interest-rate-paying currency to the high-interest-rate-paying currency (see Figure 9.6). This, however, does not always happen.

To understand why, think about the situation in the United States. The United States currently pays historically low interest rates, yet it attracts investment from other countries, even when investors have low risk aversion (i.e., they *should* be investing in the high-interest-rate countries). Why does this occur? The answer is because the United States runs a huge trade deficit (its imports are greater than its exports)—a deficit that must be financed by other countries. Regardless of the interest rates it offers, the United States attracts capital flows to finance its trade deficit.

The point of this example is to show that even when investors have low risk aversion, large trade imbalances can cause a low-interest-rate currency to appreciate (as in Figure 9.7). And when the low-interest-rate currency in a carry trade (the currency being sold) appreciates, it negatively affects the profitability of the carry trade.

Time Horizon   In general, a carry trade is a long-term strategy. Before entering into a carry trade, an investor should be willing to commit to a time horizon of at least six months. This commitment helps to make sure that the trade will not be affected by the "noise" of shorter-term currency price movements. Also, not using excessive leverage for carry trades will allow traders to hold onto their positions longer and to better weather market fluctuations by not getting stopped out.

To summarize: Carry trade investors should be aware of factors such as currency appreciation, trade balances, and time horizon before placing a trade. Any or all of these factors can cause a seemingly profitable carry trade to become unprofitable.

FUNDAMENTAL TRADING STRATEGY: STAYING ON TOP OF MACROECONOMIC EVENTS

Short-term traders seem to be focused only on the economic release of the week and how it will impact their day trading activities. This works well for many traders, but it is also important not to lose sight of the big macro events that may be brewing in the economy—or the world for that matter. The reason is because large-scale macroeconomic events will move markets and will move them big time. Their impact goes beyond a simple price change for a day or two because depending on their size and scope, these occurrences have the potential to reshape the fundamental perception toward a currency for months or even years at a time. Events such as wars, political uncertainty, natural disasters, and major international meetings are so potent due to their irregularity that they have widespread psychological and physical impacts on the currency market. With these events come both currencies that appreciate vastly and currencies that depreciate just as dramatically. Therefore, keeping on top of global developments, understanding the underlying direction of market sentiment before and after these events occur, and anticipating them could be very profitable, or at least can help prevent significant losses.

Know When Big Events Occur
- Significant G-7 or G-8 finance ministers meetings.
- Presidential elections.
- Important summits.
- Major central bank meetings.
- Potential changes to currency regimes.
- Possible debt defaults by large countries.

- Possible wars as a result of rising geopolitical tensions.
- Federal Reserve chairman's semiannual testimony to Congress on the economy.

The best way to highlight the significance of these events is through examples.

G-7 Meeting, Dubai, September 2003

The countries that constitute the G-7 are the United States, United Kingdom, Japan, Canada, Italy, Germany, and France. Collectively, these countries account for two-thirds of the world's total economic output. Not all G-7 meetings are important. The only time the market really hones in on the G-7 finance ministers meeting is when big changes are expected. The G-7 finance ministers meeting on September 22, 2003, was a very important turning point for the markets. The dollar collapsed significantly following the meeting at which the G-7 finance ministers wanted to see "more flexibility in exchange rates." Despite the rather tame nature of these words, the market interpreted this line to be a major shift in policy. The last time changes to this degree had been made was back in 2000.

In 2000, the market paid particular attention to the upcoming meeting because there was strong intervention in the EUR/USD the day before the meeting. The meeting in September 2003 was also important because the U.S. trade deficit was ballooning and becoming a huge issue. The EUR/USD bore the brunt of the dollar depreciation while Japan and China were intervening aggressively in their currencies. As a result, it was widely expected that the G-7 finance ministers as a whole would issue a statement that was highly critical of Japan's and China's intervention policies. Leading up to the meeting, the U.S. dollar had already begun to sell off, as indicated by the chart in Figure 9.9. At the time of the announcement, the EUR/USD shot up 150 pips. Though this initial move was not very substantial, between September 2003 and February 2004 (the next G-7 meeting), the dollar fell 8 percent on a trade-weighted basis, 9 percent against the British pound, 11 percent against the euro, 7 percent against the yen, and 1.5 percent against the Canadian dollar. To put the percentages into perspective, a move of 11 percent is equivalent to approximately 1,100 pips. Therefore the longer-term impact is much more significant than the immediate impact, as the event itself has the ability to change the overall sentiment in the market. Figure 9.9 is a weekly chart of the EUR/USD that illustrates how the currency pair performed following the September 22, 2003, G-7 meeting.

FIGURE 9.9   EUR/USD Post G-7 Chart
(*Source:* eSignal. www.eSignal.com)

Political Uncertainty: 2004 U.S. Presidential Election

Another example of a major event impacting the currency market is the 2004 U.S. presidential election. In general, political instability causes perceived weakness in currencies. The hotly contested presidential election in November 2004 combined with the differences in the candidates' stances on the growing budget deficit resulted in overall dollar bearishness. The sentiment was exacerbated even further given the lack of international support for the incumbent president (George W. Bush) due to the administration's decision to overthrow Saddam Hussein. As a result, in the three weeks leading up to the election, the euro rose 600 pips against the U.S. dollar. This can be seen in Figure 9.10. With a Bush victory becoming increasingly clear and later confirmed, the dollar sold off against the majors as the market looked ahead to what would probably end up being the maintenance of the status quo. On the day following the election, the EUR/USD rose another 200 pips and then continued to rise an additional 700 pips before peaking six weeks later. This entire move took place over the course of two months, which may seem like eternity to many, but this macroeconomic event really shaped the markets; for those who were following it, big profits could have been made. However, this is important even for short-term traders because given that the market was bearish

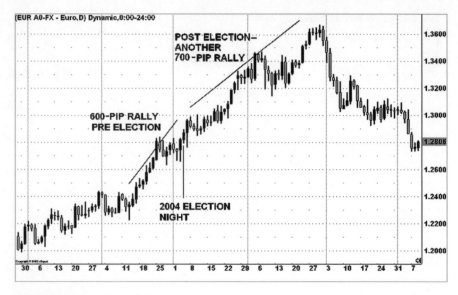

FIGURE 9.10   EUR/USD U.S. Election
(*Source:* eSignal. www.eSignal.com)

dollars in general leading up to the U.S. presidential election, a more prudent trade would have been to look for opportunities to buy the EUR/USD on dips rather than trying to sell rallies and look for tops.

Wars: U.S. War in Iraq

Geopolitical risks such as wars can also have a pronounced impact on the currency market. Figure 9.11 shows that between December 2002 and February 2003, the dollar depreciated 9 percent against the Swiss franc (USD/CHF) in the months leading up to the invasion of Iraq. The dollar sold off because the war itself was incredibly unpopular among the international community. The Swiss franc was one of the primary beneficiaries due to the country's political neutrality and safe haven status. Between February and March, the market began to believe that the inevitable war would turn into a quick and decisive U.S. victory, so they began to unwind the war trade. This eventually led to a 3 percent rally in USD/CHF as investors exited their short dollar positions.

Each of these events caused large-scale movement in the currency markets, which makes them important events to follow for all types of

FIGURE 9.11 USD/CHF War Trade
(*Source:* eSignal. www.eSignal.com)

traders. Keeping abreast of broad macroeconomic events can help traders make smarter decisions and prevent them from fading large uncertainties that may be brewing in the background. Most of these events are talked about, debated, and anticipated many months in advance by economists, currency analysts, and the international community in general. The world changes and currency traders need to be prepared for that.

COMMODITY PRICES AS A LEADING INDICATOR

Commodities, namely gold and oil, have a substantial connection to the FX market. Therefore, understanding the nature of the relationship between them and currencies can help traders gauge risk, forecast price changes, as well as understand exposure. Even if commodities seem like a wholly alien concept, gold and oil especially tend to move based on similar fundamental factors that affect currency markets. As we have previously discussed, there are four major currencies considered to be commodity currencies—the Australian dollar, the Canadian dollar, the New Zealand dollar, and the Swiss franc. The AUD, CAD, NZD, and CHF all have solid correlations with gold prices; natural gold reserves and currency laws in these countries result in almost mirror-like movements. The CAD also tends to move somewhat in line with oil prices; however, the connection here is much more complicated and fickle. Each currency has a specific correlation and reason as to why its actions reflect commodity prices so well. Knowledge of the fundamentals behind these movements, their direction, and the strength of the parallel could be an effective way to discover trends in both markets.

The Relationship

Gold   Before analyzing the relationship gold has with the commodity currencies, it is important to first understand the connection between gold and the U.S. dollar. Although the United States is the world's second largest producer of gold (behind South Africa), a rally in gold prices does not produce an appreciation of the dollar. Actually, when the dollar goes down, gold tends to go up, and vice versa. This seemingly illogical occurrence is a by-product of the perception investors hold of gold. During unstable geopolitical times, traders tend to shy away from the dollar and instead turn to gold as a safe haven for their investments. In fact, many traders call gold the "antidollar." Therefore, if the dollar depreciates, gold gets pushed up as wary investors flock from the declining greenback to the steady commodity. The AUD/USD, NZD/USD, and USD/CHF currency pairs tend to mirror gold's movements the closest because these other currencies all have significant natural and political connections to the metal.

Starting in the South Pacific, the AUD/USD has a very strong positive correlation (0.80) with gold as shown in Figure 9.12; therefore, whenever gold prices go up, the AUD/USD also tends to go up as the Australian dollar appreciates against the U.S. dollar. The reason for this relationship is that Australia is the world's third largest producer of gold, exporting about $5 billion worth of the precious metal annually. Because of this, the currency pair amplifies the effects of gold prices twofold. If instability is causing an increase in prices, this probably signals that the USD has already begun to depreciate. The pairing will then be pushed down further as importers of gold demand more of Australia's currency to cover higher costs. The New Zealand dollar tends to follow the same path in the AUD/USD pairing because New Zealand's economy is very closely linked to Australia's. The correlation in this pairing is also approximately 0.80 with gold (see Figure 9.13 for the chart). The CAD/USD has an even stronger correlation with gold prices at 0.84,

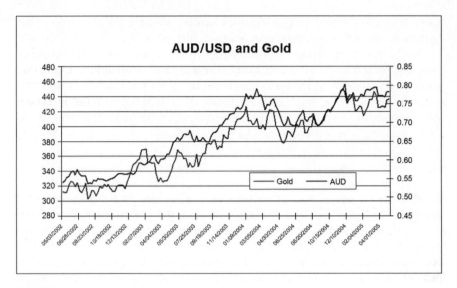

FIGURE 9.12 AUD/USD and Gold

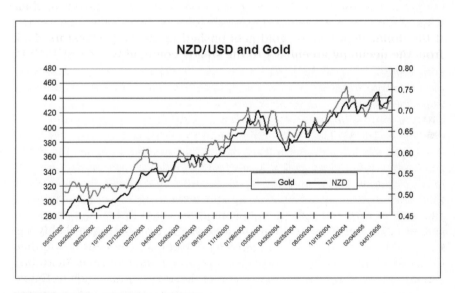

FIGURE 9.13 NZD/USD and Gold

caused in large part by analogous reasons to the AUD's connection; Canada is the fifth largest exporter of gold.

In Europe, Switzerland's currency has a strong relationship with gold prices as well. However, the CHF/USD pairing's 0.88 correlation with the metal is caused by different reasons than the NZD's, AUD's, and CAD's connections. Switzerland does not have substantial natural gold reserves like Australia or Canada and therefore it is not a notable exporter of the metal. However, the Swiss franc is one of the few major currencies that still adheres to the gold standard. A full 25 percent of Switzerland's bank issue notes are backed in gold reserves. This solid currency base makes it no mystery as to why the CHF is perceived as a currency safe haven in unstable times. During times of geopolitical uncertainties, the Swissie tends to rally. An example of this could be found in the U.S. buildup to the war in Iraq. Many investors drew their money out of the USD and invested heavily in both gold and the CHF.

Thus, a trader who notes a rising trend in gold prices (or in other metals such as copper or nickel) might be wise to go long any one of the four commodity currencies instead. One interesting incentive to go long the AUD/USD instead of gold is the unique ability of expressing the same view but also being able to earn positive carry. Gold is also usually a solid indicator of the overall picture in the metals markets.

Oil   Oil prices have a huge impact on the world economy, affecting both consumers and producers. Therefore the correlation between this commodity and currency prices is much more complex and less stable than that of gold. In fact, out of all of the commodity currencies, only one (the CAD) has any semblance of a connection with oil prices.

The USD/CAD has a correlation of –0.4, a fairly weak number indicating that a rally in oil prices will result in a rally in the Canadian dollar only some of the time. Throughout the second half of 2004 and first half of 2005, this correlation has been much stronger. Although Canada is the world's fourteenth largest producer of oil, oil's effect on its economy is much more all-encompassing than gold's. While gold prices do not have a substantial spillover into other areas, oil prices most definitely do. Canada especially has trouble due to its cold climate, which creates a large amount of demand for heating oil most of the year. Moreover, Canada is particularly susceptible to poor foreign economic conditions because it depends heavily on exports. Therefore, oil has a very mixed effect on the Canadian dollar. Most of this is dependent upon how U.S. consumer demand responds to rising oil prices. Canada's economy is closely tied to its southern neighbor since 85 percent of its exports are destined for the United States.

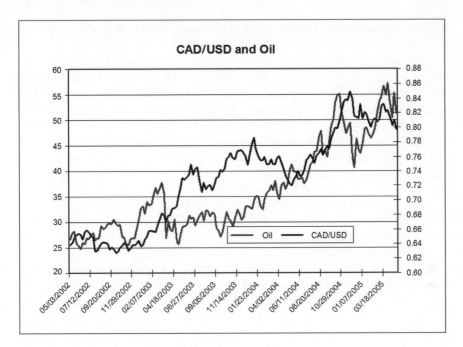

FIGURE 9.14 CAD/USD and Oil

Trading Opportunity

Now that the relationships have been explained, there are two ways to exploit this knowledge. Taking a look at Figures 9.12, 9.13, and 9.14, you can see that generally speaking, commodity prices are a leading indicator for currency prices. This is most apparent in the NZD/USD–gold relationship shown in Figure 9.13 and the CAD/USD–oil relationship shown in Figure 9.14. As such, commodity block traders can monitor gold and oil prices to forecast movements in the currency pairs. The second way to exploit this knowledge is to parlay the same view using different products, which does help to diversify risk a bit even with the high correlation. In fact, there is one key advantage to expressing the view in currencies over commodities, and that is that it offers traders the ability to earn interest on their positions based on the interest rate differential between the two countries, while gold and oil futures positions do not.

USING BOND SPREADS AS A LEADING INDICATOR FOR FX

Any trader can attest that interest rates are an integral part of investment decisions and can drive markets in either direction. FOMC rate decisions are the second largest currency-market-moving release, behind unemployment data. The effects of interest rate changes have not only short-term implications, but also long-term consequences on the currency markets. One central bank's rate decision can affect more than a single pairing in the interrelated forex market. Yield differentials fixed income instruments such as London Interbank Offered Rates (LIBOR) and 10-year bond yields can be used as leading indicators for currency movements. In FX trading, an interest rate differential is the difference between the interest rate on a base currency (appearing first in the pair) less the interest rate on the quoted currency (appearing second in the pair). Each day at 5:00 p.m. EST, the close of the day for currency markets, funds are either paid out or received to adjust for interest rate differences. Understanding the correlation between interest rate differentials and currency pairs can be very profitable. In addition to central bank overnight rate decisions, expected future overnight rates along with the expected timing of rate changes are also critical to currency pair movements. The reason why this works is that the majority of international investors are yield seekers. Large investment banks, hedge funds, and institutional investors have the ability capital-wise to access global markets. Therefore, they are actively shifting funds from lower-yielding assets to higher-yielding assets.

Interest Rate Differentials: Leading Indicator, Coincident Indicator, or Lagging Indicator?

Since most currency traders consider present and future interest rate differentials when making investment decisions, there should theoretically be some correlation between yield differences and currency pair prices. However, do currency pair prices predict rate decisions, or do rate decisions affect currency pair prices? Leading indicators are economic indicators that predict future events; coincident indicators are economic indicators that vary with economic events; lagging indicators are economic indicators that follow an economic event. For instance, if interest rate differentials predict future currency pair prices, interest rate differentials are said to be leading indicators of currency pair prices. Whether interest rate differentials are a leading, coincident, or lagging indicator of currency pair prices depends on how much traders care about future rates versus current rates. Assuming efficient markets, if currency traders care only about current interest rates and not about future rates, one would expect a coincident relationship. If currency traders consider both current and future rates, one would expect interest rate differentials to be a leading indicator of future currency prices.

The rule of thumb is that when the yield spread increases in favor of a certain currency that currency will generally appreciate against other currencies. For example, if the current Australian 10-year government bond yield is 5.50 percent and the current U.S. 10-year government bond yield is 2.00 percent, then the yield spread would be 350 basis points in favor of Australia. If Australia raised its interest rates by 25 basis points and the 10-year government bond yield appreciated to 5.75 percent, then the new yield spread would be 375 basis points in favor of Australia. Based on historical evidence, the Australian dollar is also expected to appreciate against the U.S. dollar in this scenario.

Based on a study of three years of empirical data starting from January 2002 and ending January 2005, we find that interest rate differentials tend to be a leading indicator of currency pairs. Figures 9.15, 9.16, and 9.17 are graphical representations of this finding.

These figures show three examples of currency pairs where bond spreads have the clearest leading-edge correlation. As one would expect from the fact that traders trade on a variety of information and not just interest rates, the correlation, though good, is not perfect. In general, interest rate differential analysis seems to work better over a longer period of time. However, shifts in sentiment for the outlook for the path of

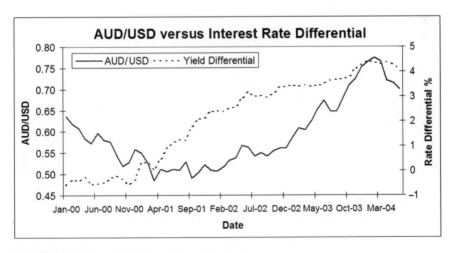

FIGURE 9.15 AUD/USD and Bond Spread

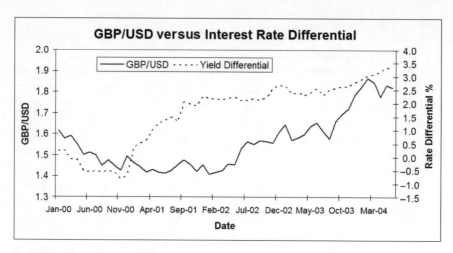

FIGURE 9.16　GBP/USD and Bond Spread

interest rates over the shorter term can still be a leading indicator for currency prices.

Calculating Interest Rate Differentials and Following the Currency Pair Trends

The best way to use interest rate differentials for trading is by keeping track of one-month LIBOR rates or 10-year bond yields in Microsoft Excel.

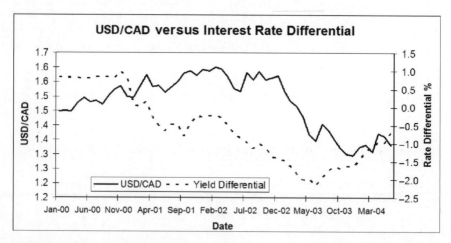

FIGURE 9.17　USD/CAD and Bond Spread

TABLE 9.1 Bond Spreads

	Date				
	10/29/2004	**11/30/2004**	**12/31/2004**	**1/31/2005**	**2/28/2005**
U.S. 10-year yield	2.00	2.29	2.40	2.59	2.71
GBP/USD	1.8372	1.9095	1.9181	1.8829	1.9210
U.K. 10-year yield	4.83	4.82	4.86	4.83	4.87
U.K.–U.S. rate differential	2.83	2.53	2.46	2.24	2.15
USD/JPY	105.81	103.07	102.63	103.70	104.63
JPY 10-year yield	0.04	0.039	0.039	0.04	0.038
U.S.–JPY rate differential	1.96	2.25	2.36	2.55	2.67

These rates are publicly available on web sites such as Bloomberg.com. Interest rate differentials are then calculated by subtracting the yield of the second currency in the pair from the yield of the first. It is important to make sure that interest rate differentials are calculated in the order in which they appear for the pair. For instance, the interest rate differentials in GBP/USD should be the 10-year gilt rate minus the 10-year U.S. Treasury note rate. For euro data, use data from the German 10-year bond. Form a table that looks similar to the one shown in Table 9.1.

After sufficient data is gathered, you can graph currency pair values and yields using a graph with two axes to see any correlations or trends. The sample graphs in Figures 9.15, 9.16, and 9.17 use the date in the x-axis and currency pair price and interest rate differentials on two y-axis graphs. To fully utilize this data in trading, you want to pay close attention to trends in the interest rate differentials of the currency pairs you trade.

FUNDAMENTAL TRADING STRATEGY: RISK REVERSALS

Risk reversals are a useful fundamentals-based tool to add to your mix of indicators for trading. One of the weaknesses of currency trading is the lack of volume data and accurate indicators for gauging sentiment. The only publicly available report on positioning is the "Commitments of Traders" report published by the Commodity Futures Trading Commission, and even that is released with a three-day delay. A useful alternative is to use risk reversals, which are provided on a real-time basis on the Forex Capital Markets (FXCM) news plug-in, under Options. As we first introduced in Chapter 7, a risk reversal consists of a pair of options for the same currency (a call and a put). Based on put/call parity, far out-of-the-money options (25 delta) with the same expiration and strike price should also have the same implied volatility. However, in reality this is not true. Sentiment is embedded in volatilities, which makes risk reversals a good tool to gauge market sentiment. A number strongly in favor of calls over puts indicates that there is more demand for calls than puts. The opposite is also true: a number strongly in favor of puts over calls indicates that there is a premium built in put options as a result of the higher demand. If risk reversals are near zero, this indicates that there is indecision among bulls and bears and that there is no strong bias in the markets.

What Does a Risk Reversal Table Look Like?

We showed a risk reversal table before in Chapter 7, (Table 7.3), but want to describe it again to make sure that it is well understood. Each of the abbreviations for the currency options are listed, and, as indicated, most risk reversals are near zero, which indicates no significant bias. For USD/JPY, though, the longer-term risk reversals indicate that the market is strongly favoring yen calls (JC) and dollar puts.

How Can You Use This Information?

For easier graphing and tracking purposes, we use positive and negative integers for call and put premiums, respectively, in Figure 9.18. Therefore a positive number indicates that calls are preferred over puts and that the market as a whole is expecting an upward movement in the underlying currency. Likewise, a negative number indicates that puts are preferred over calls and that the market is expecting a downward move in the underlying currency. Used prudently, risk reversals can be a valuable tool in judging market positioning. While the signals generated by a risk reversal system will not be completely accurate, they can specify when the market is bullish or bearish.

Risk reversals become quite important when the values are at extreme levels. We identify extreme levels as one standard deviation plus or minus the average risk reversal. When risk reversals are at these levels, they give off contrarian signals, indicating that a currency pair is overbought or oversold based on sentiment. The indicator is perceived as a contrarian signal because when the entire market is positioned for a rise in a given currency, it makes it that much harder for the currency to rally, and that much easier for it to fall on negative news or events. As a result, a strongly negative number implies oversold conditions, whereas a strongly positive number would imply overbought conditions. Although the buy or sell signals produced by risk reversals are not perfect, they can convey additional information used to make trading decisions.

Examples

Our first example of the EUR/USD is shown in Figure 9.18. Visually you can see that 25-delta risk reversals have been a leading indicator for EUR/USD price action. When risk reversals plunged to −1.39 on September 30, it was a signal that the market had a strong bearish bias. This proved to be a reliable contrarian indicator of what eventually became a 300-pip rebound in the EUR/USD over the course of nine days. When prices spiked once again almost immediately to 0.67 in favor of a continuation of the up move, the EUR/USD proved bulls wrong by engaging in an even deeper sell-off. Although there were many instances of risk reversals signaling contra-trend moves on a smaller scale, the next major spike came a year later. On August 16, risk reversals were at 1.43, which meant that bullish sentiment hit a very high level. This preceded a 260-pip drop in the EUR/USD over the course of three weeks. When risk reversals spiked

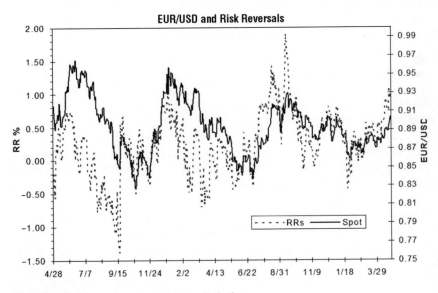

FIGURE 9.18 EUR/USD Risk Reversal Chart

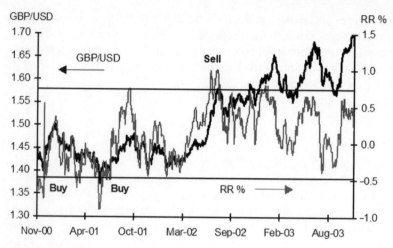

FIGURE 9.19   GBP/USD Risk Reversal Chart

once again a month later to 1.90, we saw another top in the EUR/USD, which later became a much deeper descent.

The next example is the GBP/USD. As can be seen in Figure 9.19, risk reversals do a very good job of identifying extreme overbought and oversold conditions. Buy and sell levels are added to the GBP/USD chart for further clarification of how risk reversals can also be used to time market turns. With the lack of price and volume data to give us a sense of where the market is positioned, risk reversals can be helpful in gauging general market sentiment.

USING OPTION VOLATILITIES TO TIME MARKET MOVEMENTS

Using option volatilities to time foreign exchange spot movements is a topic that we touched upon briefly in Chapter 7. Since this is a very useful strategy that is a favorite among professional hedge funds, it certainly warrants a more detailed explanation. Implied volatility can be defined as a measure of a currency's expected fluctuation over a given time period based on past price fluctuations. This is typically calculated by taking the historic annual standard deviation of daily price changes. Future prices help to determine implied volatility, which is used to calculate option premiums. Although this sounds fairly complicated, its application is not. Basically, option volatilities measure the rate and magnitude of a currency's price over a given period of time based on historical fluctuations. Therefore, if the average daily trading range of the EUR/USD contracted from 100 pips to 60 pips and stayed there for two weeks, in all likelihood short-term volatility also contracted significantly compared to longer-term volatility during the same time period.

Rules

As a guideline, there are two simple rules to follow. The first one is that if short-term option volatilities are significantly lower than long-term volatilities, one should expect a breakout, though the direction of the breakout is not defined by this rule. Second, if short-term option volatilities are significantly higher than long-term volatilities, one should expect a reversion to trading range.

Why Do These Rules Work?

During a ranging period, implied option volatilities are either low or on the decline. The inspiration for these rules is that in periods of range trading, there tends to be little movement. We care most about when option volatilities drop sharply, which could be a sign that a profitable breakout is under way. When short-term volatility is above long-term volatility, it means that near-term price action is more volatile than the long-term average price action. This suggests that the ranges will eventually contract back toward average levels. The trend is most noticeable in empirical data. Here are a few examples of when this rule accurately predicted trends or breaks.

Before analyzing the charts, it is important to note that we use one-month volatilities as our short-term volatilities and three-month volatilities as our longer-term volatilities.

In the AUD/CAD volatility chart in Figure 9.20, for the most part shorter-term volatility is fairly close to the longer-term volatility. However, the first arrow shows an instance where short-term volatility spiked well below long-term volatility, which, as indicated by our rule, suggests an upcoming breakout scenario in the currency pair. AUD/CAD did eventually break upward significantly into a strong uptrend.

The same trend is visible in the USD/JPY volatility chart in Figure 9.21. The leftmost arrow shows an instance where one-month implied volatility spiked significantly higher than three-month volatility; as expected, the spot price continued to range. The next downward arrow points to an area where short-term volatility fell below long-term volatility, leading to a breakout that sent spot prices up.

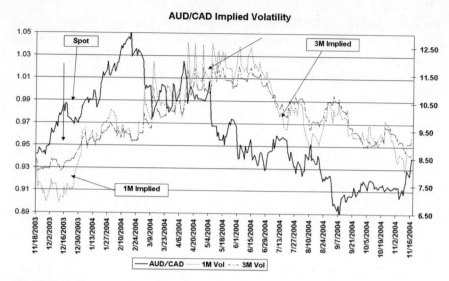

FIGURE 9.20   AUD/CAD Volatility Chart

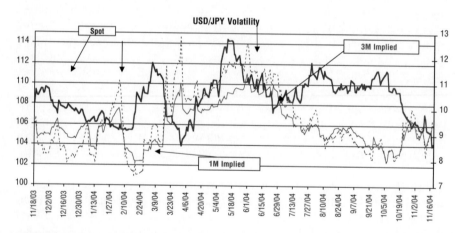

FIGURE 9.21   USD/JPY Volatility Chart

Who Can Benefit from These Rules?

This strategy is not only useful for breakout traders, but range traders can also utilize this information to predict a potential breakout scenario. If volatility contracts fall significantly or become very low, the likelihood of continued range trading decreases. After eyeing a historical range, traders should look at volatilities to estimate the likelihood that the spot will remain within this range. Should the trader decide to go long or short this range, he or she should continue to monitor volatility as long as he or she has an open position in the pair to assist them in determining when to close out that position. If short-term volatilities fall well below long-term volatilities, the trader should consider closing the position if the suspected breakout is not in the trader's favor. The potential break is likely to work in the favor of the trader if the current spot is close to the limit and far from the stop. In this hypothetical situation, it may be profitable to move limit prices away from current spot prices to increase profits from the potential break. If the spot price is close to the stop price and far from the limit price, the break is likely to work against the trader, and the trader should close the position immediately.

Breakout traders can monitor volatilities to verify a breakout. If a trader suspects a breakout, he or she can verify this breakout through implied volatilities. Should implied volatility be constant or rising, there is a higher probability that the currency will continue to trade in range than if volatility is low or falling. In other words, breakout traders should look for short-term volatilities to be significantly lower than long-term volatilities before making a breakout trade.

Aside from being a key component for pricing, option volatilities can also be a useful tool for forecasting market activities. Option volatilities measure the rate and magnitude of the changes in a currency's prices. Implied option volatilities, on the other hand, measure the expected fluctuation of a currency's price over a given period of time based on historical fluctuations.

Tracking Volatilities on Your Own

Volatility tracking typically involves taking the historic annual standard deviation of daily price changes. Volatilities can be obtained from the FXCM news plug-in available at www.fxcm.com/forex-news-software-exchange.jsp. Generally speaking, we use three-month volatilities for long-term volatilities numbers and one-month volatilities for the short term. Figure 9.22 shows how the volatilities would look on the news plug-in.

```
                             [IFR Forex Watch]
                             [FXO IMPLIED VOLS]
================================================================================
```

	EUR/USD	USD/JPY	GBP/USD	USD/CHF	AUD/USD
1 WK	8.45	7.3	7.75	10.25	8.25
1 MO	8.35	7.9	7.85	9.75	8.7
2 MO	8.5	8.1	8.05	9.75	9.15
3 MO	8.6	8.15	8.2	9.85	9.35
6 MO	8.9	8.3	8.35	10.05	9.8
1 YR	9.2	8.45	8.6	10.2	10.15
	EUR/CHF	EUR/JPY	EUR/GBP	GBP/CHF	USD/CAD
1 WK	3.65	7.4	5.6	5.7	7.35
1 MO	3.15	7.7	5.25	6.2	7.5
2 MO	3.15	7.95	5.3	6.2	7.5
3 MO	3.15	8.0	5.35	6.3	7.6
6 MO	3.3	8.2	5.6	6.5	7.7
1 YR	3.4	8.35	5.85	6.75	7.7

[LAST UPDATED 17:29 GMT May 26th 2005]

FIGURE 9.22   IFR Volatility Data

The next step is to start compiling a list of data for date, currency pair price, implied one-month volatility, and implied three-month volatility for the currency pairs you care about. The best way to generate this list is through a spreadsheet program such as Microsoft Excel, which makes graphing trends much easier. It might also be beneficial to find the difference between the one-month and three-month volatilities to look for large differentials or to calculate one-month volatility as a percentage of three-month volatility.

Once a sufficient amount of data is compiled, one can graph the data as a visual aid. The graph should use two y-axes with spot prices on one, and short- and long-term volatilities on the other. If desired, the differences in short- and long-term volatilities can be graphed as well in a separate, single y-axis graph.

FUNDAMENTAL TRADING STRATEGY: INTERVENTION

Intervention by central banks is one of the most important short-term and long-term fundamentally based market movers in the currency market. For short-term traders, intervention can lead to sharp intraday movements on the scale of 150 to 250 pips in a matter of minutes. For longer-term traders, intervention can signal a significant change in trend because it suggests that the central bank is shifting or solidifying its stance and sending a message to the market that it is putting its backing behind a certain directional move in its currency. There are basically two types of intervention, sterilized and unsterilized. Sterilized intervention requires offsetting intervention with the buying or selling of government bonds, while unsterilized intervention involves no changes to the monetary base to offset intervention. Many argue that unsterilized intervention has a more lasting effect on the currency than sterilized intervention.

Taking a look at some of the following case studies, it is apparent that interventions in general are important to watch and can have large impacts on a currency pair's price action. Although the actual timing of intervention tends to be a surprise, quite often the market will begin talking about the need for intervention days or weeks before the actual intervention occurs. The direction of intervention is generally always known in advance because the central bank will typically come across the newswires complaining about too much strength or weakness in its currency. These warnings give traders a window of opportunity to participate in what could be significant profit potentials or to stay out of the markets. The only thing to watch out for, which you will see in a case study, is that the sharp intervention-based rallies or sell-offs can quickly be reversed as speculators come into the market to fade the central bank. Whether or not the market fades the central bank depends on the frequency of central bank intervention, the success rate, the magnitude of the intervention, the timing of the intervention, and whether fundamentals support intervention. Overall, though, intervention is much more prevalent in emerging market currencies than in the G-7 currencies since countries such as Thailand, Malaysia, and South Korea need to prevent their local currencies from appreciating too significantly such that the appreciation would hinder economic recovery and reduce the competitiveness of the country's exports. The rarity of G-7 intervention makes the instances even more significant.

Japan

The biggest culprit of intervention in the G-7 markets over the past few years has been the Bank of Japan (BOJ). In 2003, the Japanese government spent a record Y20.1 trillion on intervention. This compares to the previous record of Y7.64 trillion that was spent in 1999. In the month of December 2003 (between November 27 and December 26) alone, the Japanese government sold Y2.25 trillion. The amount it spent on intervention that year represented 84 percent of the country's trade surplus. As an export-based economy, excess strength in the Japanese yen poses a significant risk to the country's manufacturers. The frequency and strength of BOJ intervention over the past few years created an invisible floor under USD/JPY. Although this floor has gradually descended from 115 to 100 between 2002 and 2005, the market still has an ingrained fear of seeing the hand of the BOJ and the Japanese Ministry of Finance once again. This fear is well justified because in the event of BOJ intervention, the average 100-pip daily range can easily triple. Additionally, at the exact time of intervention, USD/JPY has easily skyrocketed 100 pips in a matter of minutes.

In the first case study shown in Figure 9.23, the Japanese government came into the market and bought U.S. dollars and sold 1.04 trillion yen (approximately US$9 billion) on May 19, 2003. The intervention happened around 7:00 a.m. EST. Prior to the intervention, USD/JPY was trading around 115.20. When intervention occurred at 7:00 a.m., prices jumped 30 pips in one minute. By 7:30, USD/JPY was a full 100 pips higher. At 2:30 p.m. EST, USD/JPY was 220 pips higher. Intervention generally results in anywhere between 100- and 200-pip movements. Trading on the side of intervention can be very profitable (though risky) even if prices end up reversing.

The second USD/JPY example (Figure 9.24) shows how a trader could still be on the side of intervention and profit even though prices reversed later in the day. On January 9, 2004, the Japanese government came into the market to buy dollars and sell 1.664 trillion yen (approximately US$15 billion). Prior to the intervention, USD/JPY was trading at approximately 106.60. When the BOJ came into the market at 12:22 a.m. EST, prices

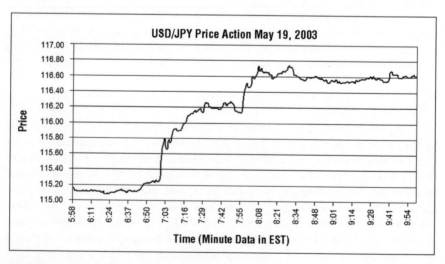

FIGURE 9.23   USD/JPY May 19, 2003

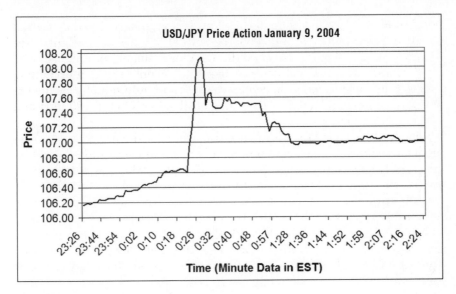

FIGURE 9.24   USD/JPY January 9, 2004

jumped 35 pips. Three minutes later, USD/JPY was 100 pips higher. Five minutes later, USD/JPY peaked 150 pips above the preintervention level. A half hour afterward, USD/JPY was still 100 pips above the 12:22 a.m. price of USD/JPY. Although prices eventually traded back down to 106.60, for those watching the markets, going in the same direction at the time of intervention still would have been profitable.

The key is not to be greedy, because USD/JPY could very well reverse if the market believes that fundamentals really warrant a stronger yen and weaker dollar in this case and that the Japanese government is simply slowing an inevitable decline or fighting a losing battle. Committing to take a solid 100-pip profit (of a 150- to 200-pip move) or using a very short-term intraday trailing stop of 15 to 20 pips, for example, can help lock in profits.

The last example of Japanese intervention, shown in Figure 9.25, is from November 19, 2003 when the Bank of Japan sold dollars and bought 948 billion yen (approximately US$8 billion). Before intervention, USD/JPY was trading around 107.90 and had dipped down to 107.65. When the BOJ came into the markets at 4:45 a.m. EST, USD/JPY jumped 40 pips in under a minute. Ten minutes later, USD/JPY was trading at 100 pips higher at 108.65. Twenty minutes following intervention, USD/JPY was trading 150 pips higher than preintervention levels.

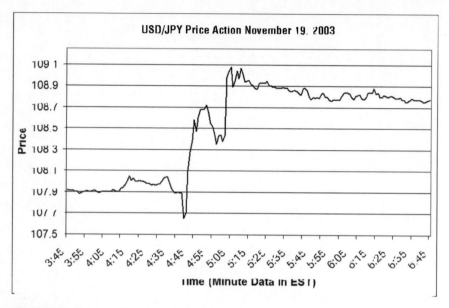

FIGURE 9.25 USD/JPY November 19, 2003

Eurozone

Japan is not the only major country to have intervened in its currency in recent years. The central bank of the Eurozone also came into the market to buy euros in 2000, when the single currency depreciated from 90 cents to 84 cents. In January 1999, when the euro was first launched, it was valued at 1.17 against the U.S. dollar. Due to the sharp slide, the European Central Bank (ECB) convinced the United States, Japan, the United Kingdom, and Canada to join it in coordinated intervention to prop up the euro for the first time ever. The Eurozone felt concerned that the market was lacking confidence in its new currency but also feared that the slide in the currency was increasing the cost of the region's oil imports. With energy prices hitting 10-year highs at the time, Europe's heavy dependence on oil imports necessitated a stronger currency. The United States agreed to intervention because buying euros and selling dollars would help to boost the value of European imports and aid in the funding of an already growing U.S. trade deficit. Tokyo joined in the intervention because it was becoming concerned that the weaker euro was posing a threat to Japan's own exports. Although the ECB did not release details on the magnitude of its intervention, the Federal Reserve reported having purchased 1.5 billion euros against the dollar on behalf of the ECB. Even though the actual

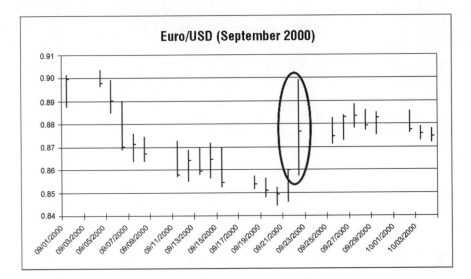

FIGURE 9.26 EUR/USD September 2000

intervention itself caught the market by surprise, the ECB gave good warning to the market with numerous bouts of verbal support from the ECB and European Union officials. For trading purposes, this would have given traders an opportunity to buy euros in anticipation of intervention or to avoid shorting the EUR/USD.

Figure 9.26 shows the price action of the EUR/USD on the day of intervention. Unfortunately, there is no minute data available dating back to September 2000, but from the daily chart we can see that on the day that the ECB intervened in the euro (September 22, 2000) with the help of its trade partners, the EUR/USD had a high-low range of more than 400 pips.

Even though intervention does not happen often, it is a very important fundamental trading strategy because each time it occurs, price movements are substantial.

For traders, intervention has three major implications for trading:

1. *Play intervention.* Use concerted warnings from central bank officials as a signal for possible intervention—the invisible floor created by the Japanese government has given USD/JPY bulls plenty of opportunity to pick short-term bottoms.

2. *Avoid trades that would fade intervention.* There will always be contrarians among us, but fading intervention, though sometimes profitable, entails a significant amount of risk. One bout of intervention by

a central bank could easily trigger a sharp 100- to 150-pip move (or more) in the currency pair, taking out stop orders and exacerbating the move.

3. *Use stops when intervention is a risk.* With the 24-hour nature of the market, intervention can occur at any time of the day. Although stops should *always* be entered into the trading platform immediately after the entry order is triggered, having stops in place is even more important when intervention is a major risk.

CHAPTER 10

Profiles and Unique Characteristics of Major Currency Pairs

It is important for all traders to have a good grasp of the general economic characteristics of each of the most commonly traded currencies in order to gauge what economic data and factors in general may have the most significant impact on a currency's movements. Some currencies tend to track commodity prices, while others may move in complete contrast. Traders also need to be aware of the difference between expected and actual data. That is, the most important aspect of interpreting news and its impact on the foreign exchange markets is the determination of whether the market is expecting a piece of news. This is known as the "market discount mechanism." The correlation between the currency markets and news is very important. News or data that are in line with expectations have less of an impact on currency movements than unexpected news or data. Therefore, short-term traders need to closely monitor expectations of the market.

CURRENCY PROFILE: U.S. DOLLAR (USD)

Broad Economic Overview

The United States is the world's leading economic power, with gross domestic product (GDP) valued at over US$11 trillion in 2004. This is the highest in the world, and, based on the purchasing power parity model, it is three times the size of Japan's output, five times the size of Germany's,

169

and seven times the size of the United Kingdom's. The United States is primarily a service-oriented country with nearly 80 percent of its GDP coming from real estate, transportation, finance, health care, and business services. Yet the sheer size of the U.S. manufacturing sector still makes the U.S. dollar particularly sensitive to developments within the sector. With the United States having the most liquid equity and fixed income markets in the world, foreign investors have consistently increased their purchases of U.S. assets. According to the International Monetary Fund (IMF), foreign direct investments into the United States are equal to approximately 40 percent of total global net inflows for the United States. On a net basis, the United States absorbs 71 percent of total foreign savings. This means that if foreign investors are not satisfied with their returns in the U.S. asset markets and they decide to repatriate their funds, this would have a significant effect on U.S. asset values and the U.S. dollar. More specifically, if foreign investors sell their U.S. dollar-denominated asset holdings in search of higher-yielding assets elsewhere, this would typically result in a decline in the value of the U.S. asset, as well as the U.S. dollar.

The import and export volume of the United States also exceeds that of any other country. This is due to the country's sheer size, as true import and export volume represent a mere 12 percent of GDP. Despite this large activity, on a netted basis, the United States is running a very large current account deficit of over $600 billion as of 2004. This is a major problem that the U.S. economy has been grappling with for more than 10 years. However, in the past two to three years, it has become an even larger problem since foreign funding of the deficit has been languishing as foreign central banks consider diversifying reserve assets out of dollars and into euros. The large current account deficit makes the U.S. dollar highly sensitive to changes in capital flows. In fact, in order to prevent a further decline in the U.S. dollar as a result of trade, the United States needs to attract a significant amount of capital inflows per day (in 2004, this number was up to $1.9 billion per day).

The United States is also the largest trading partner for most other countries, representing 20 percent of total world trade. These rankings are very important because changes in the value of the dollar and its volatility will impact U.S. trading activities with these respective countries. More specifically, a weaker dollar could boost U.S. exports to its trade partners, whereas a stronger dollar could curb foreign demand for U.S. exports. Here are the breakdowns of the most important trading partners for the United States (in order of importance).

The list of export markets is important because it ranks the importance of growth and political stability of these countries for the United

States. For example, should Canadian growth slow, its demand for U.S. exports would also fall, which would have a ripple effect on U.S. growth.

Leading Export Markets

1. Canada
2. Mexico
3. Japan
4. United Kingdom
5. European Union

Leading Import Sources

1. Canada
2. China
3. Mexico
4. Japan
5. European Union

Source: Bureau of Economic Analysis, "U.S. International Transactions," 2003 Report.

Monetary and Fiscal Policy Makers— The Federal Reserve

The Federal Reserve Board (Fed) is the monetary policy authority of the United States. The Fed is responsible for setting and implementing monetary policy through the Federal Open Market Committee (FOMC). The voting members of the FOMC are the seven governors of the Federal Reserve Board, plus five presidents of the 12 district reserve banks. The FOMC holds eight meetings per year, which are widely watched for interest rate announcements or changes in growth expectations.

The Fed has a high degree of independence to set monetary authority. It is less subject to political influences, as most members are accorded long terms that allow them to remain in office through periods of alternate party dominance in both the presidency and Congress.

The Federal Reserve issues a biannual *Monetary Policy Report* in February and July followed by the Humphrey-Hawkins testimony where the Federal Reserve chairman responds to questions from both the Congress and the Banking Committees in regard to this report. This report is important to watch, as it contains the FOMC forecasts for GDP growth, inflation, and unemployment.

The Fed, unlike most other central banks, has a mandate or "long-run objectives" of "price stability and sustainable economic growth." In order to adhere to these goals, the Fed has to use monetary policy to limit inflation and unemployment and to achieve balanced growth. The most popular tools that the Fed uses to control monetary policy are open market operations and the federal funds rate.

Open Market Operations　　Open market operations involve Fed purchases of government securities, including Treasury bills, notes, and bonds. This is one of the most popular methods for the Fed to signal and implement policy changes. Generally speaking, an increase in Fed purchases of government securities decreases interest rates, while selling of government securities by the Fed boosts interest rates.

Federal Funds Target　　The federal funds target rate is the key policy target of the Federal Reserve. It is the interest rate for borrowing that the Fed offers to its member banks. The Fed tends to increase this rate to curb inflation or decrease this rate to promote growth and consumption. Changes to this rate are closely watched by the market, tend to imply major changes in policy, and typically have large ramifications for global fixed income and equity markets. The market also pays particular attention to the statement released by the Federal Reserve, as it can offer signals for future monetary policy actions.

In terms of fiscal policy, that is in the hands of the U.S. Treasury. Fiscal policy decisions include determining the appropriate level of taxes and government spending. In fact, although the markets pay more attention to the Federal Reserve, the U.S. Treasury is the actual government body that determines dollar policy. That is, if the Treasury feels that the USD rate on the foreign exchange market is under- or overvalued, the U.S. Treasury is the government body that gives the New York Federal Reserve Board the authority and instructions to intervene in the foreign exchange market by physically selling or buying U.S. dollars. Therefore, the Treasury's view on dollar policy and changes to that view is generally very important to the currency market.

Over the past few decades, the Treasury and Fed officials have maintained a "strong dollar" bias. This was particularly true under former Treasury Secretary Paul O'Neill, who was frequently very vocal in advocating a strong dollar. Under the Bush administration, Treasury Secretary John Snow has reiterated this view and stated that he, too, favors a strong dollar. However, the Bush administration has done little to stem the dollar's slide between 2003 and 2005, which has led the market to believe that the administration actually favors a behind-the-scenes weak dollar policy and uses it as a tool to spur growth. Yet, for political reasons, it is not likely that the government would vocally change its stance to supporting a weak dollar policy.

Important Characteristics of the U.S. Dollar

- *Over 90 percent of all currency deals involve the dollar.*
  The most liquid currencies in the foreign exchange market are the EUR/USD, USD/JPY, GBP/USD, and USD/CHF. These currencies represent the most frequently traded currencies in the world, and all of these currency pairs involve the U.S. dollar. In fact, 90 percent of all currency deals involve the U.S. dollar. This explains the importance of the U.S. dollar to all foreign exchange traders. As a result, the most important economic data that usually move the market are dollar fundamentals.

- *Prior to September 11, the U.S. dollar was considered one of the world's premier safe haven currencies.*
  The reason why the U.S. dollar was previously considered one of the world's premier safe haven currencies was because prior to September 11, 2001, the risk of severe U.S. instability was very low. The United States was known to have one of the safest and most developed markets in the world. The safe haven status of the dollar allowed the United States to attract investment at a discounted rate of return, resulting in 76 percent of global currency reserves being held in dollars. Another reason why currency reserves are held in U.S. dollars is the fact that the dollar is the world's dominant factoring currency. In choosing a reserve currency, the dollar's safe haven status also played a major role for foreign central banks. However, post-9/11, foreign holders of U.S. assets, including central banks, have pared their dollar holdings as a result of increased U.S. uncertainty and decreased interest rates. The emergence of the euro has also threatened the U.S. dollar's status as the world's premier reserve currency. Many central banks have already begun to diversify their reserves by reducing their dollar holdings and increasing their euro holdings. This will continue to be a major trend that all traders should watch for in the years ahead.

- *The U.S. dollar moves in the opposite direction from gold prices.*
  As indicated in Figure 10.1, gold prices and the U.S. dollar have historically had a near perfect inverse relationship and are near perfect

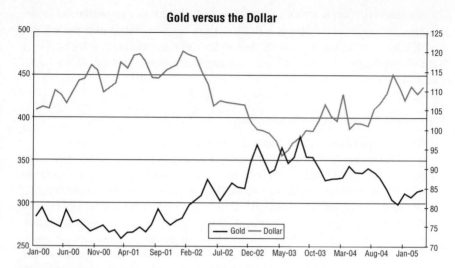

FIGURE 10.1   Gold versus Dollar Chart

mirror images of each other; this means that when gold prices rise, the dollar falls, and vice versa. This inverse relationship stems from the fact that gold is measured in dollars. Dollar depreciation due to global uncertainty has been the primary reason for gold appreciation, as gold is commonly viewed as the ultimate form of money. Gold is also seen as the premier safe haven commodity; therefore, in times of geopolitical uncertainty investors tend to flock to gold, which in essence hurts the dollar.

- *Many emerging market countries peg their local currencies to the dollar.*

    Pegging a currency to the dollar pertains to the basic idea that a government agrees to maintain the U.S. dollar as a reserve currency by offering to buy or sell any amount of domestic currency at the pegged rate for the reserve currency. These governments typically have to also promise to hold reserve currency at least equal to the amount of local currency in circulation. This is very important because these central banks have become large holders of U.S. dollars and take an active interest in managing their fixed or floating pegs. Countries with currencies pegged to the dollar include Hong Kong and, up until July 2005, China as well. China is a very active participant in the currency market because its maximum float per day is controlled within a narrow band based on the previous day's closing rate against the USD. Any fluctuations beyond this band during the day will be subject to intervention by the central bank, which will include buying or selling of U.S. dollars. Prior to July 21, 2005, China had pegged its currency at a rate of 8.3 yuan to the U.S. dollar. After years of pressure to revalue its currency, China adjusted its exchange rate to 8.11 yuan and reset the rate to the closing price of the currency each day. Along with this, China is gradually moving to a managed float referencing a basket of currencies.

Over the past year or two, the market has paid particular attention to the purchasing habits of these central banks. Talk of reserve diversification or more currency flexibility in the exchange rates of these Asian countries means that these central banks may have less of a need to own U.S. dollars and dollar-denominated assets. If this is true, it could be very negative for the U.S. dollar over the long term.

- *Interest rate differentials between U.S. Treasuries and foreign bonds are strongly followed.*

    The interest rate differential between U.S. Treasuries and foreign bonds is a very important relationship that professional FX traders follow. It can be a strong indicator of potential currency movements because the U.S. market is one of the largest markets in the world and investors are very sensitive to the yields that are offered by U.S. assets. Large investors are constantly looking for assets with the highest yields. As yields in the U.S. decrease or if yields abroad increase, this would induce investors to sell their U.S. assets and purchase foreign assets. Selling U.S. fixed income or equity assets would influence the currency market because that would require selling U.S. dollars and buying the foreign currency. If U.S. yields increase or foreign yields decrease, investors in general would be more inclined to purchase U.S. assets, therefore boosting the USD.

- *Keep an eye on the Dollar Index.*

    Market participants closely follow the U.S. Dollar Index (USDX) as a gauge of overall dollar strength or weakness. The USDX is a futures contract traded on the New York Board of Trade that is calculated using the trade-weighted geometric average of six currencies. It is important to follow this index because when market participants are reporting general dollar weakness or a decline in the trade-weighted dollar, they are typically referring to this index. Also, even though the dollar may have moved significantly against one single currency, it may not have moved as significantly on a trade-weighted basis. This is important because some central bankers may choose to focus on the trade-weighted index instead of the individual currency pair's performance against the dollar.

- *U.S. currency trading is impacted by stock and bond markets.*
  There is a strong correlation between a country's equity and fixed income markets and its currency: If the equity market is rising, generally speaking, foreign investment dollars should be coming in to seize the opportunity. If equity markets are falling, domestic investors will be selling their shares of local publicly traded firms only to seize investment opportunities abroad. With fixed income markets, economies boasting the most valuable fixed income opportunities with the highest yields will be capable of attracting foreign investment. Daily fluctuations and developments in any of these markets reflect movement of foreign portfolio investments, which in the end would require foreign exchange transactions. Cross-border merger and acquisition activities are also very important for FX traders to watch. Large M&A deals, particularly those that involve a significant cash portion, will have a notable impact on the currency markets, the reason being that the acquirer will need to buy or sell dollars to fund its cross-border acquisition target.

Important Economic Indicators for the United States

All of the following economic indicators are important for the U.S. dollar. However, since the U.S. economy is service oriented, it is important to pay particular attention to numbers for the service sector.

Employment—Nonfarm Payrolls The employment report is the most important and widely watched indicator on the economic calendar. Its importance is mostly due to political influences rather than pure economic reasons, as the Fed is under strict pressure to keep unemployment under control. As a result, interest rate policy is directly influenced by employment conditions. The monthly report consists of data from two different surveys, the Establishment Survey and the Household Survey. The Establishment Survey takes data from nonfarm payroll employment, average hourly workweek, and the aggregate hours index. The Household Survey gives information on the labor force, household employment, and the unemployment rate. Currency traders tend to focus on seasonally adjusted monthly unemployment rates and any meaningful changes in nonfarm payrolls.

Consumer Price Index   The consumer price index (CPI) is a key gauge of inflation. The index measures the prices on a fixed basket of consumer goods. Economists tend to focus more on the CPI-U or the core inflation rate, which excludes the volatile food and energy components. The indicator is widely watched by the FX markets as it drives a lot of activity.

Producer Price Index   The producer price index (PPI) is a family of indexes that measures average changes in selling prices received by domestic producers for their output. The PPI tracks changes in prices for nearly every goods-producing industry in the domestic economy, including agriculture, electricity and natural gas, forestry, fisheries, manufacturing, and mining. Foreign exchange markets tend to focus on seasonally adjusted finished goods PPI and how the index has reacted on a monthly, quarterly, and annualized basis.

Gross Domestic Product   Gross domestic product (GDP) is a measure of the total production and consumption of goods and services in the United States. The Bureau of Economic Analysis (BEA) constructs two complementary measures of GDP, one based on income and one based on expenditures. The advance release of GDP, which occurs the month after each quarter ends, contains some BEA estimates for data not yet released, inventories, and trade balance, and is the most important release. Other releases of GDP are typically not very significant unless a major revision is made.

International Trade   The balance of trade represents the difference between exports and imports of foreign trade in goods and services. Merchandise data are provided for U.S. total foreign trade with all countries, detail for trade with specific countries and regions of the world, as well as for individual commodities. Traders tend to focus on seasonally adjusted trade numbers over three-month periods as single-month trade periods are regarded as unreliable.

Employment Cost Index   The employment cost index (ECI) data is based on a survey of employer payrolls in the third month of the quarter for the pay period ending on the 12th day of the month. The survey is a probability sample of approximately 3,600 private industry employers and 700 state and local governments, public schools, and public hospitals. The big advantage of the ECI is that it includes nonwage costs, which add as much as 30 percent to total labor costs. Reaction to the ECI is often muted as it is generally very stable. It should be noted, however, that it is a favorite indicator of the Fed.

Institute for Supply Management (Formerly NAPM) The Institute for Supply Management (ISM) releases a monthly composite index based on surveys of 300 purchasing managers nationwide representing 20 different industries regarding manufacturing activity. Index values above 50 indicate an expanding economy, while values below 50 are indicative of contraction. The number is widely watched, as Fed Chairman Alan Greenspan once stated it is one of his favorite indicators.

Industrial Production The Index of Industrial Production is a set of indexes that measures the monthly physical output of U.S. factories, mines, and utilities. The index is broken down by industry type and market type. Foreign exchange markets focus mostly on the seasonally adjusted monthly change in aggregate figure. Increases in the index are typically dollar positive.

Consumer Confidence The Consumer Confidence Survey measures the level of confidence individual households have in the performance of the economy. Survey questionnaires are sent out to a nationwide representative sample of 5,000 households, of which approximately 3,500 respond. Households are asked five questions: (1) a rating of business conditions in the household's area, (2) a rating of business conditions in six months, (3) job availability in the area, (4) job availability in six months, and (5) family income in six months. Responses are seasonally adjusted and an index is constructed for each response; then a composite index is fashioned based on the aggregate responses. Market participants perceive rising consumer confidence as a precursor to higher consumer spending. Higher consumer spending is often seen as a spark that accelerates inflation.

Retail Sales The Retail Sales Index measures the total goods sold by a sampling of retail stores over the course of a month. This index is used as a gauge of consumer consumption and consumer confidence. The most important number is typically ex-autos, as auto sales can vary from month to month. Retail sales can be quite volatile due to seasonality; however, the index is an important indicator of the general health of the economy.

Treasury International Capital Flow Data (TIC Data) The Treasury international capital flow data measures the amount of capital inflow into the United States on a monthly basis. This economic release has become increasingly important over the past few years since the funding of the U.S. deficit is becoming more of an issue. Aside from the headline number itself, the market also pays close attention to the official flows, which represent the demand for U.S. government debt by foreign central banks.

CURRENCY PROFILE: EURO (EUR)

Broad Economic Overview

The European Union (EU) was developed as an institutional framework for the construction of a united Europe. The EU currently consists of 15 member countries: Austria, Belgium, Denmark, Finland, France, Germany, Greece, Ireland, Italy, Luxembourg, the Netherlands, Portugal, Spain, Sweden, and the United Kingdom. All of these countries share the euro as a common currency, except for Denmark, Sweden, and the United Kingdom. The 12 common currency countries constitute the European Monetary Union (EMU) and also share a single monetary policy dictated by the European Central Bank (ECB).

The EMU is the world's second largest economic power, with gross domestic product valued at approximately US$12 trillion in 2004. With a highly developed fixed income, equity, and futures market, the EMU has the second most attractive investment market for domestic and international investors. In the past, the EMU has had difficulty in attracting foreign direct investment or large capital flows. In fact, the EMU is a net supplier of foreign direct investments, accounting for approximately 45 percent of total world capital outflows and only 19 percent of capital inflows. The primary reason is because historically U.S. assets have had solid returns. As a result, the United States absorbs 71 percent of total foreign savings. However, with the euro becoming a more established currency and the European Monetary Union beginning to incorporate even more members, the euro's importance as a reserve currency is rising in tandem. As a result, capital flows to Europe have been increasing. With foreign central banks expected to diversify their euro reserve holdings even further, demand for euros should continue to increase.

The EMU is both a trade-driven and capital flow–driven economy; therefore trade is very important to the economies within the EMU. Unlike most major economies, the EMU does not have a large trade deficit or surplus. In fact, the EMU went from a small trade deficit in 2003 to a small trade surplus in 2004. EU exports comprise approximately 19 percent of world trade, while EU imports account for only 17 percent of total world imports. Because of the size of the EMU's trade with the rest of the world, it has significant power in the international trade arena. International clout is one of the primary goals in the formation of the EU, because it allows the individual countries to group as one entity and negotiate on an equal playing field with the United States, which is their largest trading partner. The breakdowns of the most important trading partners for the EU are:

Leading Export Markets

1. United States
2. Switzerland
3. Japan
4. Poland
5. China

Leading Import Sources

1. United States
2. Japan
3. China
4. Switzerland
5. Russia

The EMU is primarily a service-oriented economy. Services in 2001 accounted for approximately 70 percent of GDP, while manufacturing, mining, and utilities accounted for only 22 percent of GDP. In fact, a large number of the companies whose primary purpose is to produce finished products still concentrate their EU activity on innovation, research, design, and marketing, while outsourcing most of their manufacturing activities to Asia.

The EU's growing role in international trade has important implications for the role of the euro as a reserve currency. It is important for countries to have large amounts of reserve currencies to reduce exchange risk and transaction costs. Traditionally, most international trade transactions involve the British pound, the Japanese yen, and/or the U.S. dollar. Before the establishment of the euro, it was unreasonable to hold large amounts of every individual European national currency. As a result, currency reserves tended toward the dollar. At the end of the 1990s, approximately 65 percent of all world reserves were held in U.S. dollars, but with the introduction of the euro, foreign reserve assets are shifting in favor of the euro. This trend is expected to continue as the EU becomes one of the major trading partners for most countries around the world.

Monetary and Fiscal Policy Makers— The European Central Bank

The European Central Bank (ECB) is the governing body responsible for determining the monetary policy of the countries participating in the EMU. The executive board of the EMU consists of the president of the ECB, the vice president of the ECB, and four other members. These individuals along with the governors of the national central banks comprise the Governing Council. The ECB is set up so that the executive board implements the policies dictated by the Governing Council. New monetary policy decisions are typically made by majority vote, with the president having the deciding vote in the event of a tie, in biweekly meetings. Although the ECB meets on a biweekly basis and has the power to change monetary policy at each of those meetings, it is only expected to do so at meetings where an official press conference is scheduled afterward.

The EMU's primary objective is to maintain price stability and to promote growth. Monetary and fiscal policy changes are made to ensure that this objective is met. With the formation of the EMU, the Maastricht Treaty was developed by the EU to apply a number of criteria for each member country to help the EU achieve its objective. Deviations from these criteria by any one country will result in heavy fines. It is apparent, based on these criteria, that the ECB has a strict mandate focused on inflation and deficit. Generally, the ECB strives to maintain annual growth in Harmonized Index of Consumer Prices (HICP) below 2 percent and M3 (money supply) annual growth around 4.5 percent.

The EMU Criteria   In the 1992 Treaty on European Union (the Maastricht Treaty) the following criteria were formulated as preconditions for any EU member state joining the European Monetary Union (EMU).

- A rate of inflation no more than 1.5 percent above the average of the three best-performing member states, taking the average of the 12-month year-on-year rate preceding the assessment date.
- Long-term interest rates not exceeding the average rates of these low-inflation states by more than 2 percent for the preceding 12 months.
- Exchange rates that fluctuate within the normal margins of the exchange-rate mechanism (ERM) for at least two years.
- A general government debt/GDP ratio of not more than 60 percent, although a higher ratio may be permissible if it is "sufficiently diminishing."
- A general government deficit not exceeding 3 percent of GDP, although a small and temporary excess can be permitted.

The ECB and the European System of Central Banks (ESCB) are independent institutions from both national governments and other EU institutions, granting them complete control over monetary policy. This operational independence is accorded to them as per Article 108 of the Maastricht Treaty, which states that any member of the decision-making bodies cannot seek or take instructions from any community institutions, any government of a member state, or any other body. The primary tools the ECB uses to control monetary policy are:

Open Market Operations   The ECB has four main categories of open market operations to steer interest rates, manage liquidity, and signal monetary policy stance.

1. *Main refinancing operations.* These are regular liquidity-providing reverse transactions conducted weekly with a maturity of two weeks, which provide the bulk of refinancing to the financial sector.
2. *Longer-term refinancing operations.* These are liquidity-providing reverse transactions with a monthly frequency and a maturity of three months, which provide counterparties with additional longer-term refinancing.
3. *Fine-tuning operations.* These are executed on an ad hoc basis with the aim of both managing the liquidity situation in the market and steering interest rates, in particular in order to smooth the effects on interest rates caused by unexpected liquidity fluctuations.
4. *Structural operations.* These involve the issuance of debt certificates, reverse transactions, and outright transactions. These operations will be executed whenever the ECB wishes to adjust the structural position of the Eurosystem vis-à-vis the financial sector (on a regular or nonregular basis).

ECB Minimum Bid Rate (Repo Rate)   The ECB minimum bid rate is the key policy target for the ECB. It is the level of borrowing that the ECB offers to the central banks of its member states. This is also the rate that is subject to change at the biweekly ECB meetings. Since inflation is of high concern to the ECB, it is more inclined to keep interest rates at lofty levels to prevent inflation. Changes in the ECB's minimum bid rate have large ramifications for the Euro.

The ECB does not have an exchange rate target, but will factor in exchange rates in its policy deliberations, as exchange rates impact price stability. Therefore, the ECB is not prevented from intervening in the foreign exchange markets if it believes that inflation is a concern. As a result, comments by members of the Governing Council are widely watched by FX market participants and frequently move the euro.

The ECB publishes a monthly bulletin detailing analysis of economic developments and changes to its perceptions of economic conditions; it is important to follow the bulletin for signals to changes in the bias of monetary policy.

Important Characteristics of the Euro

- *The EUR/USD cross is the most liquid currency; all major euro crosses are very liquid.*

    The euro was introduced as an electronic currency on January 1, 1999. At this time, the euro replaced all pre-EMU currencies, except for Greece's currency, which was converted to the euro in January 2001. As a result, the EUR/USD cross is now the most liquid currency in the world and its movements are used as the primary gauge of the health of both the European and U.S. economies. The euro is most frequently known as the "anti-dollar" since it is dollar fundamentals that have dictated the currency pair's movements between 2003 and 2005. (See Figure 10.2.)

    EUR/JPY and EUR/CHF are also very liquid currencies that are generally used as gauges to the health of the Japanese and Swiss

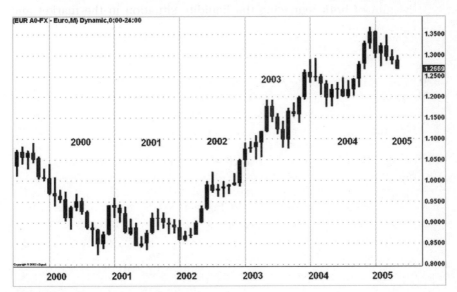

FIGURE 10.2 EUR/USD Five-Year Chart
(*Source:* eSignal. www.eSignal.com)

economies. The EUR/USD and EUR/GBP crosses are great trading currencies, as they have tight spreads, make orderly moves, and rarely gap.

- *The euro has unique risks.*

  Since the euro is a new currency, there are number of factors that need to be considered as risks to the euro that are not factors for other currencies. Namely, the ECB is frequently considered an untested central bank, due to its short history. This short history does not give market participants a good gauge to how the central bank would react under different economic and political conditions. The central bank let its Stability and Growth Pact break down in 2004 and has yet to actually impose restrictions on countries that have repeatedly breached the rules outlined by the pact. The rewritten EU constitution that has been rejected by individual countries has a number of stipulations that allow countries to escape penalization if they breach the budget deficit. This fact that the breaching of the deficits is essentially legalized has hurt confidence in the euro and the ECB. It has even prompted some countries such as Italy to consider dropping the euro and returning to the lira. In addition, since the euro is the currency for 12 member countries, it is highly sensitive to political or economical instabilities in any one country. The largest countries and the countries of the greatest importance in the Eurozone are Germany, France, Italy, and Spain.

- *The spread between 10-year U.S. Treasuries and 10-year bunds can indicate euro sentiment.*

  The 10-year government bonds serve as an important indicator of future euro exchange rates, especially against the U.S. dollar. The differential between the 10-year U.S. government bond and the 10-year German bund rates can provide a good indication for euro movement. If bund rates are higher than Treasury rates and the differential increases or the spread widens, this implies euro bullishness. A decrease in the differential or spread tightening tends to be bearish for the euro. The 10-year German bund is typically used as the benchmark bond for the Eurozone.

- *Predictions for euro area money flows.*

  Another useful interest rate is the three-month interest rate, also known as the euro interbank offer rate (Euribor rate). This is the rate offered from one large bank to another on interbank term deposits. Traders tend to compare the Euribor futures rate with the Eurodollar futures rate. Eurodollars are deposits denominated in U.S. dollars at banks and other financial institutions outside the United States. Because investors like high-yielding assets, European fixed income assets become more attractive as the spread between Euribor futures and Eurodollar futures widens in favor of the Euribors. As the spread narrows, European assets become less attractive, thereby implying a potential decrease in money flows into the euro.

Merger and acquisition activity also has important implications for EUR/USD movements. Recent years have seen increased M&A activity between EU and U.S. multinationals. Large deals, especially if in cash, often have significant short-term impacts on the EUR/USD.

Important Indicators for the Euro

All of the following economic indicators are important for the euro. However, since the EMU consists of 12 countries, it is important to keep abreast of political and economic developments such as GDP growth, inflation, and unemployment for all member countries. The largest countries within the EMU are Germany, France, and Italy. Therefore, in addition to the overall EMU economic data, the economic data of these three countries are the most important.

Preliminary GDP   Preliminary GDP is issued when Eurostat has collected data from a sufficient number of countries to produce an estimate. This usually includes France, Germany, and the Netherlands. However, Italy is not included in the preliminary release and is only added in the final number. The yearly aggregates for EU-15 and EMU-11 are a simple sum of national GDP. For the quarterly accounts, the aggregation is more complex since some countries (Greece, Ireland, and Luxembourg) do not yet produce quarterly national accounts data. Moreover, Portugal produces only partial quarterly accounts with a significant lag. Thus, both the EU-15 and EMU-11 quarterly paths are the result of estimates from quarterly data based on a group of countries accounting for more than 95 percent of total EU GDP.

German Industrial Production   The industrial production data is seasonally adjusted and includes a breakdown into four major subcategories: mining, manufacturing, energy, and construction. The manufacturing aggregate comprises four main product groups: basic and producer goods, capital goods, consumer durables, and consumer nondurables. The market tends to pay attention to the annual rate of change and the seasonally adjusted month-on-month figure. Germany's figure is most important since it is the largest country in the Eurozone; however, the market also occasionally reacts based on French industrial production. The initial industrial production release is based on a narrower data sample and hence subject to revision when the full sample has become available. The Finance Ministry occasionally indicates the expected direction of the revision in the initial data release.

Inflation Indicators

Harmonized Index of Consumer Prices   The EU Harmonized Index of Consumer Prices (HICP) published by Eurostat is designed for international comparison as required by EU law. Eurostat has published the index since January 1995. Since January 1998, Eurostat has published a specific index for the EMU-11 area called MUICP. Information on prices is retrieved by each national statistical agency. They are required to provide Eurostat with the 100 indexes used to compute the HICP. The national HICPs are totaled by Eurostat as a weighted average of these subindexes. The weights used are country specific. The HICP is released at the end of the month following the reference period, which is about 10 days after the publications of the national CPIs from Spain and France, the final EMU-5 countries to release their CPIs. Even if the information is already partly in the market when the HICP is released, it is an important release because it serves as the reference inflation index for the ECB. The ECB aims to keep Euroland consumer price inflation in a range of 0 to 2 percent.

M3   M3 is a broad measure of money supply, which includes everything from notes and coins to bank deposits. The ECB closely monitors M3, as it is viewed as a key measure of inflation. At its session in December 1998, the Governing Council of the ECB set its first reference value for M3 growth at 4.5 percent. This value supports inflation below 2 percent, trend growth of 2 to 2.5 percent, and a long-term decline in the velocity of money by 0.5 to 1 percent. The growth rate is monitored on a three-month moving average basis in order to prevent monthly volatility from distorting the information given by the aggregate. The ECB's approach to monetary targeting leaves considerable room for maneuver and interpretation. Because the ECB does not impose bands on M3 growth, as the Bundesbank used to do, there will be no automatic action when M3 growth diverges from the reference value. Moreover, although the ECB considers M3 to be the key indicator, it will also take into account the changes in other monetary aggregates.

German Unemployment   The release by the Labor Office contains information on the number of unemployed, as well as the changes on the previous month, in both seasonally adjusted (SA) and nonseasonally adjusted (NSA) terms. The NSA unemployment rate is provided, along with data on vacancies, short-shift working arrangements, and the number of employees (temporarily suspended in 1999). Within an hour after the Federal Labor Office (FLO) release, the Bundesbank releases the SA unemployment rate. The day ahead of the release, there is often a leak of the official data from a trade union source. The leak is usually of the NSA level of unemployment in millions. When a precise figure is reported on Reuters as given by "sources" for the NSA level of unemployment, the leak usually reflects the official figures. Rumors often circulate up to one week before the official release, but these are notoriously imprecise. Moreover, comments by German officials have in the past been mistranslated by the international press, so care needs to be exercised in interpreting news reports of rumors.

Individual Country Budget Deficits   The Stability and Growth Pact states that deficits must be kept below 3 percent of GDP. Countries also have targets set to further reduce their deficits. Failure to meet these targets is widely watched by market participants.

IFO (Information and Forschung [research]) Survey   Germany is by far the largest economy in Europe and is responsible for over 30 percent of total GDP. Any insight into German business conditions is seen as an insight into Europe as a whole. The IFO is a monthly survey conducted by the IFO institute in which over 7,000 German firms are asked for their assessment of the German business climate and their short-term plans. The initial publication of the results consists of the business climate headline figure and its two equally weighted subindexes: current business conditions and business expectations. The typical range is from 80 to 120, with a higher number indicating greater business confidence. The measure is most valuable, however, when measured against previous data.

CURRENCY PROFILE: BRITISH POUND (GBP)

Broad Economic Overview

The United Kingdom is the world's fourth largest economy with GDP valued at approximately US$2 trillion in 2004. With one of the most effective central banks in the world, the U.K. economy has benefited from many years of strong growth, low unemployment, expanding output, and resilient consumption. The strength of consumer consumption has in large part been due the country's strong housing market, which peaked in 2003. The United Kingdom has a service-oriented economy, with manufacturing representing an increasingly smaller portion of GDP, now equivalent to only one-fifth of national output. The capital market systems are one of the most developed in the world, and as a result finance and banking have become the strongest contributors to GDP. Although the majority of the United Kingdom's GDP is from services, it is important to know that it is also one of the largest producers and exporters of natural gas in the EU. The energy production industry accounts for 10 percent of GDP, which is one of the highest shares of any industrialized nation. This is particularly important, as increases in energy prices (such as oil) will significantly benefit the large number of U.K. oil exporters. (The United Kingdom did become a net oil importer for a brief period due to disruptions in the North Sea in 2003, but has already resumed its status as a net oil exporter.)

Overall, the United Kingdom is a net importer of goods with a consistent trade deficit. Its largest trading partner is the EU, with trade between the two constituencies accounting for over 50 percent of all of the country's import and export activities. The United States, on an individual basis, still remains the United Kingdom's largest trading partner. The breakdowns of the most important trading partners for the United Kingdom are:

Leading Export Markets

1. United States
2. Germany
3. France
4. Netherlands
5. Ireland

Leading Import Sources

1. United States
2. Germany
3. France
4. Netherlands
5. Belgium

Although the United Kingdom rejected adopting the euro in June 2003, the possibility of euro adoption will still be a factor in the backs of the minds of pound traders for many years to come. If the United Kingdom decided to join the EMU, doing so would have significant ramifications for its economy, the most important of which is that U.K. interest rates would have to be adjusted to reflect the equivalent interest rate of the Eurozone. One of the primary arguments against joining the EMU is that the U.K. government has sound macroeconomic policies that have worked very well for the country. Its successful monetary and fiscal policies have led the United Kingdom to outperform most major economies through a recent economic downturn, including the EU.

The U.K. Treasury has previously specified five economic tests that must be met prior to euro adoption.

United Kingdom's Five Economic Tests for the Euro

1. Is there sustainable convergence in business cycles and economic structures between the United Kingdom and other EMU members, so that the U.K. citizens could live comfortably with euro interest rates on a permanent basis?

2. Is there enough flexibility to cope with economic change?

3. Would joining the EMU create an environment that would encourage firms to invest in the United Kingdom?

4. Would joining the EMU have a positive impact on the competitiveness of the United Kingdom's financial services industry?

5. Would joining the EMU be good for promoting stability and growth in employment?

The United Kingdom is a very political country where government officials are highly concerned with voter approval. If voters do not support euro entry, the likelihood of EMU entry would decline. The following are some of the arguments for and against adopting the euro.

Arguments in Favor of Adopting the Euro

- Reduced exchange rate uncertainty for U.K. businesses and lower exchange rate transaction costs or risks.
- The prospect of sustained low inflation under the governance of the European Central Bank should reduce long-term interest rates and stimulate sustained economic growth.
- Single currency promotes price transparency.
- The integration of national financial markets of the EU will lead to higher efficiency in the allocation of capital in Europe.
- The euro is the second most important reserve currency after the U.S. dollar.
- With the United Kingdom joining the EMU, the political clout of the EMU would increase dramatically.

Arguments against Adopting the Euro

- Currency unions have collapsed in the past.
- Economic or political instabilities of one country would impact the euro, which would have exchange rate ramifications for otherwise healthy countries.
- Strict EMU criteria are outlined by the Stability and Growth Pact.
- Entry would mean a permanent transfer of domestic monetary authority to the European Central Bank.
- Joining a currency union with no monetary flexibility would require the United Kingdom to have more flexibility in the labor and housing markets.
- There are fears about which countries might dominate the ECB.
- Adjusting to new currency will require large transaction costs.

Monetary and Fiscal Policy Makers— Bank of England

The Bank of England (BOE) is the United Kingdom's central bank. The Monetary Policy Committee (MPC) is a nine-member committee that sets monetary policy for the United Kingdom. It consists of a governor, two deputy governors, two executive directors of the central bank, and four outside experts. The committee was granted operational independence in setting monetary policy in 1997. Despite this independence, their monetary policies are centered around achieving an inflation target dictated by the Treasury Chancellor. Currently, this target is retail price index (RPIX) inflation of 2.5 percent. The central bank has the power to change interest rates to levels that it believes will allow it to meet this target. The MPC holds monthly meetings, which are closely followed for announcements on changes in monetary policy, including changes in the interest rate (bank repo rate).

The MPC publishes statements after every meeting, along with a quarterly *Inflation Report* detailing the MPC's forecasts for the next two years of growth and inflation and justification for its policy movements. In addition, another publication, the *Quarterly Bulletin*, provides information on past monetary policy movements and analysis of the international economic environment and its impacts on the U.K. economy. All of these reports contain detailed information on the MPC's policies and biases for future policy movements. The main policy tools used by the MPC and BOE are:

Bank Repo Rate   This is the key rate used in monetary policy to meet the Treasury's inflation target. This rate is set for the bank's own operations in the market, such as the short-term lending activities. Changes to this rate affect the rates set by the commercial banks for their savers and borrowers. In turn, this rate will affect spending and output in the economy, and eventually costs and prices. An increase in this rate would imply an attempt to curb inflation, while a decrease in this rate would be to stimulate growth and expansion.

Open Market Operations   The goal of open market operations is to implement the changes in the bank repo rate, while assuring adequate liquidity in the market and continued stability in the banking system. This is reflective of the three main objectives of the BOE: maintaining the integrity and value of the currency, maintaining the stability of the financial system, and seeking to ensure the effectiveness of the United Kingdom's financial services. To ensure liquidity, the bank conducts daily open market operations to buy or sell short-term government fixed income instruments. If this is not sufficient to meet liquidity needs, the BOE would also conduct additional overnight operations.

Important Characteristics of the British Pound

- *GBP/USD is very liquid.*

    The GBP/USD is one of the most liquid currencies in the world, with 6 percent of all currency trading involving the British pound as either the base or counter currency. It is also one of the four most liquid currencies available for trading (among the EUR/USD, GBP/USD, USD/JPY, and USD/CHF). One of the reasons for the currency's liquidity is the country's highly developed capital markets. Many foreign investors seeking opportunities other than the United States have sent their funds to the United Kingdom. In order to create these investments, foreigners will need to sell their local currency and buy British pounds. (See Figure 10.3.)

- *GBP has three names.*

    The U.K.'s currency has three names—the British pound, Sterling, and Cable. All of these are interchangeable.

- *GBP is laden with speculators.*

    At the time of publication, the British pound has one of the highest interest rates among the developed nations. Although Australia and New Zealand have higher interest rates, their financial markets are not as developed as that of the United Kingdom. As a result, many investors who already have positions or are interested

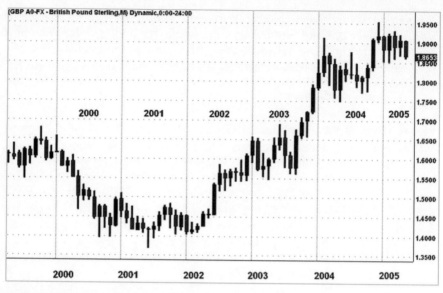

FIGURE 10.3   GBP/USD Five-Year Chart
(*Source:* eSignal. www.eSignal.com)

in initiating new carry trade positions frequently use the GBP as the lending currency and will go long the pound against currencies such as the U.S. dollar, Japanese yen, and Swiss franc. A carry trade involves buying or lending a currency with a higher interest rate and selling or borrowing a currency with a lower interest rate. In recent years, carry trades have increased in popularity, which has helped spur demand for the British pound. However, should the interest rate yield differential between the pound and other currencies narrow, an exodus of carry traders will increase volatility in the British pound.

- *Interest rate differentials between gilts and foreign bonds are closely followed.*

    Interest rate differentials between U.K. gilts/U.S. Treasuries and U.K. gilts/German bunds are widely watched by FX market participants. Gilts versus Treasuries can be a barometer of GBP/USD flows, while gilts versus bunds can be used as a barometer for EUR/GBP flows. More specifically, these interest rate differentials indicate how much premium yield U.K. fixed income assets are offering over U.S. and European fixed income assets (the German bund is usually used as a barometer for European yield), or vice versa. This differential provides traders with indications of potential capital flow or currency movements, as global investors are always shifting their capital in search for the assets with the highest yields. The United Kingdom currently provides these yields, while also providing the safety of having the same credit stability as the United States.

- *Eurosterling futures can give indications for interest rate movements.*

    Since the U.K. interest rate or bank repo rate is the primary tool used in monetary policy, it is important to keep abreast of potential changes to the interest rate. Comments from government officials is one way to gauge biases for potential rate changes, but the Bank of England is one of the few central banks that require members of the Monetary Policy Committee to publish their voting records. This personal accountability indicates that comments by individual committee members represent their own opinions and not that of the BOE. Therefore, it is necessary to look for other indications of potential BOE rate movements. Three-month eurosterling futures reflect market expectations on eurosterling interest rates three months into the future. These contracts are also useful in predicting U.K. interest rate changes, which will ultimately affect the fluctuations of the GBP/USD.

- *Comments on euro by U.K. politicians will impact the euro.*

    Any speeches, remarks (especially from the prime minister or Treasury chancellor), or polls in regard to the euro will impact the currency markets. Indication for adoption of the euro tends to put downward pressure on the GBP, while further opposition to euro entry will typically boost the GBP, the reason being that in order for the GBP to come in line with the euro, interest rates would have to decrease significantly (at the time of this writing, the United Kingdom interest rate is 4.75 percent, versus euro interest rate of 2.00 percent). A decrease in the interest rate would induce carry trade investors to close their positions, or sell pounds. The GBP/USD would also decline because of the uncertainties involved with euro adoption. The U.K. economy is performing very well under the direction of its current monetary authority. The EMU is currently encountering many difficulties with member countries breaching EMU criteria. With one monetary authority dictating 12 countries (plus the United Kingdom would be 13), the EMU has yet to prove that it has developed a monetary policy suitable for all member states.

- *GBP has positive correlation with energy prices.*

  The United Kingdom houses some of the largest energy companies in the world, including British Petroleum. Energy production represents 10 percent of GDP. As a result, the British pound tends to have a positive correlation with energy prices. Specifically, since many members of the EU import oil from the United Kingdom, as oil prices increase, they will in turn have to buy more pounds to fund their energy purchases. In addition, higher oil prices will also benefit the earnings of the nation's energy exporters.

- *GBP crosses.*

  Although the GBP/USD is a more liquid currency than EUR/GBP, EUR/GBP is typically the leading gauge for GBP strength. The GBP/USD currency pair tends to be more sensitive to U.S. developments, while EUR/GBP is a more pure fundamental pound trade since EUR is Britain's primary trade and investment partner. However, both currencies are naturally interdependent, which means that movements in the EUR/GBP cross can filter into movements in the GBP/USD. The reverse is also true; that is, movements in GBP/USD will also affect trading in EUR/GBP. Therefore it is important for pound traders to be consciously aware of the trading behavior of both currency pairs. The EUR/GBP rate should be exactly equal to the EUR/USD divided by the GBP/USD rate. Small differences in these rates are often exploited by market participants and quickly eliminated.

Important Economic Indicators for the United Kingdom

All of the following indicators are important for the United Kingdom. However, since the United Kingdom is primarily a service-oriented economy, it is particularly important to pay attention to numbers from the service sector.

Employment Situation   A monthly survey is conducted by the Office of National Statistics. The objectives of the survey are to divide the working-age population into three separate classifications—employed, unemployed, and not in the labor force—and to provide descriptive and explanatory data on each of these categories. Data from the survey provides market participants with information on major labor market trends such as shifts in employment across industrial sectors, hours worked, labor force participation, and unemployment rates. The timeliness of the survey makes it a closely watched statistic by the currency markets as it is a good barometer of the strength of the U.K. economy.

Retail Price Index   The RPI is a measure of the change in prices of a basket of consumer goods. The markets, however, focus on the underlying RPI or RPI-X, which excludes mortgage interest payments. The RPI-X is closely watched as the Treasury sets inflation targets for the BOE, currently defined as 2.5 percent annual growth in RPI-X.

Gross Domestic Product   A quarterly report is conducted by the Bureau of Statistics. GDP is a measure of the total production and consumption of goods and services in the United Kingdom. GDP is measured by adding expenditures by households, businesses, government, and net foreign purchases. The GDP price deflator is used to convert output measured at current prices into constant-dollar GDP. This data is used to gauge where in the business cycle the United Kingdom finds itself. Fast growth often is perceived as inflationary while low (or negative) growth indicates a recessionary or weak economy.

Industrial Production   The industrial production (IP) index measures the change in output in U.K. manufacturing, mining and quarrying, and electricity, gas, and water supply. Output refers to the physical quantity of items produced, unlike sales value, which combines quantity and price. The index covers the production of goods and power for domestic sales in the United Kingdom and for export. Because IP is responsible for close to a quarter of gross domestic product, IP is widely watched as it provides good insight into the current state of the economy.

Purchasing Managers Index   The purchasing managers index (PMI) is a monthly survey conducted by the Chartered Institute of Purchasing and Supply. The index is based on a weighted average of seasonally adjusted measures of output, new orders, inventory, and employment. Index values above 50 indicate an expanding economy, while values below 50 are indicative of contraction.

U.K. Housing Starts   Housing starts measure the number of residential building construction projects that have begun during any particular month. This is important data for the United Kingdom as the housing market is the primary industry that is sustaining the economy's performance.

CURRENCY PROFILE: SWISS FRANC (CHF)

Broad Economic Overview

Switzerland is the nineteenth largest economy in the world, with a GDP valued at over US$360 billion in 2004. Although the economy is relatively small, it is one of the wealthiest in the world on a GDP per capita basis. It is prosperous and technologically advanced with stability that rivals that of many larger economies. The country's prosperity stems primarily from technological expertise in manufacturing, tourism, and banking. More specifically, Switzerland is known for its chemicals and pharmaceuticals industries, machinery, precision instruments, watches, and a financial system historically known for protecting the confidentiality of its investors. This coupled with the country's lengthy history of political neutrality has created a safe haven reputation for the country and its currency. As a result, Switzerland is the world's largest destination for offshore capital. The country holds over US$2 trillion in offshore assets and is estimated to attract more than 35 percent of the world's private wealth management business. This has created a large and highly advanced banking and insurance industry that employs over 50 percent of the population and comprises more than 70 percent of total GDP. Since Switzerland's financial industry thrives on its safe haven status and renowned confidentiality, capital flows tend to drive the economy during times of global risk aversion, while trade flows drive the economy during a risk-seeking environment. Therefore trade flows are important, with nearly two-thirds of all trade conducted with Europe. Switzerland's most important trading partners are:

Leading Export Markets

1. Germany
2. United States
3. France
4. Italy
5. United Kingdom
6. Japan

Leading Import Sources

1. Germany
2. France
3. Italy

4. Netherlands
5. United States
6. United Kingdom

In recent years, merchandise trade flow has fluctuated between deficit and surplus. The current account, on the other hand, has reflected a surplus since 1966. In 2000, the current account surplus reached a high at 12.5 percent of GDP. This is the highest current account surplus among all of the industrialized countries (aside from Norway, Singapore, and Hong Kong). Most of the surplus can be attributed to the large amount of foreign direct investment into the country in search of safety of capital, despite the low yields offered by Switzerland.

Monetary and Fiscal Policy Makers— Swiss National Bank

The Swiss National Bank (SNB) is the central bank of Switzerland. It is a completely independent central bank with a three-person committee responsible for determining monetary policy. This committee consists of a chairman, a vice chairman, and one other member who constitute the Governing Board of the SNB. Due to the small size of the committee, all decisions are based on a consensus vote. The board reviews monetary policy at least once a quarter, but decisions on monetary policy can be made and announced at any point in time. Unlike most other central banks, the SNB does not set one official interest rate target, but instead sets a target range for the three-month Swiss LIBOR rate.

Central Bank's Goals   In December 1999, the SNB shifted from focusing on monetary targets (M3) to an inflation target of less than 2 percent inflation per year. This measure is taken based on the national consumer price index. Monetary targets still remain important indicators and are closely watched by the central bank, because they provide information on the long-term inflation. This new inflation focus also increases the central bank's transparency. The bank has clearly stated that "should inflation exceed 2 percent in the medium term, the SNB will tend to tighten its monetary stance." If there is a danger of deflation, the National Bank would loosen monetary policy. The SNB also closely monitors exchange rates, as excessive strength in the Swiss franc can cause inflationary conditions. This is especially true in environments of global risk aversion, as capital flows into Switzerland increase significantly during those times. As a result, the SNB typically favors a weak franc, and is not hesitant to use intervention as a liquidity tool. SNB officials intervene in the franc using a variety of methods including verbal remarks on liquidity, money supply, and the currency.

Central Bank's Tools   The most commonly used tools by the SNB to implement monetary policy include:

Target Interest Rate Range   The SNB implements monetary policy by setting a target range for their three-month interest rate (the Swiss LIBOR rate). This range typically has a 100-basis-point spread, and is revised at least once every quarter. This rate is used as the target because it is the most important money market rate for Swiss franc investments. Changes to this target are accompanied with a clear explanation in regard to the changes in the economic environment.

Open Market Operations   Repo transactions are the SNB's major monetary policy instrument. A repo transaction involves a cash taker (borrower) selling securities to a cash provider (lender), while agreeing to repurchase the securities of the same type and quantity at a later date. This structure is similar to a secured loan, whereby the cash taker must pay the cash provider interest. These repo transactions tend to have very short maturities ranging from one day to a few weeks. The SNB uses these repo transactions to manipulate undesirable moves in the three-month LIBOR rate. To prevent increases in the three-month LIBOR rate above the SNB's target, the bank would supply the commercial banks with additional liquidity through repo transactions at lower repo rates, and in essence create additional liquidity. Conversely, the SNB can reduce liquidity or induce increases in the three-month LIBOR rate by increasing repo rates.

The SNB publishes a *Quarterly Bulletin* with a detailed assessment of the current state of the economy and a review of monetary policy. A *Monthly Bulletin* is also published containing a short review of economic developments. These reports are important to watch, as they may contain information on changes in the SNB's assessment of the current domestic situation.

Important Characteristics of the Swiss Franc

- *Safe haven status.*

    This is perhaps the most unique characteristic of the Swiss franc. Switzerland's safe haven status is continually stressed because this and the secrecy of the banking system are the key advantages of

Switzerland. The Swiss franc moves primarily on external events rather than domestic economic conditions. That is, as mentioned earlier, due to its political neutrality, the franc is considered the world's premier safe haven currency. Therefore, in times of global instability and/or uncertainty, investors tend to be more concerned with capital retention than appreciation. At such times, funds will flow into Switzerland, which would cause the Swiss franc to appreciate regardless of whether growth conditions are favorable.

- *Swiss franc is closely correlated with gold.*
    Switzerland is the world's fourth largest official holder of gold. The Swiss constitution used to have a mandate requiring the currency to be backed 40 percent with gold reserves. Since then, despite the removal of the mandate, the link between gold and the Swiss franc has remained ingrained in the minds of Swiss investors. As a result, the Swiss franc has close to an 80 percent positive correlation with gold. If the gold price appreciates, the Swiss franc has a high likelihood of appreciating as well. In addition, since gold is also viewed as the ultimate safe haven form of money, both gold and the Swiss franc benefit during periods of global economic and geopolitical uncertainty.

- *Carry trades effects.*
    With one of the lowest interest rates in the industrialized world over the past few years, the Swiss franc is one of the most popular currencies used by traders in carry trades. As mentioned throughout this book, the popularity of carry trades has increased significantly over recent years, as investors are actively seeking high-yielding assets. A carry trade involves buying or lending a currency with a high interest rate and selling or borrowing a currency with a low interest rate. With CHF having one of the lowest interest rates of all industrialized countries, it is one of the primary currencies sold or borrowed in carry trades. This results in the need to sell CHF against a higher-yielding currency. Carry trades are typically done in cross-currencies such as GBP/CHF or AUD/CHF, but these trades will impact both EUR/CHF and USD/CHF. Unwinding of carry trades will involve the need for investors to purchase CHF.

- *Interest rate differentials between Euro Swiss futures and foreign interest rate futures are closely followed.*
    Interest rate differentials between three-month Euro Swiss futures and Eurodollar futures are widely watched by professional Swiss traders. These differentials are good indicators of potential

money flows as they indicate how much premium yield U.S. fixed income assets are offering over Swiss fixed income assets, or vice versa. This differential provides traders with indications of potential currency movements, as investors are always looking for assets with the highest yields. This is particularly important to carry traders who enter and exit their positions based on the positive interest rate differentials between global fixed income assets.

- *Potential changes in banking regulations.*

  Over the past few years members of the European Union have been exerting significant pressure on Switzerland to relax the confidentiality of its banking system and to increase transparency of customers' accounts. The EU is pressing this issue because of its active measures to prosecute EU tax evaders. This should be a concern for many years to come. However, this is a difficult decision for Switzerland to make because the confidentiality of customers' accounts represents the core strength of its banking system. The EU has threatened to impose severe sanctions on Switzerland if it does not comply with the proposed measures. Both political entities are currently working to negotiate an equitable resolution. Any news or talk of changing banking regulations will impact both Switzerland's economy and the Swiss franc.

- *Merger and acquisition activity.*

  Switzerland's primary industry is banking and finance. In this industry, merger and acquisition (M&A) activities are very common, especially as consolidation continues in the overall industry. As a result, these M&A activities can have significant impact on the Swiss franc. If foreign firms purchase Swiss banks or insurance companies, they will need to buy Swiss francs and in turn sell their local currencies. If Swiss banks purchase foreign firms, on the other hand, they would need to sell Swiss francs and buy the foreign currencies. Either way, it is important for Swiss franc traders to frequently watch for notices on M&A activity involving Swiss firms.

- *Trading behavior, cross-currency characteristics.*

  The EUR/CHF is the most commonly traded currency for traders who want to participate in CHF movements. (See Figure 10.4.) The USD/CHF is less frequently traded because of its higher illiquidity and volatility. However, day traders may tend to favor USD/CHF over EUR/CHF because of its volatile movements. In actuality, the USD/CHF is only a synthetic currency derived from EUR/USD and

FIGURE 10.4 USD/CHF Five-Year Chart
(*Source:* eSignal. www.eSignal.com)

EUR/CHF. Market makers or professional traders tend to use those pairs as leading indicators for trading USD/CHF or to price the current USD/CHF level when the currency pair is illiquid. Theoretically, the USD/CHF rate should be exactly equal to EUR/CHF divided by EUR/USD. Only during times of severe global risk aversion, such as the Iraq War or September 11, will USD/CHF develop a market of its own. Any small differences in these rates are quickly exploited by market participants.

Important Economic Indicators for Switzerland

KoF (Konjunkturforschungsstelle der eth, Zurich) Leading Indicators The KoF leading indicators report is released by the Swiss Institute for Business Cycle Research. This index is generally used to gauge the future health of the Swiss economy. It contains six components: (1) change in manufacturers' orders, (2) expected purchase plans of manufacturers over the next three months, (3) judgment of stocks in wholesale business, (4) consumer perception of their financial conditions, (5) backlog in the construction sector, and (6) orders backlog for manufacturers.

Consumer Price Index The consumer price index is calculated monthly on the basis of retail prices paid in Switzerland. In accordance with prevalent international practice, the commodities covered are distinguished according to the consumption concept, which includes in the calculation of the index those goods and services that are part of the private consumption aggregate according to the National Accounts. The basket of goods does not include so-called transfer expenditure such as direct taxation, social insurance contributions, and health insurance premiums. The index is a key measure of inflation.

Gross Domestic Product GDP is a measure of the total production and consumption of goods and services in Switzerland. GDP is measured by adding expenditures by households, businesses, government, and net foreign purchases. The GDP price deflator is used to convert output measured at current prices into constant-dollar GDP. This data is used to gauge where in the business cycle Switzerland finds itself. Fast growth often is perceived as inflationary while low (or negative) growth indicates a recessionary or weak economy.

Balance of Payments Balance of payments is the collective term for the accounts of Swiss transactions with the rest of the world. The current account is the balance of trade plus services portion. Balance of payments is an important indicator for Swiss traders as Switzerland has always kept a strong current account balance. Any changes to the current account, positive or negative, could see substantial flows.

Production Index (Industrial Production) The production index is a quarterly measure of the change in the volume of industrial production (or physical output by producers).

Retail Sales Switzerland's retail sales report is released on a monthly basis 40 days after the reference month. The data is an important indicator of consumer spending habits and is not seasonally adjusted.

CURRENCY PROFILE: JAPANESE YEN (JPY)

Broad Economic Overview

Japan is the third largest economy in the world with GDP valued at over US$4.6 trillion in 2004 (behind the United States and the entire Eurozone or EMU). It is the second largest single economy. The country is also one of the world's largest exporters and is responsible for over $500 billion in exports per year. Manufacturing and exports of products such as electronics and cars are the signature drivers of the economy, accounting for nearly 20 percent of GDP. This has resulted in a consistent trade surplus, which creates an inherent demand for the Japanese yen, despite severe structural deficiencies. Aside from being an exporter, Japan is also a large importer of raw materials for the production of goods. The primary trade partners for Japan in terms of both imports and exports are the United States and China. China's inexpensive goods have helped the country capture a larger share of Japan's import market. It is becoming an increasingly important trade partner, and has even surpassed the United States to become Japan's largest source of imports in 2003.

Leading Export Markets

1. United States
2. China
3. South Korea
4. Taiwan
5. Hong Kong

Leading Import Sources

1. China
2. United States
3. South Korea
4. Australia
5. Taiwan

Japan's Bubble Burst

Understanding the Japanese economy first involves understanding what led to the Japanese bubble and its subsequent burst.

In the 1980s, Japan's financial market was one of the most attractive markets for international investors seeking investment opportunities in Asia. It had the most developed capital markets in the region, and its banking system was considered to be one of the strongest in the world. At the time, the country was experiencing above-trend economic growth and near zero inflation. This resulted in rapid growth expectations, boosted asset prices, and rapid credit expansion, leading to the development of an asset bubble. Between 1990 and 1997, the asset bubble collapsed, inducing a US$10 trillion fall in asset prices, with the fall in real estate prices accounting for nearly 65 percent of the total decline, which is worth two years of national output. This fall in asset prices sparked a banking crisis in Japan. It began in the early 1990s and then developed into a full-blown systemic crisis in 1997 following the failure of a number of high-profile financial institutions. Many of these banks and financial institutions had extended loans to the builders and real estate developers at the height of the asset bubble in the 1980s, with the land as the collateral. A number of these developers defaulted after the asset bubble collapse, leaving the country's banks saddled with bad debt and collateral worth sometimes 60 to 80 percent less than when the loans were taken out. Due to the large size of these banking institutions and their role in corporate funding, the crisis had profound effects on both the Japanese economy and the global economy. Enormous bad debts, falling stock prices, and a collapsing real estate sector have crippled the Japanese economy for almost two decades.

In addition to the banking crisis, Japan also has the highest debt level of all of the industrialized countries, at over 140 percent of GDP. As a result of the country's deteriorating fiscal position and rising public debt, the country experienced over 10 years of stagnation. With this high debt burden, Japan still stands at risk of a liquidity crisis. The banking sector has become highly dependent on a government bailout. As a result, the Japanese yen is very sensitive to political developments and to any words in speeches by government officials that may indicate potential changes in monetary and fiscal policy, attempted bailout proposals, and any other rumors.

Monetary and Fiscal Policy Makers— Bank of Japan

The Bank of Japan (BOJ) is the key monetary policy making body in Japan. In 1998, the Japanese government passed laws giving the BOJ operational independence from the Ministry of Finance (MOF) and complete control over monetary policy. However, despite the government's attempts to decentralize decision making, the MOF still remains in charge of foreign exchange policy. The BOJ is responsible for executing all official Japanese foreign exchange transactions at the direction of the MOF. The Bank of Japan's Policy Board consists of the BOJ governor, two deputy governors, and six other members. Monetary policy meetings are held twice a month with briefings and press releases provided immediately. The BOJ also publishes a *Monthly Report* issued by the Policy Board and a *Monthly Economic Report*. These reports are important to watch for changes in BOJ sentiment and signals of new monetary or fiscal policy measures, as the government is constantly trying to develop initiatives to stimulate growth.

The MOF and the BOJ are very important institutions that both have the ability to impact currency movements. Since the MOF is the director of foreign exchange interventions, it is important to watch and keep abreast of the comments made from MOF officials. Being an export-driven economy, the government tends to favor a weaker Japanese yen. Therefore, if the Japanese yen appreciates significantly or too rapidly against the dollar, members of the BOJ and MOF will become increasingly vocal about their concerns or disapproval in regard to the current level or movements in the Japanese yen. These comments do tend to be market movers, but it is important to note that if government officials flood the market with comments and no action, the market would start to become immune to these comments. However, the MOF and BOJ do have a lengthy history of interventions in the currency markets to actively manipulate the JPY in Japan's best interests; therefore, their comments cannot be completely disregarded. The most popular tool that the BOJ uses to control monetary policy is open market operations.

Open Market Operations   These activities are focused on controlling the uncollateralized overnight call rate. The Bank of Japan has maintained a zero interest rate policy for some time now, which means that the Bank of Japan cannot further decrease this rate to stimulate growth, consumption, or liquidity. Therefore in order to maintain zero interest rates, the BOJ has to manipulate liquidity through open market operations, targeting zero interest on the overnight call rate. It manipulates liquidity by the outright buying or selling of bills, repos, or Japanese government bonds. A repo transaction involves a cash taker (borrower) selling securities to a cash provider (lender), while agreeing to repurchase securities of the same type and quantity at a later date. This structure is similar to a secured loan, whereby the cash taker must pay the cash provider interest. These repo transactions tend to have very short maturities ranging from one day to a few weeks.

In terms of fiscal policy, the Bank of Japan continues to consider a number of methods to deal with its nonperforming loans. This includes inflation targeting, nationalizing a portion of private banks, and repackaging the banks' bad debt and selling it at a discount. No policies have been decided upon, but the government is aggressively considering all of these and other alternatives.

Important Characteristics of the Japanese Yen

- *Proxy for Asian strength/weakness.*

  Japan tends to be seen as a proxy for broad Asian strength because the country has the largest GDP in Asia. With the most developed capital markets, Japan was once the primary destination for all investors who wanted access into the region. Japan also conducts a significant amount of trade with its Asian partners. As a result, economic problems or political instability in Japan tend to spill over into the other Asian countries. However, this spillover is not one-sided. Economic or political problems in other Asian economies can also have dramatic impacts on the Japanese economy and hence movements in the Japanese yen. For example, North Korean political instability poses a great risk to Japan and the Japanese yen since of the G-7 nations Japan has the strongest ties to North Korea.

- *Bank of Japan intervention practices.*

  The BOJ and MOF are very active participants in the FX markets. That is, they have a lengthy history of entering the FX markets if they are dissatisfied with the current JPY level. As Japan is a very political economy, with close ties between government officials and principals of large private institutions, the MOF has a very narrow segment in mind when it decides to depreciate a strong JPY. Since the BOJ is such an active participant, it is very much in tune with the market's movements and other participants. Periodically the BOJ receives information on large hedge fund positions from banks and is likely to intervene when speculators are on the other side of the market, allowing them to get the most bang for the buck. There are typically three main factors behind BOJ and MOF intervention:

  1. *Amount of appreciation/depreciation in JPY.* Intervention has historically occurred when the yen moves by seven or more yen in less than six weeks. Using the USD/JPY as a barometer, 7 yen would be equivalent to 700 pips, which would represent a move from 117.00 to 125.00. (See Figure 10.5)

  2. *Current USD/JPY rate.* Historically, only 11 percent of all BOJ interventions to counter a strong JPY have occurred above the 115 level.

  3. *Speculative positions.* In order to maximize the impact of intervention, the BOJ and MOF will intervene when market participants hold positions in the opposite direction. Traders can find a gauge for the positions of market participants by viewing the

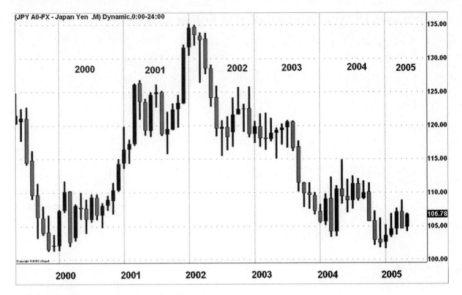

FIGURE 10.5   USD/JPY Five-Year Chart
(*Source:* eSignal. www.eSignal.com)

International Monetary Market (IMM) positions from the CFTC web site at www.cftc.gov.

- ***JPY movements are sensitive to time.***

    JPY crosses can become very active toward the end of the Japanese fiscal year (March 31), as exporters repatriate their dollar-denominated assets. This is particularly important for Japanese banks because they need to rebuild their balance sheets to meet Financial Services Authority (FSA) guidelines, which require the banks to mark to market their security holdings. In anticipation of the need for repatriation-related purchases of the Japanese yen, speculators frequently also bid the yen higher in an attempt to take advantage of this increased inflow. As a result, following fiscal year-end, the Japanese yen tends to have a bias toward depreciation as speculators close their positions.

    Aside from the fiscal year-end, time is also a factor on a day-to-day basis. Unlike traders in London or New York who typically have lunch at their trading desk, Japanese traders tend to take hourlong lunches between 10 and 11 p.m. EST, leaving only a junior trader in the office. Therefore, the Japanese lunchtime can be volatile, as the market gets very illiquid. Aside from that time frame, the JPY tends to move in a fairly orderly way during Japanese and London hours, unless breaking announcements or government official comments are made or surprising economic data is released. During U.S. hours, however, the JPY tends to have higher volatility, as U.S. traders are actively taking both USD and JPY positions.

- **Banking stocks are widely watched.**

  Since the crux of Japan's economic crisis stems from the nonperforming loan (NPL) problems of the Japanese banks, banking sector stocks are closely watched by FX market participants. Any threat of default by these banks, disappointing earnings, or further reports of significant NPLs can indicate even deeper problems for the economy. Therefore, bank stock movements can lead movements in the Japanese yen.

- **Carry trade effects.**

  The popularity of carry trades has increased in recent years, as investors are actively seeking high-yielding assets. With the Japanese yen having the lowest interest rate of all industrialized countries, it is the primary currency sold or borrowed in carry trades. The most popular carry trade currencies included GBP/JPY, AUD/JPY, NZD/JPY, and even USD/JPY. Carry traders would go short the Japanese yen against the higher-yielding currencies. Therefore reversal of carry trades as a result of spread narrowing would actually be beneficial for the Japanese yen, as the reversal process would involve purchasing the yen against the other currencies.

Important Economic Indicators for Japan

All of the following economic indicators are important for Japan. However, since Japan is a manufacturing-oriented economy, it is important to pay particular attention to numbers from the manufacturing sector.

Gross Domestic Product   Gross domestic product is a broad measure of the total production and consumption of goods and services measured over quarterly and yearly periods in Japan. GDP is measured by adding total expenditures by households, businesses, government, and net foreign purchases. The GDP price deflator is used to convert output measured at current prices into constant-dollar GDP. Preliminary reports are the most significant for FX market participants.

Tankan Survey The Tankan is a short-term economic survey of Japanese enterprises published four times a year. The survey includes more than 9,000 enterprises, which are divided into four major groups: large, small, and medium-sized as well as principal enterprises. The survey gives an overall impression of the business climate in Japan and is widely watched and anticipated by foreign exchange market participants.

Balance of Payments Balance of payments information gives investors insight into Japan's international economic transactions that include goods, services, investment income, and capital flows. The current account side of BOJ is most often used as a good gauge of international trade. Figures are released both monthly and semiannually.

Employment Employment figures are reported on a monthly basis by the Management and Coordination Agency of Japan. The employment release is a measure of the number of jobs and unemployment rate for the country as a whole. The data is obtained through a statistical survey of the current labor force. This release is a closely watched economic indicator because of its timeliness and its importance as a leading indicator of economic activity.

Industrial Production The industrial production (IP) index measures trends in the output of Japanese manufacturing, mining, and utilities companies. Output refers to the total quantity of items produced. The index covers the production of goods for domestic sales in Japan and for export. It excludes production in the agriculture, construction, transportation, communication, trade, finance, and service industries; government output; and imports. The IP index is then developed by weighting each component according to its relative importance during the base period. Investors feel IP and inventory accumulation have strong correlations with total output and can give good insight into the current state of the economy.

CURRENCY PROFILE: AUSTRALIAN DOLLAR (AUD)

Broad Economic Overview

Australia is the fifth largest country in terms of GDP in the Asia-Pacific region. Its gross domestic product is approximately US$750 billion in 2004. Although its economy is relatively small, on a per capita basis it is comparable to many industrialized Western European countries. Australia has a service-oriented economy with close to 79 percent of GDP coming from industries such as finance, property, and business services. However, the country has a trade deficit, with manufacturing dominating the country's exporting activities. Rural and mineral exports account for over 60 percent of all manufacturing exports. As a result, the economy is highly sensitive to changes in commodity prices. The breakdowns of Australia's most important trading partners are important because downturns or rapid growth in Australia's largest trade partners will impact demand for the country's imports and exports.

Largest Export Markets

1. Japan
2. United States
3. China
4. New Zealand
5. Republic of Korea
6. United Kingdom

Largest Import Sources

1. United States
2. Japan
3. China

Japan and the Association of Southeast Asian Nations (ASEAN) are the leading importers of Australian goods. The ASEAN includes Brunei, Cambodia, Indonesia, Laos, Malaysia, Myanmar, Philippines, Singapore, Thailand, and Vietnam. Therefore, it may be logical to assume that the Australian economy is highly sensitive to the performance of the countries in the Asian-Pacific region. However, during the Asian crisis, Australia grew at an average rate of 4.7 percent per year from 1997 to 1999 despite the fact that Asia is the central destination for the bulk of Australian exports. Australia was able to maintain strength as a result of the country's sound foundation of strong domestic consumption. As a result, the economy has been able to withstand past crises. Consumption has been on a steady rise since the 1980s. Therefore consumer consumption is an important indicator to watch during times of global economic slowdown for signals of the slowdown's spillover effects onto Australia's domestic consumption.

Monetary and Fiscal Policy Makers—
Reserve Bank of Australia

The Reserve Bank of Australia (RBA) is the central bank of Australia. The monetary policy committee within the central bank consists of the governor (chairman), the deputy governor (vice chairman), secretary to the treasurer, and six independent members appointed by the government. Changes on monetary policy are based on consensus within the committee.

Central Bank's Goals   The RBA's charter states that the mandate of the Reserve Bank Board is to focus monetary and banking policy on ensuring:

- The stability of the currency of Australia.
- The maintenance of full employment in Australia.
- The economic prosperity and welfare of the people of Australia.

In order to achieve these objectives, the government has set an informal consumer price inflation target of 2 to 3 percent per year. The RBA believes that the key to long-term sustainable growth in the economy is to control inflation, which would preserve the value of money. In addition, an inflation target provides a discipline for monetary policy making and guidelines for private sector inflation expectations. This also increases the transparency of the bank's activities. Should inflation or inflation expectations exceed the 2 to 3 percent target, traders should know that it would raise red flags at the RBA and prompt the central bank to favor a tighter monetary policy—in other words, further rate hikes.

Monetary policy decisions involve setting the interest rate on overnight loans in the money market. Other interest rates in the economy are influenced by this interest rate to varying degrees, so that the behavior of borrowers and lenders in the financial markets is affected by monetary policy (though not only by monetary policy). Through these channels, monetary policy affects the economy in pursuit of the goals outlined earlier.

Cash Rate   This is the RBA's target rate for open market operations. The cash rate is the rate charged on overnight loans between financial intermediaries. As a result, the cash rate should have a close relationship with the prevailing money market interest rates. Changes in monetary policy directly impact the interest rate structure of the financial system, and also impact sentiment in a currency. The chart in Figure 10.6 graphs the

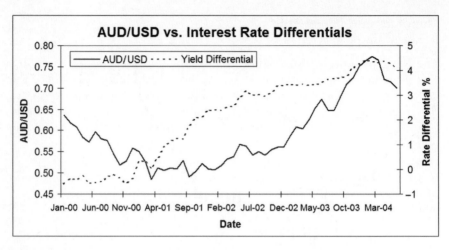

FIGURE 10.6   AUD/USD and Bond Spread

AUD/USD against the interest rate differential between Australia and the United States. Broadly speaking, there is a clear positive correlation between the interest rate differential and the movement in the currency. That is, between 1990 and 1994 Australia aggressively cut interest rates from a high of 17 percent to 4.75 percent, leading to a sharp decline in the AUD/USD. A different scenario was seen between 2000 and 2004. At the time, Australia was raising interest rates while the United States was cutting interest rates. This divergence in monetary policies led to a very strong rally in the AUD/USD over the next five years. (See Figure 10.7.)

Maintaining the Cash Rate: Open Market Operations   The focus of daily open market operations is to keep the cash rate close to the target by managing money market liquidity provided to commercial banks. If the Reserve Bank wishes to decrease the cash rate, it would increase the supply of short-dated repurchase agreements at a lower interest rate than the prevailing cash rate, which would in essence decrease the cash rate. If the Reserve Bank wishes to increase the cash rate, it would decrease the supply of short-dated repurchase agreements, which would in essence increase the cash rate. A repurchase agreement involves a cash taker (commercial bank) selling securities to a cash provider (RBA), while agreeing to repurchase securities of the same type and quantity at a later date. This structure is similar to a secured loan, whereby the cash taker must pay the cash provider interest. These repo transactions tend to have very short maturities ranging from one day to a few weeks.

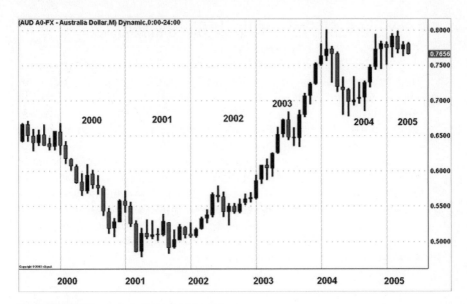

FIGURE 10.7 AUD/USD Five-Year Chart
(*Source:* eSignal. www.eSignal.com)

Australia has had a floating exchange rate since 1983. The Reserve Bank of Australia may undertake foreign exchange market operations when the market threatens to become excessively volatile or when the exchange rate is clearly inconsistent with underlying economic fundamentals. The RBA monitors a trade-weighted index as well as the cross-rate with the U.S. dollar. Intervention operations are invariably aimed at stabilizing market conditions rather than meeting exchange rate targets.

Monetary Policy Meetings The RBA meets every month (except for January) on the first Tuesday of the month to discuss potential changes in monetary policy. Following each meeting, the RBA issues a press release outlining justifications for its monetary policy changes. If rates are left unchanged, no statement is published. The RBA also publishes a monthly *Reserve Bank Bulletin*. The May and November issues of the *Reserve Bank Bulletin* include the semiannual statement on the Conduct of Monetary Policy. The February, May, August, and November issues contain a Quarterly Report on the Economy and Financial Markets. It is important to read these bulletins for signals on potential monetary policy changes.

Important Characteristics of the Australian Dollar

- *Commodity-linked currency.*

     Historically, the Australian dollar has had a very strong correlation (approximately 80 percent) with commodity prices and, more specifically, with gold prices. The correlation stems from the fact that Australia is the world's third largest gold producer, and gold represents approximately $5 billion in exports for the nation each year. As a result, the Australian dollar benefits when commodity prices increase. Of course, it also decreases when commodity prices decline. If commodity prices are strong, inflationary fears start to appear and the RBA would be inclined to increase rates to curb inflation. However, this is a sensitive topic, as gold prices tend to increase in times of global economic or political uncertainty. If the RBA increases rates during those conditions, it leaves Australia more vulnerable to spillover effects.

- *Carry trade effects.*

     Australia has one of the highest interest rates among the developed countries. With a fairly liquid currency, the Australian dollar is one of the most popular currencies to use for carry trades. A carry trade involves buying or lending a currency with a high interest rate and selling or borrowing a currency with a low interest rate. The popularity of the carry trade has contributed to the 57 percent rise of the Australian dollar against the U.S. dollar between 2001 and 2005. Many foreign investors were looking for high yields when equity investments offered minimal returns. However, carry trades last only as long as the actual yield advantage remains. If global central banks increase their interest rates and the positive interest rate differentials between Australia and other countries narrow, the AUD/USD could suffer from an exodus of carry traders.

- *Drought effects.*

     Since the majority of Australia's exports are commodities, the country's GDP is highly sensitive to severe weather conditions that may damage the country's farming activities. For example, 2002 was a particularly difficult year for Australia, because the country was experiencing a severe drought. The drought had taken an extreme toll on Australia's farming activities. This is especially important because agriculture accounts for 3 percent of the country's GDP. The RBA estimates that the "decline in farm production could directly reduce GDP growth by around 1 percentage point." Aside from exporting activities, a drought also has indirect effects on other aspects of Australia's economy. Industries that supply and service agriculture, such as the wholesale and transport sectors, as well as retail operations in rural farming areas may also be negatively affected by a drought. However, it is important to note that the Australian economy has a history of recovering strongly after a drought. The 1982–1983 drought first subtracted, then subsequently added, around 1 to 1.5 percentage points to GDP growth. The 1991–1995 drought reduced GDP by around 0.5 to 0.75 percentage points in 1991–1992 and 1994–1995, but eventually boosted GDP by 0.75 percentage points.

- **Interest rate differentials.**
    Interest rate differentials between the cash rates of Australia and the short-term interest rate yields of other industrialized countries should also be closely watched by professional traders of the Australian dollar. These differentials can be good indicators of potential money flows as they indicate how much premium yield Australian dollar short-term fixed income assets are offering over foreign short-term fixed income assets, or vice versa. This differential provides traders with indications of potential currency movements, as investors are always looking for assets with the highest yields. This is particularly important to carry traders who enter and exit their positions based on the positive interest rate differentials between global fixed income assets.

Important Economic Indicators for Australia

Gross Domestic Product   Gross domestic product is a measure of the total production and consumption of goods and services in Australia. GDP is measured by adding expenditures by households, businesses, government, and net foreign purchases. The GDP price deflator is used to convert output measured at current prices into constant-dollar GDP. This data is used to gauge where in the business cycle Australia finds itself. Fast growth often is perceived as inflationary while low (or negative) growth indicates a recessionary or weak economy.

Consumer Price Index   The consumer price index (CPI) measures quarterly changes in the price of a basket of goods and services that account for a high proportion of expenditure by the CPI population group (i.e., metropolitan households). This basket covers a wide range of goods and services, including food, housing, education, transportation, and health. This is the key indicator to watch as monetary policy changes are made based on this index, which is a measure of inflation.

Balance of Goods and Services   This number is a monthly measure of Australia's international trade in goods and services on a balance of payments basis. General merchandise imports and exports are derived mainly from international trade statistics, which are based on Australian Customs Service records. The current account is the balance of trade plus services.

Private Consumption   This is a national accounts measure that reflects current expenditure by households, and producers of private nonprofit services to households. It includes purchases of durable as well as nondurable goods. However, it excludes expenditures by persons on the purchase of dwellings and expenditures of a capital nature by unincorporated enterprises. This number is important to watch, as private consumption or consumer consumption is the foundation for resilience in the Australian economy.

Producer Price Index   The producer price index (PPI) is a family of indexes that measures average changes in selling prices received by domestic producers for their output. The PPI tracks changes in prices for nearly every goods-producing industry in the domestic economy, including agriculture, electricity and natural gas, forestry, fisheries, manufacturing, and mining. Foreign exchange markets tend to focus on seasonally adjusted finished goods PPI and how the index has reacted on a month-on-month, quarter-on-quarter, half-year-on-half-year, and year-on-year basis. Australia's PPI data is released on a quarterly basis.

CURRENCY PROFILE: NEW ZEALAND DOLLAR (NZD)

Broad Economic Overview

New Zealand is a very small economy with GDP valued at approximately US$86 billion in 2004. In fact, at the time of publication the country's population is equivalent to less than half of the population of New York City. It was once one of the most regulated countries within the Organization for Economic Cooperation and Development (OECD), but over the past two decades the country has been moving toward a more open, modern, and stable economy. With the passing of the Fiscal Responsibility Act of 1994, the country is shifting from an agricultural farming community to one that seeks to become a leading knowledge-based economy with high skills, high employment, and high value-added production. This Act sets legal standards that hold the government formally responsible to the public for its fiscal performance. It also sets the framework for the country's macroeconomic policies. The following are the principles outlined under the Fiscal Responsibility Act:

- Debt must be reduced to prudent levels by achieving surpluses on the operating budget every year until such a level is reached.
- Debt must be reduced to prudent levels and the government must ensure that expenditure is lower than revenue.
- Sufficient levels of Crown net worth must be achieved and maintained to guard against adverse future events.
- Reasonable taxation policies must be followed.
- Fiscal risks facing the government must be prudently managed.

New Zealand also has highly developed manufacturing and services sectors, with the agricultural industry driving the bulk of the country's exports. The economy is strongly trade oriented, with exports of goods and services representing approximately one-third of GDP. Due to the small size of the economy and its significant trade activities, New Zealand is highly sensitive to global performance, especially of its key trading partners, Australia and Japan. Together, Australia and Japan represent 30 percent of New Zealand's trading activity. During the Asian crisis, New Zealand's GDP contracted by 1.3 percent as a result of reduced demand for exports, as well as two consecutive droughts that reduced agricultural and related production. New Zealand's most important trading partners are:

Leading Export Markets

1. Australia
2. United States
3. Japan

Leading Import Sources

1. Australia
2. United States
3. Japan

Monetary and Fiscal Policy Makers—
Reserve Bank of New Zealand

The Reserve Bank of New Zealand (RBNZ) is the central bank of New Zealand. The Monetary Policy Committee is an internal committee of bank executives who review monetary policy on a weekly basis. Meetings to decide on changes to monetary policy occur eight times a year or approximately every six weeks. Unlike most other central banks, the decision for rate changes rests ultimately on the bank's governor. The current Policy Target Agreements set by the minister and the governor focus on maintaining policy stability and avoiding unnecessary instability in output, interest rates, and the exchange rate. Price stability refers to maintaining the annual CPI inflation at 1.5 percent. If the RBNZ does not meet this target, the government has the ability to dismiss the governor of the RBNZ, though this is rarely done. This serves as a strong incentive for the RBNZ to meet its inflation target. The most common tools used by the RBNZ to implement monetary policy changes are:

Official Cash Rate   The official cash rate (OCR) is the rate set by the RBNZ to implement monetary policy. The bank lends overnight cash at 25 basis points above the OCR rate and receives deposits or pays interest at 25 basis points below this rate. By controlling the cost of liquidity for commercial banks, the RBNZ can influence the interest rates offered to individuals and corporations. This effectively creates a 50-basis-point corridor that bounds the interbank overnight rate. The idea is that banks offering funds above the upper bound will attract few takers, because funds can be borrowed for a lower cost from the RBNZ. Banks offering rates below the lower bound also will attract few takers, because they are offering lower yields than the RBNZ. The official cash rate is reviewed and manipulated to maintain economic stability.

Objectives for Fiscal Policy   Open market operations are used to meet the cash target. The cash target is the targeted amount of reserves held by registered banks. The current target is NZ$20 million. The RBNZ prepares forecasts of daily fluctuations on the cash target and will then use these forecasts to determine the amount of funds to inject or withdraw in order to meet the cash target. The following objectives from the New Zealand Treasury provide a guideline for fiscal policy measures:

- *Expenses*. Expenses will average around 35 percent of GDP over the horizon used to calculate contributions toward future New Zealand superannuation (NZS) costs. During the buildup of assets to meet future NZS costs, expenses plus contributions will be around 35 percent of GDP. In the longer term, expenses less withdrawals to meet NZS costs will be around 35 percent of GDP.

- *Revenue.* Raise sufficient revenue to meet the operating balance objective: a robust, broad-based tax system that raises revenue in a fair and efficient way.
- *Operating balance.* Operating surplus on average over the economic cycle sufficient to meet the requirements for contributions toward future NZS costs and ensure consistency with the debt objective.
- *Debt.* Gross debt below 30 percent of GDP on average over the economic cycle. Net debt, which excludes the assets to meet future NZS costs, below 20 percent of GDP on average over the economic cycle.
- *Net worth.* Increase net worth consistent with the operating balance objective. This will be achieved through a buildup of assets to meet future NZS costs.

Important Characteristics of the New Zealand Dollar

- ### Strong correlation with AUD.
  Australia is New Zealand's largest trading partner. This, coupled with the proximity of the countries and the fact that New Zealand is highly trade oriented, creates strong ties between the economies of the two countries. When the Australian economy does well and Australian corporations increase their importing activities, New Zealand is one of the first to benefit. In fact, since 1999, the Australian economy has performed extremely well with a booming housing market that created a need to increase imports of building products. As a result, this strength translated into a 10 percent increase in Australia's imports from New Zealand between 1999 and 2002. Figure 10.8 illustrates how these two currency pairs are near-perfect mirror images of each other. In fact, over the past five years, the two currency pairs have had a positive correlation of approximately 97 percent.

- ### Commodity-linked currency.
  New Zealand is an export-driven economy with commodities representing over 40 percent of the country's exports. This has resulted in a 50 percent positive correlation between the New Zealand dollar and commodity prices. That is, as commodity prices increase, the New Zealand dollar also has a bias for appreciation. The correlation between the Australian dollar and the New Zealand dollar contributes to the currency's status as a commodity-linked currency. However, the

FIGURE 10.8   AUD/USD vs. NZD/USD Chart

New Zealand dollar's correlation with commodity prices is not limited to its own trade activities. In fact, the performance of the Australian economy is also highly correlated with commodity prices. Therefore, as commodity prices increase, the Australian economy benefits, translating into increased activity in all aspects of the country's operations, including trade with New Zealand.

- *Carry trades.*

   With one of the highest interest rates of the industrialized countries, the New Zealand dollar has traditionally been one of the most popular currencies to purchase for carry trades. A carry trade involves buying or lending a currency with a high interest rate and selling or borrowing a currency with a low interest rate. The popularity of the carry trade has contributed to the rise of the New Zealand dollar in an environment where many global investors are looking for opportunities to earn high yields. However, this also makes the New Zealand dollar particularly sensitive to changes in interest rates. That is, when the United States begins increasing interest rates while New Zealand stays on hold or reduces interest rates, the carry advantage of the New Zealand dollar would narrow. In such situations, the New Zealand dollar could come under pressure as speculators reverse their carry trader positions. (See Figure 10.9.)

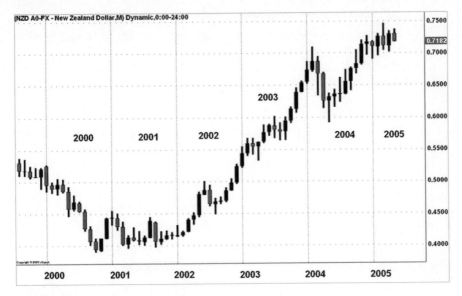

FIGURE 10.9 NZD/USD Five-Year Chart
(*Source:* eSignal. www.eSignal.com)

- *Interest rate differentials.*

    Interest rate differentials between the cash rates of New Zealand and the short-term interest rate yields of other industrialized countries are closely watched by professional NZD traders. These differentials can be good indicators of potential money flows as they indicate how much premium yield NZD short-term fixed income assets are offering over foreign short-term fixed income assets, or vice versa. This differential provides traders with indications of potential currency movements, as investors are always looking for assets with the highest yields. This is particularly important to carry traders who enter and exit their positions based on the positive interest rate differentials between global fixed income assets.

- *Population migration.*

    As mentioned earlier, New Zealand has a very small population, equal to less than half that of New York City. Therefore, increases in migration into the country can have significant effects on the economy. Between 2002 and 2003, the population of New Zealand increased by 37,500 people versus an increase of 1,700 between 2001 and 2002. Although these absolute numbers appear small, for New

Zealand they are fairly significant. In fact, this strong population migration into New Zealand has contributed significantly to the performance of the economy, because as the population increases, the demand for household goods increases, leading to an increase in overall consumption.

- *Drought effects.*

    Since the bulk of New Zealand's exports are commodities, the country's GDP is highly sensitive to severe weather conditions that may damage the country's farming activities. In 1998, droughts cost the country over $50 million. In addition, droughts are also very frequent in Australia, New Zealand's largest trading partner. These droughts have cost Australia up to 1 percent in GDP, which also translated into a negative impact on the New Zealand economy.

Important Economic Indicators for New Zealand

New Zealand does not release economic indicators often, but the following are the most important.

Gross Domestic Product   GDP is a quarterly measure of the total production and consumption of goods and services in New Zealand. GDP is measured by adding expenditures by households, businesses, government, and net foreign purchases. The GDP price deflator is used to convert output measured at current prices into constant-dollar GDP. This data is used to gauge where in the business cycle New Zealand finds itself. Fast growth often is perceived as inflationary while low (or negative) growth indicates a recessionary or weak economy.

Consumer Price Index   The consumer price index (CPI) measures quarterly changes in the price of a basket of goods and services that account for a high proportion of expenditure by the CPI population group (i.e., metropolitan households). This basket covers a wide range of goods and services including food, housing, education, transportation, and health. This is the key indicator to watch as monetary policy changes are made based on this index, which is a measure of inflation.

Balance of Goods and Services   New Zealand's balance of payments statements are records of the value of New Zealand's transactions in goods, services, income, and transfers with the rest of the world, and the changes in New Zealand's financial claims on the rest of the world (assets) and liabilities to the rest of the world. New Zealand's International

Investment Position statement shows, at a particular point in time, the stock of a country's international financial assets and international financial liabilities.

Private Consumption   This is a national accounts measure that reflects current expenditure by households, and producers of private non-profit services to households. It includes purchases of durable as well as nondurable goods. However, it excludes expenditures by persons on the purchase of dwellings and expenditures of a capital nature by unincorporated enterprises.

Producer Price Index   The producer price index (PPI) is a family of indexes that measures average changes in selling prices received by domestic producers for their output. The PPI tracks changes in prices for nearly every goods-producing industry in the domestic economy, including agriculture, electricity and natural gas, forestry, fisheries, manufacturing, and mining. Foreign exchange markets tend to focus on seasonally adjusted finished goods PPI and how the index has reacted on a month-on-month, quarter-on-quarter, half-year-on-half-year, and year-on-year basis. New Zealand's PPI data is released on a quarterly basis.

CURRENCY PROFILE: CANADIAN DOLLAR (CAD)

Broad Economic Overview

Canada is the world's seventh largest country with GDP valued at US$980 billion in 2004. The country has been growing consistently since 1991. It is typically known as a resource-based economy, as the country's early economic development hinged upon exploitation and exports of the country's natural resources. It is now the world's fifth largest producer of gold and the fourteenth largest producer of oil. However, in actuality nearly two-thirds of the country's GDP comes from the service sector, which also employs three out of every four Canadians. The strength in the service sector is partly attributed to the trend by businesses to subcontract a large portion of their services. This may include a manufacturing company subcontracting delivery services to a transportation company. Despite this, manufacturing and resources are still very important for the Canadian economy, as they represent over 25 percent of the country's exports and are the primary source of income for a number of provinces.

   The Canadian economy started to advance with the depreciation of its currency against the U.S. dollar and the Free Trade Agreement that came into effect on January 1, 1989. This agreement eliminated almost all trade tariffs between the United States and Canada. As a result, Canada now exports over 85 percent of their goods to the United States. Further negotiations to incorporate Mexico created the North American Free Trade Agreement (NAFTA), which took effect on January 1, 1994. This more advanced treaty eliminated most tariffs on trading between all three countries. Canada's close trade relationship with the United States makes it particularly sensitive to the health of the U.S. economy. If the U.S. economy sputters, demand for Canadian exports would suffer. The same is true for the opposite scenario: if U.S. economic growth is robust, Canadian exports will benefit. The following is a breakdown of Canada's trading partners:

Leading Export Markets

1. United States
2. Eurozone
3. Japan
4. United Kingdom
5. China

Leading Import Sources

1. United States
2. China
3. Mexico
4. Japan
5. United Kingdom

Monetary and Fiscal Policy Makers— Bank of Canada

Canada's central bank is known as the Bank of Canada (BOC). The Governing Council of the Bank of Canada is the board that is responsible for setting monetary policy. This council consists of seven members: the governor and six deputy governors. The Bank of Canada meets approximately eight times per year to discuss changes in monetary policy. It also releases a monthly monetary policy update every quarter.

Central Bank Goals   The Bank of Canada's focus is on maintaining the "integrity and value of the currency." This primarily involves ensuring price stability. Price stability is maintained by adhering to an inflation target agreed upon with the Department of Finance. This inflation target is currently set at 1 to 3 percent. The bank believes that high inflation can be damaging to the functioning of the economy, while low inflation on the other hand equates to price stability, which can help to foster sustainable long-term economic growth. The BOC controls inflation through short-term interest rates. If inflation is above the target, the bank will apply tighter monetary conditions. If it is below the target, the bank will loosen monetary policy. Overall, the central bank has done a pretty good job of keeping the inflation target within the band since 1998.

The bank measures monetary conditions using its Monetary Conditions Index, which is a weighted sum of changes in the 90-day commercial paper rate and G-10 trade-weighted exchange rate. The weight of the interest rate versus the exchange rate is 3 to 1, which is the effect of a change in interest rates on the exchange rate based on historical studies. This means that a 1 percent increase in short-term interest rates is the same as a 3 percent appreciation of the trade-weighted exchange rate. In order to change monetary policies, the BOC would manipulate the bank rate, which would in turn affect the exchange rate. If the currency appreciates to undesirable levels, the BOC can decrease interest rates to offset the rise. If it depreciates, the BOC can raise rates. However, interest rate changes are not used for the purposes of manipulating the exchange rate. Instead, they are used to control inflation. The following are the tools most commonly used by the BOC to implement monetary policy.

Bank Rate   This is the main rate used to control inflation. It is the rate of interest that the Bank of Canada charges to commercial banks. Changes to this rate will affect other interest rates, including mortgage rates and prime rates charged by commercial banks. Therefore changes to this rate will filter into the overall economy.

Open Market Operations   The Large Value Transfer System (LVTS) is the framework for the Bank of Canada's implementation of monetary policy. It is through this framework that Canada's commercial banks borrow and lend overnight money to each other in order to fund their daily transactions. The LVTS is an electronic platform through which these financial institutions conduct large transactions. The interest rate charged on these overnight loans is called the overnight rate or bank rate. The BOC can manipulate the overnight rate by offering to lend at rates lower or higher than the current market rate if the overnight lending rate is trading above or below the target banks.

On a regular basis, the bank releases a number of publications that are important to watch. This includes a biannual *Monetary Policy Report* that contains an assessment of the current economic environment and implications for inflation and a quarterly *Bank of Canada Review* that includes economic commentary, feature articles, speeches by members of the Governing Council, and important announcements.

Important Characteristics of the Canadian Dollar

- *Commodity-linked currency.*

  Canada's economy is highly dependent on commodities. As mentioned earlier, they are currently the world's fifth largest gold producer and the fourteenth largest oil producer. The positive correlation between the Canadian dollar and commodity prices is close to 60 percent. Strong commodity prices generally benefit domestic producers and increase their income from exports. There is a caveat, though, and that is eventually strong commodity prices will hurt external demand from places like the United States, which could filter into reduced demand for Canadian exports.

- *Strong correlation with the United States.*

  The United States imports 85 percent of Canada's exports. Canada has been running merchandise trade surpluses with the United States since the 1980s. The current account surplus with the United States reached a record high of $90 billion in 2003. Strong demand from the United States and strong energy prices led to record highs in the value of energy exports of approximately $36 billion in 2001. Therefore the Canadian economy is highly sensitive to changes in the U.S. economy. As the U.S. economy accelerates, trade increases with Canadian companies, benefiting the performance of the overall economy. However, as the U.S. economy slows, the Canadian economy will be hurt significantly as U.S. companies reduce their importing activities.

- *Mergers and acquisitions.*

  Due to the proximity of the United States and Canada, cross-border mergers and acquisitions are very common, as companies worldwide strive for globalization. These mergers and acquisitions lead to money flowing between the two countries, which ultimately impact the currencies. Specifically, the significant U.S. acquisition of Canadian energy companies in 2001 led to U.S. corporations injecting over $25 billion into Canada. This led to a strong rally in USD/CAD, as the U.S. companies needed to sell USD and buy CAD in order to pay for their acquisitions. (See Figure 10.10.)

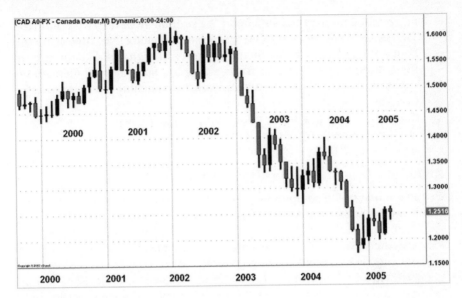

FIGURE 10.10   USD/CAD Five-Year Chart
(*Source:* eSignal. www.eSignal.com)

- *Interest rate differentials.*

    Interest rate differentials between the cash rates of Canada and the short-term interest rate yields of other industrialized countries are closely watched by professional Canadian dollar traders. These differentials can be good indicators of potential money flows as they indicate how much premium yield Canadian dollar short-term fixed income assets are offering over foreign short-term fixed income assets, or vice versa. This differential provides traders with indications of potential currency movements, as investors are always looking for assets with the highest yields. This is particularly important to carry traders who enter and exit their positions based on the positive interest rate differentials between global fixed income assets.

- *Carry trades.*

    The Canadian dollar became a popular currency to use for carry trades after its three-quarter-point rate increases between April and July of 2002. A carry trade involves buying or lending a currency with a high interest rate and selling or borrowing a currency with a low interest rate. When Canada has a higher interest rate than the United States, the short USD/CAD carry trade becomes one of the more popular carry trades due to the proximity of the two countries. The carry trade is a popular trade, as many foreign investors and hedge funds look for opportunities to earn high yields. However, if the United States embarks on a tightening campaign or Canada begins to lower rates, the positive interest rate differential between the Canadian dollar and other currencies would narrow. In such situations, the Canadian dollar could come under pressure if the speculators begin to exit their carry trades.

Important Economic Indicators for Canada

Unemployment   The unemployment rate represents the number of unemployed persons expressed as a percentage of the labor force.

Consumer Price Index   This measures the average rate of increase in prices. When economists speak of inflation as an economic problem, they generally mean a persistent increase in the general price level over a period of time, resulting in a decline in a currency's purchasing power. Inflation is often measured as a percentage increase in the consumer price index (CPI). Canada's inflation policy, as set out by the federal government and the Bank of Canada, aims to keep inflation within a target range of 1 to 3 percent. If the rate of inflation is 10 percent a year, $100 worth of purchases last year will, on average, cost $110 this year. At the same inflation rate, those purchases will cost $121 next year, and so on.

Gross Domestic Product   Canada's gross domestic product (GDP) is the total value of all goods and services produced within Canada during a given year. It is a measure of the income generated by production within Canada. GDP is also referred to as economic output. To avoid counting the same output more than once, GDP includes only final goods and services—not those that are used to make another product: GDP would not include the wheat used to make bread, but would include the bread itself.

Balance of Trade   The balance of trade is a statement of a country's trade in goods (merchandise) and services. It covers trade in products such as manufactured goods, raw materials, and agricultural goods, as well as travel and transportation. The balance of trade is the difference between the value of the goods and services that a country exports and the value of the goods and services that it imports. If a country's exports exceed its imports, it has a trade surplus and the trade balance is said to be positive. If imports exceed exports, the country has a trade deficit and its trade balance is said to be negative.

Producer Price Index   The producer price index (PPI) is a family of indexes that measures average changes in selling prices received by domestic producers for their output. The PPI tracks changes in prices for nearly every goods-producing industry in the domestic economy, including agriculture, electricity and natural gas, forestry, fisheries, manufacturing, and mining. Foreign exchange markets tend to focus on seasonally adjusted finished goods PPI and how the index has reacted on a month-on-month, quarter-on-quarter, half-year-on-half-year, and year-on-year basis.

Consumer Consumption   This is a national accounts measure that reflects current expenditure by households, and producers of private non-profit services to households. It includes purchases of durable as well as nondurable goods. However, it excludes expenditures by persons on the purchase of dwellings and expenditures of a capital nature by unincorporated enterprises.

About the Author

Kathy Lien is the Chief Currency Strategist at Forex Capital Markets (FXCM). Kathy is responsible for providing research and analysis for DailyFX.com, the most comprehensive free currency research and news site online. She writes both technical and fundamental research reports, market commentaries, and trading strategies. A seasoned FX analyst and trader, prior to joining FXCM Kathy was an associate at JPMorgan Chase where she worked in cross-markets and foreign exchange trading. Kathy has vast experience within the interbank market using both technical and fundamental analysis to trade FX spot and options. Kathy also has experience trading a number of products outside of FX, including interest rate derivatives, bonds, equities, and futures. She holds a bachelor degree in finance from New York University. Kathy has written for *Stocks & Commodities*, CBS MarketWatch, ActiveTrader, *Futures*, and *SFO* magazine. She is frequently quoted on CBS MarketWatch and Reuters, appeared on CNBC, and has taught seminars across the country. She has also hosted trader chats on EliteTrader, eSignal, and FXStreet, sharing her expertise in both technical and fundamental analysis.

Index